Understanding Buddhism

Teaching Religions and Worldviews

Series Editor: James D. Holt

This series explores the beliefs and practices of the different religions and worldviews alongside pedagogically supported approaches of how knowledge of each religion or worldview could be taught within the primary and secondary classroom, and to enhance teaching of those students in the classroom who practice that particular religion or worldview.

Books in the series explore the beliefs and practices of each religion or worldview as a lived experience in the UK. Aspects of each religion or worldview are explored including the concepts that form the central beliefs, and then the expression of these beliefs in worship, daily life and the ethics of believers in the modern day. Each chapter will utilize the authentic voice of those who identify with the religion or worldview today through the use of vignettes and provide reflective tasks for the reader to consider the concepts and how they can be taught in the classroom.

Also available in the series:
Understanding Sikhism, James D. Holt

Forthcoming in the series:
Understanding Hinduism, James D. Holt

Understanding Buddhism

A Guide for Teachers

James D. Holt

BLOOMSBURY ACADEMIC
LONDON • NEW YORK • OXFORD • NEW DELHI • SYDNEY

BLOOMSBURY ACADEMIC
Bloomsbury Publishing Plc
50 Bedford Square, London, WC1B 3DP, UK
1385 Broadway, New York, NY 10018, USA
29 Earlsfort Terrace, Dublin 2, Ireland

BLOOMSBURY, BLOOMSBURY ACADEMIC and the Diana logo are trademarks
of Bloomsbury Publishing Plc

First published in Great Britain 2024

Copyright © James D. Holt, 2024

James D. Holt has asserted his right under the Copyright, Designs and Patents Act, 1988,
to be identified as Author of this work.

For legal purposes the Acknowledgements on p. xvi constitute an extension of this copyright page.

Series design by Charlotte James
Cover image © Philippe Lissac / Godong / Getty Images

All rights reserved. No part of this publication may be reproduced or transmitted in
any form or by any means, electronic or mechanical, including photocopying,
recording, or any information storage or retrieval system, without prior
permission in writing from the publishers.

Bloomsbury Publishing Plc does not have any control over, or responsibility for, any
third-party websites referred to or in this book. All internet addresses given in this book
were correct at the time of going to press. The author and publisher regret any
inconvenience caused if addresses have changed or sites have ceased to exist, but can
accept no responsibility for any such changes.

A catalogue record for this book is available from the British Library.

A catalog record for this book is available from the Library of Congress.

ISBN: HB: 978-1-3503-3023-8
PB: 978-1-3503-3027-6
ePDF: 978-1-3503-3024-5
eBook: 978-1-3503-3025-2

Series: Teaching Religions and Worldviews

Typeset by Newgen KnowledgeWorks Pvt. Ltd., Chennai, India

To find out more about our authors and books visit www.bloomsbury.com
and sign up for our newsletters.

For Holly

This is the entire holy life, Ananda, that is, good friendship, good companionship, good comradeship

– *Upaddhasutta*

Contents

List of figures	ix
List of tables	x
Series editor's foreword	xi
Acknowledgements	xvi
Note on text	xvii

Introduction   1

Part 1   Key concepts in Buddhism

1   **The nature of existence**   21

2   **The nature of humanity**   47

3   **The Buddha**   67

4   **The Middle Way and the Threefold Path**   91

5   **The bodhisattva and arahant ideals**   105

6   **The dhamma/dharma and the sangha**   119

7   **Expressions of belief**   141

Part 2   Contemporary issues

8   **The ethical dimension**   165

| 9 | **Authority and diversity in the Buddhist world** | 187 |
| 10 | **Buddhism and contemporary Britain** | 207 |

Notes	215
Reference list	217
Glossary	231
Index	239

Figures

1.1	The Wheel of Life	32
2.1	Nineteenth-century painting of Buddhist cosmology	59
4.1	The Noble Eightfold Path	93
6.1	Budai	133
7.1	The teaching Buddha	154
9.1	Gohonzon	191
9.2	Similar and different	205

Tables

1.1	The Twelve Nidanas in the Tibetan Wheel of Life	33
1.2	The Twelve Nidanas in Theravada Buddhism	34
2.1	The Fourteen Dalai Lamas	55
2.2	The Thirty-One Planes of Existence and Three Realms of Rebirth in Theravada Cosmology	60
3.1	The Experience of the Bodhisattva (Future Buddha Gautama) with Previous Buddhas	73
3.2	The Thirty-Two Marks of a Great Being (Mahapurusa)	78
3.3	The Thirty-Two Portents of the Buddha's Birth	79
4.1	The Threefold Way and the Eightfold Path	94
4.2	Comparison of the Eightfold Path and Student Views	103
8.1	The Paramitas of Mahayana and Theravada Buddhism	168
8.2	Three Approaches to the Five Precepts	169
9.1	The Ten Precepts and Ten Positive Precepts of Triratna Buddhism	199
10.1	Census Data. Buddhism in England and Wales	208

Series editor's foreword
James D. Holt

The teaching of religion in schools has an interesting history in the UK. It has been through various iterations and paradigm shifts. There is a suggestion, and quite a loud one, at the moment that we are in the midst of a change of paradigm as it moves from a world religions approach to one that is focussed on religion and worldviews. Much is made of this shift, suggesting that it is a seismic landscape-altering approach within the classroom. Against this background it may seem odd to write a series of books that focuses on subject knowledge for teachers of what can be seen as reified religious structures that could be seen to be artificial creations.

Although the nomenclature used in the systematization of religions has changed to include worldviews, I am not convinced that the change is as seismic as has been suggested. The religion and worldviews approach to the teaching of religion and beliefs in schools is, in some ways, a rebranding rather than anything substantive. Effective teaching of religion and belief in schools has, in the recent past, always taken account of worldviews, maybe without recognizing that this is what has been happening. The 'change' to religion and worldviews will still rely on essential aspects of religions/structural worldviews and it is for this reason that this series of books are being written. What is meant by the 'essential' aspects? That will differ between religions and worldviews; it is at this point that a discussion of the positive contributions of a religion and worldviews approach will help frame the writing of this, and subsequent, books.

There are many ways to discuss what is entailed in a religion and worldviews approach to the teaching of religion and belief in schools and other settings. I often speak about the 'messiness' of religion and worldviews, and this messiness has to do with two terms: religions and worldviews.

In exploring the term 'religion', it becomes evident very quickly that the neat structures that we have in our minds, or that are taught in the classroom, are not reflective of the reality that we find in the world today. The various elements that we use in comparative religion enable us to line religions up next to each other and compare various elements, but in some ways in trying to get them to conform to a particular structure of religion, we have tried to fit square pegs into round holes. Jonathan Z. Smith noted this:

> 'Religion' is not a native category. It is not a first person term of self-characterization. It is a category imposed from the outside on some aspect of native culture. It is the other,

in these instances colonialists, who are solely responsible for the content of the term. (2004, 179–80)

In having religions fit an artificially constructed paradigm it is possible to see that both the constituent parts and the whole have been made less and their vibrancy and meaning have been lost. One such example in the development of the idea of what Buddhism is in relation to Christianity or, at least to the religious structure of Christianity, has meant that the person of the Buddha, Siddhartha Gautama, has developed as the central focus of Buddhism in the West, and this is reflected in the way that Buddhism is taught in classrooms. Authors such as Tomoko Masuzawa (2005) highlight that original Buddhism was mined and reified in the nineteenth century with reference to texts in India, with little reference to the lived reality of different Buddhisms in other countries. As a result Donald Lopez (1995) suggests that Buddhism is a 'hypostatised object … created by Europe, [which, in turn] could also be controlled by it, and it was against this Buddhism that all the Buddhisms of the modern Orient were to be judged' (7). Further exploration of this can be found later on, but it remains true to say that the Enlightenment understanding of religion was reinforced as colonial powers sought to make sense of the beliefs and practices that they found among the peoples of the Empire.

In establishing religion as an observable and static phenomenon, the religions themselves began to reflect the structures and emphases of those who studied and wrote about them. While it is possible to see a continued diversity of expression and understanding, certain principles began to be perceived as normative, and as such an orthodoxy (even if only from the outsider's perspective) began to develop and deviance from the constructed norms began to be seen to be peripheral, where in the past was part of a vast panoply of loosely related beliefs and practices. This normafication continues today; in 2021 it was argued, by Kalpana Jain, that Indian prime minister Modi was attempting to normalize a particular understanding of the Ramayana and by association the celebration of Diwali. Establishing a Hindu canon or orthodoxy could be seen to be unifying, yet at the same time eroding the diversity and vibrancy of the Hindu community.

It is this approach that, it is argued, developed a post-enlightenment view of religion and religions. The history of Sikhism, for example, can also be seen to be a reflection of this process where boundaries were established and norms enforced. The typology of religions, in the Western mind, prior to the nineteenth century tended to reflect a fourfold model: that of Christian, Jewish, Muslim and Heathen/Pagan. Christianity was the 'norm' while Judaism and Islam were seen to be related (but ultimately wrong), and everything else was put into the equivalent of the 'other' category. During the nineteenth century religious classifications began to develop further with the first recorded use of terminology such as Buddhism (Boudhism) in 1801, Hinduism (Hindooism) in 1829, Taoism (Taouism) in 1839, Zoroastrianism in 1854 and Confucianism in 1862 (see Josephson, 2012). The nuance of difference within and between religions were not explored in great depth, as is illustrated in the classification of Sikhs as Hindus in the earliest Indian colonial censuses.

Up until this point in Sikh history, the self-identification and practice undertaken by Sikhs as followers of the Gurus was seen to be fairly diverse, but also not a matter that needed to be delineated. There was evidence of practices more associated with Hinduism being followed by Sikhs alongside what could be seen to be more Sikh-like elements. It was in the classification of such that provided the impetus for some Sikhs to begin to establish an orthodoxy that separated the Panth from Hinduism. The publication of *Ham Hindu Nahin* (We Are Not Hindus) in 1899 is evidence of Sikhs feeling the need to establish boundaries where previously they were not perceived to be important (greater exploration of this Sikh 'orthodoxy' is explored in the Sikh volume of this series).

To some extent the development of a focus on worldviews within the classroom can be seen to be an effort to counter the colonialization of religions and return the understanding of them to a richer and more diverse expression that allows for individual expressions of religion. In exploring worldviews the Commission on Religious Education (2018) has suggested what they mean:

> The English word 'worldview' is a translation of the German *weltanschauung*, which literally means a view of the world. A worldview is a person's way of understanding, experiencing and responding to the world. It can be described as a philosophy of life or an approach to life. This includes how a person understands the nature of reality and their own place in the world. A person's worldview is likely to influence and be influenced by their beliefs, values, behaviours, experiences, identities and commitments. (Commission on RE, 2018, 4)

The Theos Think Tank (2021) video *No One Stands Nowhere* suggests that a worldview is a complex amalgam of various influences that are constantly shifting and developing. This means that there are personal and institutional worldviews, and that in these institutional worldviews there is a wide variety of experiences and interpretations. This can be seen to build the world of writers such as Kimberlé Crenshaw (1989) and bell hooks (1994) who have explored aspects of intersectionality. Crenshaw explored what is was to be a Black woman and how race and gender intersect. This develops into a discussion of worldviews and how they are held by individuals; Trevor Cooling suggests that people 'inhabit' their worldview (Cooling et al., 2020, 29).

This is an important development in the study of religion but, as suggested earlier, is not new. People like Robert Jackson (1997) have long suggested a listening to the insider or individual voice as a way to understand the complexity of religion. This ethnographic approach recognizes the rich diversity of lived religion. In the wider academic field of Religious Studies writers such as McGuire (2008) and Ammerman (2021) have similarly advocated for a focus on the lived experience of religion in the lives of individuals. If this is what is meant by 'worldviews' then it could be argued that teaching about religion in schools has been doing this. The focus on worldviews as a concept is a timely reminder that the religions that we explore are not neatly packaged, but they are messy and a result of the confluence of influences and identities in a person's life.

In trying to understand I imagine a prism, similar to that found on the cover of Pink Floyd's *Dark Side of the Moon* album. The prism is the receptacle where our backgrounds, cultures, experiences coalesce to help make sense of life and the expressions and interpretations of new experiences and the development of values and the like form. These form a different spectrum of colours for each individual. This intersectionality recognizes and emphasizes that no two people are alike. Simply speaking, in the context of this book, a Sikh brother and sister in the UK would have different perceptions of Sikhism despite similar upbringings, because of their gender as well as other experiences that may have coloured their view.

This approach could be seen to problematize the very concept of religion and worldviews to such an extent that religion could be seen to lose all meaning. It reduces religion to an individual expression of individual belief system.

The argument and purpose of this series of books is to recognize the messiness, intersectionality and worldviews approach to religions, but in a way that does not dismiss everything that is useful about a world religions paradigm. It will recognize the diversity within each tradition, but will also use what can be commonly termed the 'essential' aspects of a religion or worldview that enables diversity to be recognized. The essential aspects are needed to frame the discussions that are taking place. Ben Wood (2020) argues:

> Some argue that 'essentialism' narrows and limits understanding and fails to provide a realistic picture of the world and religion and belief. Others, myself included, accept this to a point, arguing that 'essentialism' may be limited, but it is a necessary part of the process of learning about religions in a progressive manner, in that what is learnt in this phase is essential for progress to more sophisticated learning. (Wood, 2020)

The Commission on RE (2018) suggest that:

> We need to move beyond an essentialised presentation of six 'major world faiths' and towards a deeper understanding of the complex, diverse and plural nature of worldviews at both institutional and personal levels. (Commission on RE, 2018, 6)

Although it may not be what they intended, I would suggest that a 'moving beyond' essentialism does not mean that we need to dismiss the existence of the central elements of a religion or institutionalized worldview; rather, that we should utilize aspects that are helpful to frame our study. Moving beyond is studying religion in a framework of intersectionality or worldviews that recognizes the problems inherent in the world religions paradigm. This means that adopting a categorization of all religions as having set commonalities is out of date and does not reflect the lived reality of many people in the world. Any study of religion in schools must begin with a recognition of the diversity that is found within the world.

I argue elsewhere (Holt, 2022) that this diversity is appropriate at every level of the school experience. At the very youngest of ages it is possible to use language such as 'many', 'most', and 'some' when speaking of religious belief and practice. As pupils get older it is possible to introduce the nuances and specifics of diversity. It also serves the purpose of exercising a humility of knowledge when we teach; in the intersectional world of religions it is impossible to know everything about the beliefs and practices of all aspects of a religion; using qualifiers ensures that we are not unconsciously establishing boundaries and norms in religions that do not exist.

One of the consequences of exploring religion and worldviews as a paradigm is the inclusion of systems of belief that are not seen to be religious. For many years, groups such as Humanists UK have argued for a recognition and inclusion of non-religious worldviews within the classroom. Many schools, syllabi and specifications now include non-religious worldviews; the worldviews approach can be seen to have expanded what might be explored in the curriculum. In recognizing that the 'big six' have traditionally been prioritized, it is possible that this shift in paradigm will expand what traditions and worldviews should be studied. I have explored the arguments for the inclusion of religions 'beyond the big six', and also the inclusion of expressions of the big six beyond the mainstream, and that we should expand what we understand and teach (Holt, 2019). It is against this background that this series of books works; while recognizing what can be perceived as the 'normative' it will also recognize and explore aspects of diversity within the religious tradition.

It is at this point I feel that it is important that I recognize my own positionality with respect to the religions and worldviews that will be covered in this series. For most of the religions I will be coming from the perspective of an outsider. I recognize both the benefits and hindrances this may bring. I cannot fully understand what it is to live as a Sikh, or as a Buddhist. The spirituality of Islam or of Hinduism is not something that I have experienced as a believer. This does not mean, though, that I am unsympathetic. When I present the beliefs and practices of the individual religions I will do so, as best I can, in a way that they would be understood by believers. I understand and appreciate the impact that religions and worldviews can have on the lives of individuals and communities. As an outsider I am also able to recognize debates within the community that may be given short shrift by an insider.

As a teacher, lecturer and professor of religious education over many years I am also able to understand the nuances of what is needed to teach religion and worldviews in the classroom. I will not be able to cover everything, and the selection of material may leave out things that some people think are important. That is the beauty of intersectionality and worldviews; there are a myriad of ways that religion can be understood and presented. It is my hope that this series of books will provide a basis on which to build in the future. I would encourage to discuss the contents of this book with fellow professionals, your students, but perhaps most importantly with followers of the religions and worldviews explored. The authentic voice is central to understanding the beliefs, practices and impact of religion. This book should provide you with a good knowledge on which to develop your teaching and those conversations.

Acknowledgements

There are many people who contribute to the writing of a book. At many different points throughout my life there are people I have met, worked with and become friends with, who have contributed to my understanding of religion and especially, in terms of this book, of Buddhism.

There are many members of the Buddhist community who have helped with the answering of questions over the years that have assisted in my understanding that enabled this book to be written. I will not be able to name them all, but Natalie Bowler, Robin Hayter, Jack Nolan and Joyce Miller have been particularly helpful over the years. I take complete responsibility for anything that might not quite be as understood within the Buddhist community.

Within my teaching community so many people challenge me, and inspire me, to be better and understand more. John Rudge, Lesley Wakefield, Martin Fahey, Diane Kolka and Christine Paul have particularly been helpful in my understanding of Buddhism. Special thanks are also due to colleagues and students at the University of Chester, especially Wendy Dossett who is a constant support and source of understanding.

The biggest thanks of all are reserved for my wife Ruth, and our children, Eleanor, Abi, Ethan, Gideon and Martha, who know that sometimes I disappear and hibernate for a while as I write. I am so grateful for their love and support.

As with everything I do, all credit goes to God. I am nothing without the influence of God in my life.

Note on text

There are different translations available of some of the texts used throughout this book. Although they are in the public domain, I am grateful to dhammatalks.org for their efforts in making these works available for free and for allowing me to quote freely from them. Where certain suttas/sutras were not available on dhammatalks, suttacentral.net was used unless otherwise stated. Again, I am grateful for the availability of these texts in English.

In transliterating from Sanskrit or Pali there are often different spellings in English. The words have been chosen based on their being one of the most frequent ways of spelling. Many Sanskrit and Pali words have been italicized the first time they are used, and for many of these, the meaning will be found alongside usage and in the Glossary.

It should also be noted that in translating the words into English, some of the meaning may be lost. There is a tendency to try and translate one word into another, and this does not always get the meaning across. I have tried, as far as possible, to recognize the incompleteness of these translations.

In some areas there is a use of the Pali spelling, and in others the Sanskrit. This is not to suggest a priority of one over the other; it is for ease of reading and discussion. I have tried, as far as possible, to use Pali spelling when discussing Theravada, and Sanskrit when discussing Mahayana. Diacritic marks have not been used.

Note on text

There are different translations available of some of the texts used throughout this book. Although they are in the public domain, I am grateful to dhammatalks.org for their efforts in making these works available for free and for allowing me to quote freely from them. Where certain suttas/sutras were not available on dhammatalks, suttacentral.net was used unless otherwise stated. Again, I am grateful for the availability of these texts in English.

In transliterating from Sanskrit or Pali there are often different spellings in English. The words have been chosen based on their being one of the most frequent ways of spelling. Many Sanskrit and Pali words have been italicized the first time they are used, and for many of these, the meaning will be found alongside usage and in the Glossary.

It should also be noted that in translating the words into English, some of the meaning may be lost. There is a tendency to try and translate one word into another, and this does not always get the meaning across. I have tried, as far as possible, to recognize the incompleteness of these translations.

In some areas there is a use of the Pali spelling, and in others the Sanskrit. This is not to suggest a priority of one over the other; it is for ease of reading and discussion. I have tried, as far as possible, to use Pali spelling when discussing Theravada, and Sanskrit when discussing Mahayana. Diacritic marks have not been used.

Introduction

What is Buddhism? Who is a Buddhist? These seem like straightforward questions that are simple to answer. Buddhism is the religion founded by the Buddha, and a Buddhist is someone who follows that religion, or the teachings of the Buddha. While these answers might have been acceptable in the past, and I am not sure they would have, it is impossible to utilize such reductive answers to understand Buddhism or Buddhists. As a teacher of Buddhism in schools, it might be tempting to approach definitions and experience in this way so as to provide clarity and certainty. This provides what I have called elsewhere a 'chocolate box' view of religion (Holt, 2022), or Buddhism, where all Buddhists believe the same thing and fit into the neat structures that we have produced them in a colonial worldview. This leads to a simplistic view of Buddhism that fits neatly into a table that shares characteristics of all other religions such as founder, holy book, places of pilgrimage.

In trying to define Buddhism a person is faced with many issues, not least those explored in the Series Editor's Foreword. When we approach Buddhism through a 'world religions' or chocolate box lens we realize that there are many issues with a one-size-fits-all approach to religion in general and Buddhism more specifically. The challenge of Buddhism to a normative definition of religion is shown in the UK Government's 2020 review into how the government should best engage with faith groups in England. In this call for evidence Colin Bloom defined religion thus:

> Religion is a particular and organised system of faith and *worship in a supreme being or entity or supreme beings or entities* … Typically, religions will have places of worship such as Churches, Temples, Mosques and Synagogues, and will often have a national and international hierarchy. In almost every case, the world's major religions will have a creed, Holy Scriptures and other ancient texts. (emphasis added) (Williams, 2020)

In the final report Bloom (2023, 18) added the qualifiers 'generally' and 'often'. These definitions reinforced the approaches that have been criticized in the Series Editor's Foreword. Buddhism does not neatly fit into the category of religion as defined by the UK Government. This does not mean that Buddhism is not a religion, rather that the UK Government's definition in 2020 was out of date and reliant on a colonial and Christocentric view of religion. In some ways the discussion of whether Buddhism is a religion should have been relegated to the scrap heap many years ago. We recognize religion not as a one-size–fits-all concept, but as a word or concept that is used to best fit the phenomenon that we are exploring. David Brazier (2014) has articulated this very clearly when he suggested that 'Buddhism is, has always been, and needs to continue to be understood as a religion' (xvii). Why this needs stating this bluntly will be explored further on, but two important points arise from its recognition as such:

1. Buddhism is a religion that seeks to answer life's questions.
2. Buddhism is a religion that influences the lives of many around the world.

I should note at this stage, and will return to this later, that while the chocolate box view of religion would have Buddhism rejecting the idea of 'a supreme being or entity or supreme being and entities', a *Pew Research Center Report* (2021) suggests that in India 43 per cent of Buddhists believe in God with absolute certainty, 23 per cent with less certainty and 33 per cent do not believe in God (7). This is a very blunt statistic as it doesn't unpack what is meant by God, and whether the respondents were thinking about the realm of gods, rather than a more Western idea of an omnipotent God. This will be unpacked further (see Chapter 2) but at this point it highlights the multifaceted nature of Buddhism. Indeed, John Strong (2015) suggests that it is more correct to speak of Buddhisms rather than a singular Buddhism – an approach that could be seen to have echoes of Richard Gombrich (1988) who recalls an experience where a group of British scholars failed to find any commonalities between any of the forms of Buddhism. Gombrich suggests that they went too far in this conclusion, and that there are some, but it does highlight that as teachers we need to recognize the limits of the Buddhism(s) we teach in the classroom. As highlighted in the Series Editor's Foreword, elements of 'Buddhism' that we now teach are an inheritance of a colonial approach to religion, rather than the history and structure of the Buddhist experience.

Beginning our understanding and teaching of Buddhism with the knowledge that it is messy and diverse enables students to engage with many different forms and experiences of Buddhism, or at least recognize that there is more than what they are learning. There is, however, still a need to establish a working definition of Buddhism and who is a Buddhist, as in the end there is a way of life that can be seen to be Buddhist.

What is Buddhism?

The appending of *ism* in Buddhism suggests that there is a body of beliefs, knowledge and practices associated with the Buddha that is worthy of study. Wilfred Cantwell Smith suggested that the defining of religions and their boundaries in the colonial period

> normally took the form of adding the Greek suffix '-ism' to a word used to designate the persons who are members of the religious community or followers of a given tradition. (1991, 62)

In some ways, it is a codifying of the aspects of a Buddhist way of life. It is, in its simplest form, a way of life and series of beliefs that is based on the teachings of the Buddha. As suggested earlier, this is only partially correct and could be seen to be the headline definition underneath which there is much more going on. Such a definition raises the question as to 'Who is the Buddha?' and what are the series of beliefs and practices which can be seen to be Buddhist in nature?

In exploring the codification or presentation of Buddhism in the classroom it would appear that the most common approach begins with an exploration of the life of the Buddha, Siddhartha Gautama. The religion of Buddhism is a religion that is based on his example and his teachings. Indeed, it has been expressed that his life is a suitable starting point because it encapsulates many of the aspects of Buddhist teaching and practice (Holt, 2022). This may be true, but it could be seen to be a justification of a view of Buddhism that was created through the Christian lens of colonialism. A religion that focussed around the life and example of an individual was intelligible and familiar to those Christians who observed the religions of India and other areas of the British Empire. It is important to recognize that Buddhism is not restricted to, nor was it originally founded by, the person of Siddhartha Gautama or Shakyamuni Buddha. In a Buddhist worldview, Siddhartha Gautama, *the* Buddha is the latest in a line of Buddhas over the aeons of time to have found the path to enlightenment and established the framework for others to follow. This does not negate his importance or impact, but it helps people realize that it is the truths that are of most importance as they seek for enlightenment. Karen Armstrong (2000) has noted that the nature of the path 'discovered' by the Buddha was, in reality, a rediscovery:

> [The Buddha] always insisted that he had simply discovered 'a path of great antiquity, an ancient trail, travelled by human beings in a far-off, distant era.' The other Buddhas, his predecessors, had taught this path an immeasurably long time ago, but this ancient knowledge had faded over the years and had been entirely forgotten. Gautama insisted that this insight was simply a statement of things 'as they really are'; the path was written into the very structure of existence. (75)

The focus of the study of Buddhism shifts ever so slightly, or significantly, with the knowledge that while the Buddha is central to the articulation of Buddhism in this aeon of existence, the truths elucidated are woven into the fabric of existence.

A Buddha (enlightened being) is significant within Buddhism as a being who has discovered the path to enlightenment for themselves. Within Theravada Buddhism (see Chapter 5) there is a separate designation of *arahant* (Skt: *arhat*) for someone who attains enlightenment by following the teachings of the Buddha. The *Samyutta Nikaya* records this distinction:

> The Tathagata – the worthy one, the rightly self-awakened one, who from disenchantment with consciousness, from dispassion, from cessation, from lack of clinging (for

consciousness) is released – is termed 'rightly self-awakened.' And a discernment-released monk – who from disenchantment with consciousness, from dispassion, from cessation, from lack of clinging (for consciousness) is released – is termed 'discernment-released'. (Samyutta Nikaya 22:58)

The major role of a Buddha, having attained enlightenment, is to teach others, as the teacher who is fully enlightened (*sattha*) gives their teaching (*sasana*) to those who would seek to follow the path of the Buddha (*savaka* or *sravaka*). As such, while fundamental to Buddhism, a focus on the Buddha to introduce or define Buddhism is to confuse the teaching with the teacher. The two are connected but are not necessarily synonymous. Without the Buddha, the truth of existence would still exist but would lie undiscovered.

With this as a background it is possible to move towards a qualified understanding of what Buddhism is. It bears repeating that any attempt at defining Buddhism is subject to the lens through which we view it. Donald Lopez (1995a) suggests that in exploring Buddhism we recognize the lens through which we view it and remove anything that clouds our understanding as much as possible:

> The question is not one of purging some contamination from our knowledge so that we might understand 'Buddhism' better, that (to use a Buddhist metaphor) by removing a cataract from our eye our vision of Buddhism may correspond more closely to its truth, our image gradually approximating its reality. (21)

This links very much with the concept of disciplinary lenses and worldviews within the classroom teaching of religion. Recognizing that we all have a positionality that brings with it assumptions, we are able to recognize that people who are defining Buddhism are doing so through their own lenses. As teachers, our responsibility is not so much to help students remove those lenses from themselves and others but to critically recognize them in their study of Buddhism. Rather than one accepted Buddhism there are many Buddhisms that are lived in the world today, and throughout history. There should not be one accepted Buddhism against which all others are judged.

Richard Gombrich (2006) fuses an approach to Buddhism that tries to strip the lenses with which we approach Buddhism and defines Buddhism as a religion thus:

> For Buddhists, religion is purely a matter of understanding and practising the Dhamma [Sanskrit: Dharma], understanding and practice which constitute progress towards salvation. They conceive salvation – or liberation, to use a more Indian term – as the total eradication of greed, hatred and delusion. To attain it is open to any human being, and it is ultimately the only thing worth attaining, for it is the only happiness which is not transient. (24)

This is a useful definition for teachers, as it provides an essentialist approach to Buddhism, that most Buddhists would recognize or at least not disagree with. This definition itself has issues. Gombrich notes that the use of the word 'salvation' is problematic, as it is using

Christocentric language to make sense of terminology that is translated in new contexts. David McMahan (2008) notes that this is perhaps an inevitable feature of Buddhism as it transforms in new contexts. Indeed, he notes that this has taken place throughout the history of Buddhism, as it has moved into new countries and cultures. It begins with the translation of words and continues in the transformation of Buddhism:

> There can never be a translation that carries all possible meanings and associations seamlessly from the original language and refuses all novel meanings and associations in the new context. Translation and transmission is inevitably – word-by-word, text-by-text, culture-by-culture – transformation. (18)

Thus, when we are defining Buddhism we must be aware of which Buddhism it is that we define. This adaptation of Buddhism to the context in which it finds itself makes the underlying message intelligible for those who receive it. Thus Japanese Buddhism has different expressions to Tibetan, and also to those found in the UK and other Western countries. The breadth of Buddhism means that while the message of the Buddha can be found at its heart there are many different ways that it finds expression.

This returns to the discussion earlier about the attempt to find that which is shared by all Buddhists. For many commentators and writers, the defining characteristic of Buddhism across all contexts is the going for refuge in the Three Refuges or Three Jewels:

- The *Buddha*
- The *dhamma* (*dharma*): teachings of the Buddha
- The *sangha*: the community of Buddhists

The Dalai Lama and Thubten Chodron (2014) have suggested that 'all Buddhist traditions agree that taking refuge in the Three Jewels is the demarcation of becoming a Buddhist' (17). It is important to note, however, that the understanding of each of these refuges may differ between traditions, and these will be explored in greater detail in Chapters 3 and 6. The concept of 'refuge' is highlighted in the declaration:

> I take refuge in the Buddha.
> I take refuge in the Dharma.
> I take refuge in the Sangha [English].

The statements are generally repeated three times and highlight the value (treasures/jewels) and safety (refuge) that can be found through taking refuge in these three things. In exploring the importance of the concept of refuge in the Three Jewels a Buddhist commented:

> A Buddhist takes refuge in *the Buddha*, Which means: one who is awake, one's own wakefulness, one who knows, one's own sense of knowing (it is not about worshipping the historical Buddha who is only one who came to know), One who knows what? *The dhamma*, which means: the way things are, that which is actual, that which is true when

realised leads to a Transformative insight that is beneficial to oneself, other and All ... the way to peace, the way to tie a shoe lace, the way to light a fire, the way to find facts, the way of peace, Alongside who? *The sangha*: the community, namely, the noble community. This is known as the triple gem principle. Ones goes to refuge. (emphasis in the original)

The taking of refuge in the Buddha, the dhamma and the sangha is not only a statement of belief, but a call to action. One Buddhist has suggested:

Being a Buddhist means you take refuge in the Buddha, Dharma and Sangha. This means you don't seek lasting happiness in worldly circumstances, but look inside your own mind. The purpose of Buddhist practice is to free oneself from suffering and find lasting happiness, and to help others to do likewise.

As such it is impossible to speak of Buddhism as a purely theoretical approach to life; it is a call to action. In writing this book it was a dilemma as to whether to begin a discussion with beliefs or actions, as the two are intertwined in understanding what Buddhism is. Many people see Buddhism as a way of life which is only understood in its expressions, while others suggest that in order to understand the expressions a knowledge of the beliefs and concepts is necessary.

The Buddha, the dhamma and the sangha will be explored in much greater detail; but as three unifying aspects of Buddhism, at least at a superficial level, they provide a framework in which we can find a working definition of Buddhism that is able to be used in the classroom. Against this background it is imperative that even this 'definition' is subject to interpretation across the Buddhist community. It is to the diversity that we now turn.

History and the definition of Buddhism

History is an important aspect of the definition of any religion. The shared history of a people and a community is often used to delineate the boundaries of such a community. Buddhism is no less reliant on history to establish the boundaries of who can be considered a Buddhist, but is used alongside/as part of the definitions and borders of the different schools and traditions.

As noted earlier the history of Buddhism begins aeons ago; however, within this time frame Buddhism can be seen to begin with Shakyamuni Buddha; the Buddha of the Shakyas, Siddhartha Gautama, who lived approximately 566 BCE to 486 BCE (Gethin, 1998, 14). These dates are not confirmed but are those that are usually accepted based on Pali sources that Ashoka was consecrated as king in 168 BCE, 218 years after the Buddha's death. Other sources place Ashoka's consecration 100 years after the Buddha's death. Rupert Gethin (1998) notes that 'there is no scholarly consensus' (14) but that most would now place his death closer to 400 BCE. Prior to the Buddha's death, one of his chief disciples, Ananda, has a conversation with him about the leadership of the sangha following his death. The Buddha signifies that people should be led by his teachings (the dharma/dhamma) and it is to those teachings that they should go for wisdom, and seek guidance from.

On first impression the delineation of Buddhism into the various traditions that arose from the Buddha's teachings which are taught within schools today seems very straightforward. It is often taught in terms of the three vehicles as a way to understand the various approaches to Buddhism that have developed through the centuries since the Buddha. The traditional threefold grouping suggests three main traditions within Buddhism: Nikaya, Mahayana and Vajrayana.

Hinayana/Nikaya Buddhism which is often translated as the 'lesser' or 'common' vehicle. This appellation has been given by those from the Mahayana tradition. Theravada, or Way of the Elders, is the only surviving school of Nikaya Buddhism and is to be found mainly within South and Southeast Asia. In light of this there are scholars who prefer to use geographical distinctions and developments in their description of the various Buddhisms (see, e.g. Hinnells, 2010 and Cantwell and Kawanami, 2013). The importance of geography in shaping different Buddhisms will be discussed in greater detail further on.

The idea of the three vehicles is rejected by Theravada Buddhists. Nikaya Buddhism is the oldest surviving form of Buddhism. Theravada Buddhists only accept the historical Buddha and teachings that can be historically linked to him. The beliefs about the Buddha reflect his place as the main focus of devotion and as a guide, teacher and exemplar. Although many see Mahayana 'the great vehicle' to have developed in India somewhere between the second century BCE and the first century CE it is not as clear-cut as might be suggested by some commentators. Sometimes Theravada is seen to be the 'original' Buddhism, but as is seen by the appellation of lesser, this does not always seem to be a positive aspect.

Though often described as a later development, perhaps even as a reclamation of Buddhism, it is possible to suggest that this threefold typology is seen by many, especially Mahanyana Buddhists, to trace its lineage back to the Buddha himself. This is most evident in the *Lotus Sutra*. The *Lotus Sutra's* full title, translated from Chinese, is 'wonderful Dharma lotus flower sutra' (Reeves, 2008, 1). The *Lotus Sutra* begins with the Buddha on Vulture Peak. He is surrounded by deities, monks, nuns and also many bodhisattva. The Buddha delivers a speech that uses the phrase 'skilful means' which causes some to question what he means. It is at this point that 5,000 thousand people leave the meeting. The Buddha declares that while in the past he has taught three paths or vehicles (see Chapter 5), there is really only one path, *buddhayana* (the Buddha vehicle). He illustrates this with the telling of a parable of a father enticing his children out of a burning building with the promise of three great vehicles, one pulled by goats, the second by deer and the final one by oxen. Although they are placated and happy with these vehicles, the Buddha reveals that there is really only one vehicle that is satisfactory. They may have set out on the path with one of three vehicles, but in reality there is only one:

> Therefore I use skilful means,
> Telling them of three vehicles,
> Enabling all living beings
> To understand the suffering of the threefold world ...
>
> It is for the sake of all beings,
> That by means of this parable
> I teach the One Buddha-Vehicle. (*Lotus Sutra*, 127)

Although there is a later suggested date for the *Lotus Sutra*, it illustrates a belief within Mahayana Buddhism that rather than a later development the teachings and practices found therein are an authentic teaching of the Buddha. This was missed by some because they left the audience with the Buddha, or because they did not understand. This will be explored in greater depth in Chapter 5.

The development of the three-vehicle typology is expanded with the inclusion of *Vajrayana* (the Diamond Vehicle) as a school or tradition of Buddhism. Simplistically Vajrayana (also known as Tantric Buddhism) developed in India in approximately the fifth century. Vajrayana can be seen to be a part of Mahayana Buddhism, and the four main schools of Tibetan Vajrayana Buddhism identify themselves as belonging to Mahayana. Mahayana itself can be seen as a precursor for the practice of Vajrayana with its focus on compassion. Rather than the promise of buddhahood in the future, Vajrayana highlights the importance of the teacher who shows the student the path to enlightenment and the possibility of buddhahood in this lifetime. For many, this can be seen as a further linear development of Buddhist teaching and practice. Using a framework developed from Peter Harvey's (2021b) work it is possible to suggest a historically linear development of the different vehicles:

Stage 1   The life of the Buddha

Stage 2   First Council after the Buddha's passing established his teachings and the vinaya for the ordained monks and nuns

Stage 3   Second and Third Councils and the first of many schisms eighty-six years later. At this time disagreements began usually over the rules of monastic discipline, though there were disagreements about doctrine too. At the time of the Second Council the *Sthaviras* (Pali: Theras) split from the majority of the Buddhist tradition identified as *Mahasamghikas* (those belonging to the universal sangha). Theravada Buddhists today would identify themselves as being the inheritors of Sthaviras. A fourth-century text the Dipavamsa identifies Theravada as original and supreme:

> These 17 sects are schismatic,
> only one is non-schismatic.

With the non-schismatic sect,
there are eighteen in all.
Like a great banyan tree,
the Theravada is supreme,
The Dispensation of the Conqueror,
complete, without lack or excess.
The other sects arose
like thorns on the tree. (Dipavamsa, 4:90–1; Sujato, 2012a)

Stage 4 Third century BCE. The Sthaviras developed three separate schools of thought: the Pudgalavada, the Sarvastivada and Vibhajyavada. The Sthaviras tended to be conservative in terms of discipline, but there were differences between the groups in terms of belief. There was an increase in the spread of Buddhism during the reign of Ashoka.

Stage 5 Second century BCE. Between approximately 150 BCE and 100 CE Mahayana is seen to have developed, perhaps arising out of *Mahasamghika* and *Sarvastivada* traditions and teachings. It then 'developed many sub-strands, which led to forms of Buddhism in China and the rest of East Asia, and in Tibet' (Harvey, 2021b, 191). These Mahayana traditions tended to arise around new texts attributed to the Buddha that emphasized the buddha-nature of all and a more compassion-based focus to Buddhism. Mahayana Buddhism spread in India, East Asia, China and many other lands.

Stage 6 circa Fifth-century Vajrayana Buddhism developed with a focus on tantric exercises and mantras.

Stage 7 Sixth century. Buddhism arrived in Japan via Korea.

It should be noted that there was much more happening within the Buddhist world within these years, and the timeline is rather crude, as is the decision to stop the timeline in the sixth century. Exploration of Buddhism in particular contexts will be developed throughout this book.

One problem of the exploration of the threefold typology as a linear development with the clear divisions that we see in today's world is the shared histories and developments that can be seen to be within Nikaya and Mahayana forms of Buddhism. Indeed, many monks were within the Nikaya tradition but following what could be seen to be a Mahayana path. Indeed, Shantideva, the eighth-century author of *A Guide to the Bodhisattva's Way of Life*, wrote at a time in India when 'Mahayana was well established' (Batchelor, 2015, vii). Despite it being well established, Tshering (2015) suggests that 'outwardly, Shantideva was a [Theravada] monk strictly observing the code of monastic discipline, secretly he was a realized tantric adept. But most importantly of all he was a Bodhisattva' (iii). Lopez highlights that the traditional view of decline and rejuvenation is too simplistic and not borne out by the facts:

One difficulty with such an approach is the almost unavoidable propensity to see the Hinayana-Mahayana-Vajrayana sequence as a value-laden development of one kind or another, in which one member of the triad is exalted above the others. (Lopez, 1995, 6)

Such an approach suggests that 'one vehicle ceases before the next becomes fully formed' (Lopez, 1995, 7). There is overlap in terms of history and geography. It can be seen that the various traditions of Buddhism develop somewhat independently in different geographical locations. It is the emphasis, and influence, of adherents in these areas that sees developments in Buddhism. It is not that Buddhism was subsumed by local customs and beliefs, but that through interplay between Buddhist teaching and the local culture, beliefs and customs that a Buddhism intelligible to its immediate context ultimately developed.

Despite this fluidity of movement, it is possible to see the influence of geography on the development of the different Buddhisms. John Strong (2015) further recognizes not only historical differences that find their manifestation in the Buddhisms of today but also cultural and geographical diversity. He begins his exploration of the various traditions through a narration of the design of Lumbini, the birthplace of the Buddha and a UNESCO World Heritage Site. He outlines the different monasteries, temples,[1] meditation centres, pagodas and other buildings that can be found within Lumbini and uses them to understand the modern diversity of Buddhism. The buildings that can be found in Lumbini include:

- Mahamaya World Peace Buddhist Monastery established by the Maha Bodhi Society of India
- The Sri Lanka Monastery
- The Gautami Centre for Nuns (international in outlook but established by a Nepalese Theravada bhikkhuni)
- Lokamani Pagoda Vipassana Centre established by Satya Narayan Goenka
- The Panditarama International Vipassana Centre
- Zhonghua si (the Chinese monastery)
- Dae Sung Suk Ga Sa (the Korean monastery)
- Nippondera (Japan Temple) established by the Sokyo (Whole Teaching) Temple
- The World Peace Buddha Relic Stupa/World Peace Pagoda established by Nipponzan Myohoji, a Nicheren tradition
- Linh Son Buddhist Temple funded by French/Vietnamese Buddhists
- Viet Nam Phat Quoc Tu Temple (the Vietnam Buddhist monastery)
- The Great Lotus Stupa of Tibetan style funded by the Tara Foundation of Germany
- The Lumbini Udyana Mahachaitya from the Kagyu school with funding from the United Trungram Buddhist Foundation. Also called the World Centre for Peace and Unity

There are many other buildings, but the unmistakable point that is being made is that although this is a place of unity, there is much diversity even within the divisions that may have traditionally been accepted. Many of these are based on geographic and cultural differences rather than the central aspects of Buddhist teaching. This is important to note; as we explore different expressions of Buddhism we must be aware of vast differences within traditions, and between countries. One example of this that is emblematic of the diversity of expression within other countries is the place of Buddhism within Japan. The points that I make here will be illustrative and necessarily brief. Further exploration will be undertaken at different points within the remainder of this book. One of the largest schools of Buddhism within Japan is Nichiren Buddhism and was established based on the teachings of Nichiren in the thirteenth century. The main focus of Nichiren's teachings surrounded the *Lotus Sutra* and in the centuries since there can be seen to have been divisions within the Nichiren community that led to different groups. These divisions have often surrounded the assimilation of Japanese traditions and thoughts into the practice of Buddhism. For example, in one of the earlier schisms one point of division was the honouring of local kami (deities) and the adoption of Tendai thought (see Stone, 1999). In the twentieth century a Nichiren-inspired Japanese Buddhism developed, illustrating the symbiotic nature of the relationship with Nichiren Buddhism and Japan. Paul Williams (2009) has highlighted how, for some, this has been seen to be a weakness of Buddhism, but in reality it was so for many Buddhists:

> Mahayanists in particular see adaptation, and perhaps even syncretism, as a virtue in the Dharma, enabling the teachings to be adapted to the needs of hearers, and thereby indicating the wisdom and compassion of the Omniscient Buddha. (2)

This symbiotic relationship can be seen to be replicated in various countries and contexts. Indeed, Triratna Buddhism (originally Friends of the Western Buddhist Order) can be seen as a recasting of Buddhist principles for the modern world in the West, where perhaps a hard division between the ordained and lay sangha was not practicable, or the touching of money would be a necessity for all (see Chapter 10). Throughout history, these cultural adaptations have ensured that Buddhism flourished in certain areas, but for many Buddhist observers it would have maintained its essence that enabled the Buddha's teachings to continue to be followed. This recognizes the 'messiness' of religion and will help teachers explain the *Pew Research Center Report* (2021) which suggested that in India 43 per cent of Buddhists believe in God with absolute certainty, 23 per cent with less certainty and 33 per cent do not believe in God. Though their immediate expression may differ, it is not that Buddhists would accept the existence of a 'personal' God, but there are 'gods' both in terms of the Buddha's experiences (see Chapter 3) and also in terms of the utilization of existing beliefs to help understand and frame Buddhism in different countries.

It is perhaps unsatisfactory that in seeking to define Buddhism we have only briefly touched upon the traditional three-vehicle typology, and the history and development of

Buddhism has only been superficially touched on at this point. In rejecting the different approaches to the defining of Buddhism, this book also accepts the different ways of defining boundaries. The three vehicles are a useful shorthand which will incorporate significant differences in the purpose of life (see Chapter 5) and in the view of the nature of existence. However, to suggest that there is a linear development that culminates in clearly defined boundaries today would be to miss the vibrancy and diversity within each of these. There will undoubtedly be areas of agreement and disagreement. There will be some who are termed 'Mahayana' who will have more in common with some 'Theravada' Buddhists than some fellow Mahayana Buddhists. No typology seems to fit nicely; yet as Buddhist develops in the modern world the delineations are becoming more obvious and perhaps important to those within Buddhism.

Modern Buddhism

As Buddhism has moved into the 'West' and encountered modernism, there has been a shift in the way Buddhism has been understood. Sometimes this has been within the context of the search for the original and authentic Buddhism. In some ways as we explore the Buddhism that we teach within the classroom, it could be argued that we focus on Modern Buddhism and the inheritance that we have received through this modernizing process. This 'modernizing' of Buddhism is within the context of the 'Modernism' movement; David McMahan (2008) has suggested that:

> Many modernizing interpreters of Buddhism, both Asian and western, have proffered the theme of the rescue of the modern West – which they claimed has lost its spiritual bearings through modernization – by the humanizing wisdom of the East. In order for the rescue to succeed, however, Buddhism itself had to be transformed, reformed and modernized – purged of mythological elements and 'superstitious' cultural accretions. (5)

Reflecting on McMahan's argument it is possible to observe that the wider discussion about Buddhism's appeal to the modern world is that it is countercultural and an antidote to the materialism that can be found within many societies. It is also possible to see evidence of the point that he makes, that Buddhism has been transformed to fit the demands of the modern world.

In the previous section of this chapter we drew on the work of John Strong to highlight the cultural and geographic diversity of Buddhism. Buddhism is a religion that has incorporated elements of its 'host' countries in a way that might be rejected by other religions. The objective truths that it teaches can find expression in the context of existing beliefs and traditions. Thus we see differing expressions and practices within Tibetan and Japanese Buddhism. For many Buddhists this is a strength as it enabled Buddhist teachings and principles to be understood within the context of their cultural identity. There are many in the modern world, however, who would see such developments as additions to the message of the Buddha, and a form of syncretism that should be rejected.

As such, there are what McMahan (2008) identified as 'superstitious cultural accretions' that modern Buddhism has sought to remove from the message and practice of Buddhism. One such example that will be discussed further on in Chapter 3 is in the narration of the story of Siddhartha Gautama's life and his past lives. On exploring 'traditional' narratives of the Buddha's lives, there are many of the gods, such as Brahma, who are involved at different points. The mystical and more miraculous elements of the Buddha's lives seem to be overlooked in favour of the more rational aspects of the message. This will be explored at various points throughout the book, where stories, beliefs and expressions are discussed in terms of 'traditional' and 'modern' understandings.

At this point, we are faced with a dilemma as teachers. I feel it is important to teach religion in the way that it is understood and lived today (see the next section) rather than as a historical anthropological study. If, in the contexts that we teach, a modern understanding of Buddhism is the largest expression then should that be the one that receives most attention in the classroom? In some ways, yes; but we also need to be prepared to explore the fact that this is not the only expression of Buddhism that is in the modern world, and also that it is not necessarily the Buddhism that was first taught by the Buddha, and has been reclaimed in the modern world. As with all expressions of religions and worldviews, we need to explore their historical developments and influences. For younger age-group classrooms this may be the recognition of 'some' and 'many' in our language; as the students we teach get older it is possible to interrogate the influences and inheritance of Buddhism today.

The lived reality of Buddhism

Even within the different traditions of Buddhism there is also the lived reality for individuals. This is an important aspect of the teaching of any religion or worldview. As explored in the Series Editor's Foreword earlier on, when we are teaching religions and worldviews we need to recognize the diversity, and this is most effectively done through an exploration of the lived experience of followers. We have similarly recognized that there are 'essential' aspects of belief or practices that are Buddhist and these will be discussed in subsequent chapters. At this point it is important to note the lived experience as this will frame the teachings and practices that we explore. David McMahan (2008) illustrates this vividly with his description of very different individuals who would all consider themselves to be Buddhist. Perhaps in our own experiences we could list a similar mix of Buddhists that we know and associate with. Individuals who he describes include:

- 'A Western Buddhist sympathizer' who practices meditation on a daily basis and attends meditation retreats all focussed around a statue of the Buddha. She is still an Anglican and sees no conflict between her meditation and her Christianity, as she has no formal links with Buddhist groups. This lady has begun to develop a Buddhist ethic with a focus on an increasing vegetarianism and a desire to attain peace in her life and the world. Indeed, she seeks to live 'more deeply, richly, and compassionately' rather than seeking to escape the world (McMahan, 2008, 30). Mahan suggests that this is the type of 'Buddhist' people are most likely to meet within the Western world.

- 'A Thai laywoman' who follows the prescribed ethical rules that she sees as Buddhist, as they are taught within the sangha. She observes rules and rituals in the hope of gaining karmic merit to produce a positive rebirth for herself and her family. She gives dana to the monastery and observes rituals around stupas. She believes in spirits and wears tokens and amulets imbued with power. Although not able to describe complex beliefs she is immersed in Buddhism 'through her family, her modest schooling, and … Buddhist culture' (McMahan, 2008, 31).

- 'An American Dharma teacher' who first encountered Buddhism while travelling in India. She attended weekly *zazen* meditation meetings with a Zen teacher. Through many years of practice she became a Zen master and teaches others zazen. While she bows to the Buddha she recognizes that this is 'bowing to the Buddha nature on oneself' (McMahan, 2008, 32). She tries to make Zen teachings accessible to all, and to remove cultural accretions that included patriarchal and hierarchical structures. She feels it an important aspect of her worldview to speak out for human rights.

- 'A traditional Monk'; although Tibetan he lives in exile in India in a monastery where his 'primary activities are participating in rituals and pursuing [a] rich intellectual life' (McMahan, 2008, 33). In his ritual life he offers prayers to different deities, recites sutras, performs rites for the guardians of the monastery, casts out evil spirits and cures illness. There are non-material entities who are an integral part of his worldview including 'ghosts, local spirits, … and … deities, as well as Buddhas and bodhisattvas of the traditional Mahayana pantheon' (McMahan, 2008, 34).

These four people are emblematic of Buddhists who can be found around the world. It is theirs and others' voices that need to be heard in the classroom to help students understand the multifaceted nature of Buddhism. A Buddhism which, as referred to earlier, is both atheistic but also has over 66 per cent of adherents in India believing in a deity. One of the approaches to teaching religion and worldviews within the classroom referred to earlier is the ethnographic approach that takes account and utilizes the voices of individuals in our teaching.

The question will quite naturally arise as to how there can be so much diversity within Buddhism. There is the intellectually demanding approach to Buddhism where people seek to understand every aspect of belief such as the nature of the self or no-self and what that really means. In contrast there is the so-called popular Buddhism where people live a life of belief and trust. The rules are in place and the virtues extolled; little more is needed in knowing how to live. This diversity of approach to Buddhism is evidenced in the Simpsons episode where Lisa becomes a Buddhist. 'She of Little Faith' is Episode 6 of Season 13. In this episode Lisa becomes disenchanted with the commercialism of her local church and searches for a new faith. She stumbles upon the Springfield Buddhist Temple where she meets the characters Lenny and Carl, along with 'the world's most famous Buddhist': Richard Gere. Various elements of the beliefs and practices of Buddhism and the individuals involved are explored.

- Lenny follows Buddhism to achieve inner peace as it's the only way to deal with the children.
- The buddharupa as the focus in the 'temple' is Budai or the future Maitreya Buddha.
- Richard Gere is raking the sand in a Zen garden.
- The Dalai Lama is identified as the fourteenth reincarnation of Avalokitesvara.
- Freedom from desire enables a person to be free from suffering.
- Richard Gere desires a free Tibet.
- Carl desires a meatball sandwich.
- All things are impermanent and empty of inherent existence.
- Buddhism is concerned with the pursuit of enlightenment as there are no creator gods.
- Lisa plants her own bodhi tree to meditate beneath.
- While Lisa chants *om mani padme hum*, Lenny and Carl are chanting 'Who likes short shorts'.
- Buddhism respects the diversity of other traditions and it is possible to celebrate Christmas, and worship at church with her family.

When I have used this excerpt in the classroom, I have had students look for elements that are Buddhist and those that are at odds with the Buddhism we have studied. The expected responses of inaccuracies would surround the use of Budai as a focus for the entire temple, the eating of a meatball sandwich and the syncretism of attending church while adopting a Buddhist worldview. Other aspects may have elements of accuracy but the combining of them all could be seen to create a pastiche that is not sympathetic to, or even disrespectful of, Buddhist tradition. One Buddhist has suggested that Buddhism is not about outward action or even being labelled a Buddhist:

> Some people have fixed ideas as to what a Buddhist, Christian, Muslim or Jew is and so if I say I am one of them things, the person who does not think critically may associate me with their belief of what they think it means to be a Buddhist, Christian, Jew or Muslim And so I am careful.

Essentially, that a person cannot be judged by labels that are commonly applied. This highlights the problematic nature of teaching Buddhism within the classroom. Whose Buddhism do we teach?

Referring back to the Series Editor's Foreword, it is necessary for the teacher to recognize this diversity but also to establish the 'essential' aspects of Buddhism that should form the central aspects of a curriculum.

Thoughts for the classroom

Throughout this chapter we have tried to define Buddhism and to outline who is a Buddhist. To an extent it has been purposeful to problematize these questions. The moment that we think we have codified an approach to, or understanding of, Buddhism there can be an exception found that develops the definition that we are working with. In exploring the history, the three vehicles, modern Buddhism and the lived reality of Buddhist life, we begin to recognize that there is no objectively ideal way to define Buddhism. Whatever boundaries are drawn or definition developed, they are all at best approximations. Many teachers will have spent their careers teaching the threefold typology where Theravada is seen to be the 'original'; or that Mahayana was a later doctrinal development that expanded the concept of Buddha and shifted the goal of Buddhists, and that Vajrayana sought the same goal as Mahayana but through different means. This approach could be seen to privilege certain Buddhist expressions found throughout the world. Very early on in my career I attended a meeting to discuss the curriculum in the local area. One Buddhist became very cross as she realized that the Buddhism to be taught established Theravada as the orthodox expression, and that Mahayana was schismatic.

As teachers we need to be very careful as to how we speak of and teach about Buddhism. With all of the differences that we have explored within Buddhism in this chapter, there are numerous traditions to be found within the UK that have not been mentioned, though some will be found within the umbrella appellations of the three vehicles, which as an approach to Buddhism would be rejected by many Theravada Buddhists. Groups that will find expression within the UK, in addition to those termed 'non-sectarian', according to buddhanet.info include:

- Bodhicharaya
- Chinese Zen Buddhism
- Community of Interbeing
- Dechen
- Forest Sangha
- Gudo Nishijima Roshi
- Humanistic Buddhism
- Japanese Soto
- Japanese Tendai
- Kadampa

- Karma-Kagyu
- Korean Chogye
- Mahasi Sayadaw
- New Kadampa
- Nichiren
- Nichiren Daishonin
- Nichiren Shu
- Order of Buddhist Contemplation
- Pure Land
- Sakya Tibetan Tradition
- Soka Gakkai International
- Soto Zen
- Thai Western Forest Monastery
- Theravada
- Theravada Forest Sangha
- Thich Nhat Hahn Tradition
- Tibetan
- Tibetan Gelugpa
- Tibetan Nyingma
- Vajrayana
- Vietnamese
- Western Chan Fellowship
- Zen

It is impossible for a teacher to cover each of these or even make a cursory mention of aspects of the different beliefs, practices and emphases that delineate them from others. This is in addition to the expressions of Buddhism particular to an individual. It is for this reason that at the start of an exploration of Buddhism that the diversity should be discussed, and then movement is made into an exploration of the essential aspects of such. The subsequent chapters of this book will adopt this approach, and then in tandem with suggestions for the classroom, differences will be noted as applicable that could be for the interest of the teacher, and also for application in the classroom.

Part 1

Key concepts in Buddhism

1

The nature of existence

Having established the complexity of defining Buddhism, it then becomes problematic to know where to begin a study of its expression in the twenty-first century. In the classroom the study of Buddhism often begins with an exploration of the life of the Buddha, Siddhartha Gautama or Shakyamuni Buddha. In some ways, as explored in the Introduction and also developed in further detail in Chapter 3, this is the result of a Western Christian Colonial understanding of religion which begins with a 'figure'. Indeed, in an introduction to Buddhism elsewhere (see Holt, 2022) I have suggested that the Buddha's life is a useful starting place as it is an allegory for the most important aspects of Buddhist belief. It is a conscious decision in this book to begin elsewhere. The Buddha is important, but he has shown the way and as he suggested prior to his death it is the dhamma/dharma that is the most important source of beliefs and how to live.

This is the second problem in the decision of where to start; do we start with the practices of Buddhism as these are the most important aspects of life? Or do we start with the beliefs that can be seen to underpin these expressions? A knowledge of the teachings of the Buddha is insufficient to be Buddhist, or realize the truth of reality. Thich Nhat Hanh (1998a) suggests that people must 'remember that a sutra or a Dharma talk is not insight in and of itself. It is a means of presenting insight, using words and concepts … The Buddha said many times, "My teaching is like a finger pointing to the moon. Do not mistake the finger for the moon"' (17). One of the stories told of the Buddha relates to the futility of beliefs by themselves, which also illustrates why some 'big questions' that many want answering by religion remain unanswered in Buddhism. In this parable a man is wounded by a poisoned arrow. His family wish to take him to a doctor, but he refuses treatment until he knows who shot the arrow, the background of the archer, the kind of bow used and so on. Only with these answers would he accept the treatment offered. But the man might well die before receiving these answers. Just so, with many answers about the machinations of the universe and many of the more metaphysical issues that occupy the minds of many.

It is against this background that this, and subsequent chapters, discuss aspects of the beliefs and practices of Buddhism. The aim of these chapters is to articulate the beliefs and practices of Buddhism as typically understood, though with the recognition of the diversity of understanding that will necessarily be a part of religion. It is also with the acknowledgement that these beliefs lead to different expressions and way to live as a Buddhist today.

The choice of the nature of existence as the first belief to be explored is motivated by the fact that understanding the nature of reality will enable all other aspects of Buddhism to be put into perspective. This chapter will provide the context for other aspects of the Dharma that will be explored in subsequent chapters.

The Four Noble Truths

In the *Dhammacakkappavattana Sutta* (Setting the Wheel of Dhamma in Motion) the Buddha is seen to have set the Wheel of Dhamma in motion through his realization of the Four Noble Truths. The Four Noble Truths are the first things that the Buddha is believed to have taught. Indeed in his telling of the parable of the poisoned arrow he suggests that many things lie undisclosed by him; he then elucidates what has been disclosed by him and the reasons behind their disclosure:

> And what is disclosed by me? 'This is stress,' is disclosed by me. 'This is the origination of stress,' is disclosed by me. 'This is the cessation of stress,' is disclosed by me. 'This is the path of practice leading to the cessation of stress,' is disclosed by me. And why are they disclosed by me? Because they are connected with the goal, are fundamental to the holy life. They lead to disenchantment, dispassion, cessation, calming, direct knowledge, self-awakening, unbinding. That's why they are disclosed by me. (*Culamalukya Sutta*)

The Buddha used a well-known Indian medical formula to help explain the Four Noble Truths to his friends. Buddhists believe that the Buddha's teaching is a cure for the world's illnesses.

- What is the illness?
- What has caused the illness?
- Does a cure exist?
- The remedy – what does the patient need to do in order to be cured?

This might lead teachers to present the Four Noble Truths as simple and straightforward; the Buddha suggests otherwise, to Ananda. In using the examples of shooting an arrow to hit a target, he asks Ananda if that is easier than splitting a horsehair into seven. He further elaborates in the *Horsehair Vala Sutta* that understanding the Four Noble Truths requires much more care, even more than splitting horsehair. The realization of the Four Noble Truths is not a one-time event that then influences each act or belief afterwards. Rather, the understanding of the Four Noble Truths and their impact on a person's life is a process that will underpin every outworking in acts and beliefs. One Buddhist has commented that these Truths lie at the heart of what Buddhism is and what it means to be a Buddhist:

One versed in the dhamma has realised:

- The four noble truths: within life is the potential for suffering,
- That there are general and unique causes to suffering – namely, attachment, ignorance, and aversion (three poisons) – the 5 hindrances (ill-will, sloth-torpor, restlessness/unhelpful remorsefulness, infatuation with sense desires, and doubt of one's own abilities and in the dhamma – the way things are).
- That there is a way to uproot these factors.
- That there is a path that leads to the uprooting of suffering which comprises of: reflection, thinking, critical thought, meditation (awareness of breath and loving kindness meditation), discipline, noble friendship and an openness to learning.

At the same time, however, it should be noted that for Buddhists the Noble Truths are not just beliefs but objective truths that highlight the nature of existence. The Buddha did not create the Four Noble Truths, they always existed; in a Buddhist worldview he realized them (though there are differences surrounding the understanding of such which are explored in Chapter 3). The Truths themselves are not that which are 'noble'; rather, they are truths that are realized by the 'noble ones', those who grasp the reality of existence. Teachers need to be careful in presenting the Four Noble Truths as first this, then that. They may appear simple, but their implications are vast.

The First Noble Truth: Dukkha

The First Noble Truth is *dukkha*, or the reality of suffering. This is understood and taught in different ways in the classroom. The teacher needs to be careful to be precise in their explanations as it will be easy to slip into lazy descriptions that are not completely incorrect but do not recognize the diversity and depth of the reality of dukkha and suffering within Buddhism.

The Buddha is reported to have taught in the *Dhammacakkappavattana Sutta*:

Now this, monks, is the noble truth of stress: Birth is stressful, aging is stressful, death is stressful; sorrow, lamentation, pain, distress, and despair are stressful; association with the unbeloved is stressful, separation from the loved is stressful, not getting what is wanted is stressful. In short, the five clinging-aggregates are stressful.

It is notable in this translation that dukkha is translated as 'stress' rather than the more common 'suffering' and highlights the limitations of translation in aiding understanding of specific concepts. Glenn Wallis (2007) suggests that in translating dukkha into English we have accepted 'suffering' as the default, but that it is imperfect and only refers to one expression of dukkha. He suggests that solely using suffering as the translation is 'drama-queenish'. He prefers the term 'unease' but recognizes that the concept is much wider than this and that the lexicon is an unending continuum that includes words such as:

faint unsettledness
irritation
impatience
annoyance
frustration
disappointment
dissatisfaction
aggravation
tension
stress
anxiety
vexation
pain
desperation
sorrow
sadness
suffering
misery
agony
anguish (120–1).

Recognizing the wider scope of the term 'dukkha' enables Buddhists to develop a greater understanding of suffering and how this is found in life. Walpola Rahula (1997) suggests something similar when he writes:

> It is admitted that the term dukkha in the First Noble Truth contains, quite obviously, the ordinary meaning of 'suffering', but in addition it also includes deeper ideas such as 'imperfection', 'impermanence', 'emptiness', 'insubstantiality'. It is difficult therefore to find one word to embrace the whole conception of the term dukkha as the First Noble Truth, and so it is better to leave it untranslated, than to give an inadequate and wrong idea of it by conveniently translating it as 'suffering' or 'pain'. (17)

The expansiveness and nature of dukkha is similarly diverse within Buddhism. The truth of suffering has led to some suggesting that 'everything is suffering' or 'life is suffering.' Thich Nhat Hanh (1998a) rejects this interpretation of the Buddha's teaching and suggests that it is a later interpolation. Hanh notes that this approach may be helpful in realizing when one may be becoming too attached to suffering but that it is not the original teaching of the Buddha. Rather, the Buddha 'says that he only wants us to recognize suffering when it is present and to recognize joy when suffering is absent' (21). Thanissaro Bhikkhu (2022) similarly notes that the Buddha never actually said that 'life is suffering'; rather, he outlined aspects of life that were 'stressful' such as birth and aging.

This understanding is somewhat at odds with the received understanding of the First Noble Truth, but it serves to recognize a more positive view of existence, and also of the Buddhist worldview. This is not to suggest that Buddhism is optimistic, neither is it considered pessimistic. Rahula indeed rejects both of these in favour of 'realistic', with neither an exaggeration of suffering or offering false hope.

Utilizing suffering as a truth or fact of existence helps people understand the unsatisfactoriness of the life experience. As such, the suffering that exists or that people experience helps in developing an understanding of experience, and the impermanence of everything (anicca) (which will be explored further on). In many Buddhist understandings of suffering there tend to be three types of dukkha that people experience in their lives:

1. *Dukkha-dukkha* – the suffering of suffering. In this understanding this aspect of suffering is that which is identified universally as such. These might include the pains of illness, injury, old-age, painful experiences and so on.

2. *Viparinama-dukkha* – the suffering of change. This is linked with anicca (one of the Three Marks of Existence – see further on), where people suffer because of the changing nature of things, relationships and life in general. The change that occurs means that there is frustration in life, and also the associated view that because everything changes a person can never be satisfied.

3. *Sankhara-dukkha* – the suffering of existence, sometimes described as the suffering of conditioned existence (this will be explored in greater detail further on when discussing dependent origination). In some ways this can be seen to be a peculiarly Buddhist understanding of dukkha and the recognition that everything that exists is dependent on something else. This is the truth of dukkha, that life is unsatisfactory and impermanent. With this lying beyond everything, then it is possible to understand that everything comes to an end and may ultimately be unsatisfactory in terms of existence.

Melvin McLeod (2022) utilizes a shorthand to outline these three types of suffering: 'Losing what we want, getting what we don't want, and our underlying feelings of fear and unease.' He then adds a fourth: 'The suffering caused by other people and their egos' (38). Recognizing the different types of dukkha will enable Buddhists to be clearer as they seek to establish the Four Noble Truths in their lives, and seek to find a solution to dukkha.

This threefold typology is not the only understanding of the nature of dukkha that can be found within Buddhism. The Dalai Lama and Thubten Chodron (2014) outline that in Pali and Sanskrit traditions there are sixteen attributes of the Four Noble Truths, meaning that there are four aspects to each. For the truth of dukkha the four attributes are:

Sanskrit

1. The aggregates (see the Five Skandhas/Khandas further on) are impermanent and constantly changing.
2. The aggregates are subject to pain, passions and karma.
3. The aggregates are empty (see further on: sunyata) because they are impermanent.
4. The aggregates do not have a self-sufficient existence (see further on: anatta).

Pali

1. The aggregates are oppressive, or weighed down by the cycle of samsara.
2. The aggregates are conditioned, meaning that acts performed for positive karma are unsatisfactory.
3. The aggregates burn like fire because of desires.
4. The aggregates are subject to change.

Utilizing the threefold typology of suffering mentioned earlier, and also the focus on the aggregates as one of the main aspects of dukkha, Thich Nhat Hanh (1998a) suggests that their delineation is 'an attempt to justify the universalization of suffering', and in so doing, we could be led to ask the question: 'Where is the joy?' (22). Thich Nhat Hanh's point is well-taken; if we focus on suffering in our teaching of Buddhism we present a very pessimistic view of existence. Whereas, in his view, a dukkha, as one of the Three Marks of Existence, is replaced by nirvana in many writings, and changes completely the focus of existence. Rather than seeking for the truth of suffering in every experience, Buddhists would seek for the positive outworking of such.

Despite this suggestion for the Three Marks of Existence, it is important to recognize that the First Noble Truth is that of dukkha. Although suffering might be a first port of call in our explanations for students, it should not be the end. There is a vast difference between saying that 'life is suffering' instead of 'life is unsatisfactory' or that 'suffering is a characteristic of life'. In a theme that will be returned to in every chapter of this book, there is a middle way between pessimism and optimism, and Buddhism, through its recognition of dukkha as the First Noble Truth, would find its place there.

Dependent origination

This understanding of the Four Noble Truths links very clearly with dependent origination/arising (pratityasamutpada/paticcasamuppada). The centrality of dependent origination in helping to understand the nature of dukkha and also to link it to the Second Noble Truth is a central aspect of dharma. The Buddha is reported to have said:

> I shall teach you the Dhamma: 'When this exists, that is; due to the arising of this, that arises. When this doesn't exist, that is not; due to the cessation of this, that ceases.'
> (*Cuḷasakuludayi Sutta*, 79:8)

This belief highlights the belief that everything is interconnected, and dependent (i.e. not independent), on other aspects and events in the universe. Everything that occurs does so dependent on causes and conditions that pre-exist. The Dalai Lama and Thubten Chodron (2014) suggest:

> Contemplating causal dependence leads us to understand that all functioning things do not exist by their own power. That they arise dependent on causes and conditions indicate that they exist. Thus they are both empty and existent. (177)

The belief in dependent origination is inherently linked with the belief of emptiness or sunyata. The end of the quotation mentioned earlier suggests that all things are both empty and yet existent. The *Heart Sutra* indicates that everything is empty:

> The Bodhisattva Avalokita,
> while moving in the deep course
> of Perfect Understanding,
> shed light on the five skandhas and
> found them equally empty. (Thich Nhat Hanh, 2017b, 128)

It is important to note that, in discussing, sunyata emptiness does not mean nothingness. For something to be empty there needs to be something that it is empty of. Thich Nhat Hanh (2012a) suggests an answer to what existence is empty of:

> When Avalokita says that our sheet of paper is empty, he means it is empty of a separate, independent existence. It cannot just be by itself. It has to inter-be with the sunshine, the cloud, the forest, the logger, the mind, and everything else. It is empty of a separate self. But, empty of a separate self means full of everything … 'Emptiness' means empty of a separate self. It is full of everything, full of life. The word 'emptiness' should not scare us. It is a wonderful word. To be empty does not mean to be non-existent. (416–17)

In this understanding, while the form may be 'empty' it is actually full of everything. Sunyata thus becomes an important aspect of existence and the nature of dependent origination. This aspect of sunyata is exemplified in the Six Elements Practice of meditation, taught by the Buddha in the *Dhatu-Vibhanga Sutta* (see Chapters 7 and 9). Bodhipaksa (2007) highlights that as each element is reflected upon, it is given back to whence it came: earth to earth, water to water and so on. The resultant emptiness is a realization of everything being interconnected and that emptiness is full of everything: 'I'm no longer separate and small, but an intimate part of the vast cycle of the elements.'

The idea of the piece of paper is a very evocative image. When one looks through it and sees its emptiness, a person is also able to see its fullness as it contains the efforts of the logger, the tree from which it came, the water and the sun that gave it life, and so on. When extended to the existence of a person, the memories, the experiences, the people, the physical moments and so on are all part of the idea of emptiness and no permanent self (see Chapter 2). The positive nature of sunyata is central to the way that a Buddhist should view life. Emptiness enables a person to recognize the changing and impermanent nature of themselves and of existence more widely. It is this that highlights the first of the Three Marks of Existence (*trilakshana*) or *anicca* (Skt: *anitya*), meaning impermanence. Without anicca and the attendant sunyata then there would be no existence.

Sunyata and dependent origination are ways to understand how the cycle of rebirth continues, and how nothing has an independent existence:

> They cannot come to be by their own strength,
> Or yet maintain themselves by their own strength; Relying for support on other states,
> Weak in themselves, and formed, they come to be;
> They come to be with others as condition. They are aroused by others as their objects,
>   They are produced by object and condition, And each by something other than itself.
>   (*Visuddhimagga*, 18:36)

In both Theravada and Mahayana traditions there are twelve nidanas (links) of dependent origination (see *Paticcasamuppada Vibhanga Sutta*). It is tempting to see them as linear; rather, they are all interconnected. Indeed, in their description of them the Dalai Lama and Chodron (2014) reverse the order in which they are listed further on. The nidanas are:

- Ignorance (*avidya*)

   And which ignorance? Not knowing stress, not knowing the origination of stress, not knowing the cessation of stress, not knowing the way of practice leading to the cessation of stress: This is called ignorance. (*Paticcasamuppada Vibhanga Sutta*)

   It is evident from this saying of the Buddha that ignorance is rooted in not knowing the Four Noble Truths. It is this ignorance that means people are unable to realize the truth of dukkha and the reality of existence. Ignorance does not mean understanding the interconnectedness of all things, and thus, everything is seen to have inherent and independent existence. Only in recognizing that everything is dependent on other things can a person move from ignorance and live an awakened life.

- Formation (*samskara*)

   And which fabrications? These three are fabrications: bodily fabrications, verbal fabrications, mental fabrications. These are called fabrications. (*Paticcasamuppada Vibhanga Sutta*)

These are sometimes termed formative actions. In these a person seeks karma to determine a positive rebirth. The intentions of such ensure that the cycle of rebirth continues. Only through a realization and reorientation towards the intention of being free from dukkha can a person hope for freedom from rebirth

- Consciousness (*vijnana*)

  And which consciousness? These six are classes of consciousness: eye-consciousness, ear-consciousness, nose-consciousness, tongue-consciousness, body-consciousness, intellect-consciousness. This is called consciousness. (*Paticcasamuppada Vibhanga Sutta*)

  Here consciousness 'refers to the mental consciousness that initiates the new life, connecting the mainstream from the previous life with the new life' (Dalai Lama and Chodron, 2014, 167–8). These are the external awareness factors of a being: eye, ear, nose, tongue, body and intellect. These consciousness and the attendent consciousnesses animate a being and enable thought and existece. This will be explored in greater detail in Chapter 2.

- Name and form (*nama-rupa*)

  And which name-and-form? Feeling, perception, intention, contact, and attention: This is called name. The four great elements, and the form dependent on the four great elements: This is called form. This name and this form are called name-and-form. (*Paticcasamuppada Vibhanga Sutta*)

  Name and form is indicative of when the name (the mind) and the form (matter) coalesce to bring together the five khandas (see Chapter 2) to form a being. Between Mahayana and Theravada there can be seen to be a difference in the understanding of name and form. In Theravada traditions the name refers to five mental factors that enable beings to make sense of the world around them, these are: feeling, discrimination, intention, contact and attention. Whereas in the Mahayana traditions name refers to the non-form/material skandhas that animate the body.

- The six ayatanas (*sadayatana*)

  And which six sense media? These six are sense media: the eye-medium, the ear-medium, the nose-medium, the tongue-medium, the body-medium, the intellect-medium. These are called the six sense media. (*Paticcasamuppada Vibhanga Sutta*)

  The six ayatanas are sometimes referred to as senses or sources. They are inextricably linked with the six consciousnesses outlined earlier on, in the sense that individually they are the source of the arising of each.

- Contact (*sparsa*)

    And which contact? These six are classes of contact: eye-contact, ear-contact, nose-contact, tongue-contact, body-contact, intellect-contact. This is called contact. (*Paticcasamuppada Vibhanga Sutta*)

    This is the contact between each of the individual senses and the outer environment. One example is when the sense of the 'eye' sees an object, the consciousness and ayatana come together to create a perception, sensation or feeling.

- Sensation (*vedana*)

    And which feeling? These six are classes of feeling: feeling born from eye-contact, feeling born from ear-contact, feeling born from nose-contact, feeling born from tongue-contact, feeling born from body-contact, feeling born from intellect-contact. This is called feeling. (*Paticcasamuppada Vibhanga Sutta*)

    Sometimes referred to as perceptions or feelings, within Buddhism there tend to be only three types of feeling: pleasure, pain and neutral. These naturally arise based on a person's experience and karma. It is for the individual to decide whether to crave for each of these. It may be that a person craves for pleasurable feelings, craves to avoid painful ones or craves for neutral ones to persist. Only through mindfulness can a feeling arise and dissipate without any desire to crave or grasp.

- Craving (*tanha/trsna*)

    And which craving? These six are classes of craving: craving for forms, craving for sounds, craving for smells, craving for tastes, craving for tactile sensations, craving for ideas. This is called craving. (*Paticcasamuppada Vibhanga Sutta*)

    This brings dissatisfaction to a person's life as a person craves for three things: sensual cravings, renewed existence and non-existence. In this state a person is always desiring attachments which make them continually enmeshed in the cycle of rebirth.

- Grasping (*upadana*)

    And which clinging/sustenance? These four are clingings: sensuality-clinging, view-clinging, habit-and-practice-clinging, and doctrine-of-self-clinging. This is called clinging. [Or: These four are sustenances: sensuality-sustenance, view-sustenance, habit-and-practice-sustenance, and doctrine-of-self-sustenance.]. (*Paticcasamuppada Vibhanga Sutta*)

    Linked very much with the idea of craving, is the grasping to sensual pleasures, to wrong views, to the efficacy of rules and practice and to the idea of the self. A person consumed by attachment is consumed by the desire for more, and the idea of the self and the ego as the purpose of this life.

- Becoming (*bhava*)

    And which becoming? These three becomings: sensual becoming, form becoming, and formless becoming. This is called becoming. (*Paticcasamuppada Vibhanga Sutta*)

    Karma keeps a person rooted in the cycle of rebirth. The karma determined by the intentions of a person lead to a rebirth is often termed an active kamma of renewed existence. Meaning that the karma accumulated and intended propels that consciousness to a rebirth. The second type of rebirth, or becoming, could be termed resultant rebirth existence, which is a natural consequence of karma, rather than a result of intention. A person is subject to the chains of karma until they are released by non-attachment and an awakening.

- Rebirth (*jati*)

    And which birth? Whatever birth, taking birth, descent, coming-to-be, coming-forth, appearance of aggregates, and acquisition of (sense) media of the various beings in this or that group of beings, that is called birth. (*Paticcasamuppada Vibhanga Sutta*)

    Birth refers to the moment of creation, the moment when the consciousness and khandas form a new being. This is seen by many to be at the moment of conception which involves the sperm, the egg and the consciousness. Unless the chain of dependent origination is broken the cycle of rebirth will continue.

- Old age and death (*jara-marana*)

    Now which aging-and-death? Whatever aging, decrepitude, brokenness, graying, wrinkling, decline of life force, weakening of the faculties of the various beings in this or that group of beings, that is called aging. Whatever deceasing, passing away, breaking up, disappearance, dying, death, completion of time, break up of the aggregates, casting off of the body, interruption in the life faculty of the various beings in this or that group of beings, that is called death. (*Paticcasamuppada Vibhanga Sutta*)

    Immediately upon being born a person is aging and dying. It is the cycle of life and rebirth that continues, and can only be broken by realizing dependent origination and the need to escape the cycle.

Each of these are interconnected with each other, as although they may be interpreted or described as linear they each have interplay with the others. Illustrations of these twelve nidanas can be found around the outside of the Tibetan Wheel of Life (see Figure 1.1). The corresponding illustration is shown in Table 1.1.

Figure 1.1 The Wheel of Life.

Source: Stephen Shephard, CC BY-SA 3.0 (http://creativecommons.org/licenses/by-sa/3.0/) via Wikimedia Commons.

Table 1.1 The Twelve Nidanas in the Tibetan Wheel of Life

Nidana	Illustration in the Wheel of Life
Ignorance (*avidya*)	A blind man or woman.
Formation (*samskara*)	Potters making pots.
Consciousness (*vijnana*)	A monkey.
Name and form (*nama-rupa*)	People in a boat, travelling through samsara.
The six ayatanas/senses (*sadayatana*)	A house with six windows.
Contact (*sparsa*)	An embracing couple.
Sensation (*vedana*)	An arrow piercing an eye.
Craving (*trsna*)	A man drinking beer, usually surrounded by empty bottles.
Grasping (*upadana*)	A monkey or a person reaching for fruit.
Becoming (*bhava*)	A pregnant woman or a couple making love.
Rebirth (*jati*)	A woman in childbirth.
Old age and death (*jara-marana*)	A corpse.

Thus, in the classroom, the Wheel of Life becomes an important teaching tool in helping students understand the nature of dependent origination and the twelve interconnected links. The temptation may be to only use the Wheel of Life when exploring concepts of the afterlife, but every element can be used to support the teaching of other principles.

The Theravada tradition places them into four groups to try and understand how they function in life (see Table 1.2). Each life enables the arising of the next stage. For example, in the past life ignorance and formation, combined with craving, grasping and becoming, lead to the present life. In the present life, the five results bring aspects of existence together. The five causes then give rise to a further rebirth and future results.

Rupert Gethin (1998) outlines the importance of dependent origination when he highlights that it does not only 'hold the key to the way in which beings become enmeshed in suffering, it also points to the way in which they can free themselves from suffering' (157).

Although included under the First Noble Truth, dependent origination is inherent in each of the Four Noble Truths. A realization of the nature of dependent origination helps people understand the nature of suffering, and also how it can be overcome, which is central to the subsequent Noble Truths.

When exploring the First Noble Truth within the classroom there is a temptation to summarize it as 'all life is suffering', and then move onto the Second Noble Truth. While, in some situations and with some classes, this may be appropriate, there is an opportunity

Table 1.2 The Twelve Nidanas in Theravada Buddhism

	Links	Twenty modes	
Five past causes	Ignorance (avidya)	Ignorance (avidya)	Past life
	Formation (samskara)	Formation (samskara)	
		Craving (trsna)	
		Grasping (upadana)	
		Becoming (bhava)	
First transition			
Present results	Consciousness (vijnana)	Consciousness (vijnana)	Present rife
	Name and form (nama-rupa)	Name and form (nama-rupa)	
	The six ayatanas/senses (sadayatana)	The six ayatanas/senses (sadayatana)	
	Contact (sparsa)	Contact (sparsa)	
	Sensation (vedana)	Sensation (vedana)	
Second transition			
Present causes	Craving (trsna)	Craving (trsna)	
	Grasping (upadana)	Grasping (upadana)	
	Becoming (bhava)	Becoming (bhava)	
		Ignorance (avidya)	
		Formation (samskara)	
		Consciousness (vijnana)	
Third transition			
Future results	Rebirth (jati)	Consciousness (vijnana)	Future life
	Old age and death (jara-marana)	Name and form (nama-rupa)	
		The six ayatanas/senses (sadayatana)	
		Contact (sparsa)	
		Sensation (vedana)	

for the teacher to pause and consider the meaning of the word 'dukkha' and its various translations and meanings.

Within the classroom dukkha is a rich vein for exploration in terms of its meanings and expressions. There are many stories from the life of the Buddha that explore the universality of dukkha. One such story is that of a young woman called Krisha Gotami whose firstborn child died. Overcome with grief she searched for a way to restore him to life. At length she was told that the only person who could possibly perform this miracle was the Buddha. She went to the Buddha who listened to her with compassion. He told her that the cure could be found by bringing him a mustard seed from a house which has never encountered death.

Excited by this, she set off for the city. She stopped at the first house to be told that many people had died in that family. This was repeated at every house in the city. No house had been untouched by death. She realized that the task she had been given could not be fulfilled.

She buried her child and then returned to the Buddha to explain to him that she was beginning to understand. She asked him to teach her the truth of death. The Buddha told her that all things are impermanent and change. The importance of storytelling in the teaching of Buddhism is explored further in Chapter 3.

An exploration of sunyata and dependent origination may seem to be too complex for many students, but there are different levels at which they can be understood. These concepts can serve as a springboard for many other aspects of Buddhism, whether it is each of the Four Noble Truths or the concepts of anatta and anicca (see Chapter 2). Understanding how everything is empty yet interconnected to everything in the universe is an important aspect of Buddhism. Buddhism is not a way of life that is nihilistic; everything has inherent meaning and all aspects of existence are brought together in a way that points forward, to an ever-changing and ever-progressing view of life and existence.

The Second Noble Truth: Samudaya and tanha

The Second Noble Truth explores the origin, cause source or arising (*samudaya*) of dukkha, which is *tanha* (Skt: *trsna*), which is commonly translated as thirst, desire or craving suggesting more than wanting, but that there is a need within a being that is exhibited through tanha. Importantly, in Buddhism suffering or dukkha is caused rather than just existing. As explored in the discussion of dependent origination mentioned earlier it is evident that tanha is inextricably linked with dukkha and the continued existence of it through attachment with its root in ignorance of its true causes and the true nature of things. The 'Present Causes' of dependent origination as outlined in Theravada Buddhism include:

- Craving

- Grasping
- Becoming

In a further relation to the Wheel of Life (see Figure 1.1), the three animals that lie at its centre are the pig, the cockerel and the snake. These interlinked animals (symbolized by the biting of each other's tails) drive the continued cycle of rebirth, and are symbolic of ignorance, greed and aversion (collectively known as the Three Poisons).

It is important to note that tanha is merely the immediately identifiable cause of dukkha. Rahula (1997) has suggested, and the discussion about dependent origination would support this, that although tanha is the immediate cause of suffering, the actual source of suffering goes much deeper. He suggests:

> So tanha, 'thirst', is not the first or the only cause of the arising of dukkha. But it is the most palpable and immediate cause, the 'principal thing' and the 'all-pervading thing'. (290)

It is, therefore, important to recognize the interrelatedness of all things as shown in the teaching of dependent origination that helps Buddhists understand the causes of suffering and the tanha that is a result of ignorance.

In the *Dhammacakkappavattana Sutta* the Buddha taught the link between tanha and continued dukkha in the cycle of rebirth:

> And this, monks, is the noble truth of the origination of stress: the craving that makes for further becoming – accompanied by passion and delight, relishing now here and now there – i.e., craving for sensuality, craving for becoming, craving for non-becoming.

The Buddha identifies the three types of tanha or craving:

1. Craving for sensuality (*kama-tanha*)

   The temptation when speaking of 'sensuality' is the limiting of this craving to that which the modern world describes as 'sensual' in terms of sexual pleasure. It is important to note that in this context 'sensuality' refers to the desire for sensory experience – referring to the senses of a person. Indeed, it has been expanded further to include a desire for 'wealth and power, but also desire for, and attachment to, ideas and ideals, views, opinions, theories, conceptions and beliefs (*dhamma-tanha*)' (Rahula, 1997, 30).

   These are the base cravings of a person who is dissatisfied with what they have. This craving goes beyond the suffering that is caused for individuals but lies at the heart of the causes of suffering exemplified in the wider world, such as global inequalities, global warming, wars, famine and so on. Each of these can be seen to be caused by greed for things, including power and wealth, which will continue to provide unsatisfactoriness in life and in society. This greed is driven by ignorance of the true nature of existence. That everything is empty and is related to everything else through dependent origination.

2. Craving of becoming (sometimes translated as existence) (*bhava-tanha*)

This aspect of tanha can be understood as the desire or craving for continued existence or rebirth. This leads people to perform actions for the purpose of gaining good *kamma* (Skt: *karma*) and therefore a positive rebirth. The ignorance that lies at the heart of continued existence means that a person is focused on the perpetuation of the self, desiring the rebirth of such.

'Karma' is a term that many observers of Buddhism believe that they understand, perhaps based on its adoption into the everyday vernacular of the Western world. Examples include television series' such as *My Name is Earl* whose whole premise is based around karma as a law of cause and effect of 'what goes around comes around'. Karma, in Buddhism, is not an immutable law that is controlled by the universe or by a deity, rather it is something that drives the cycle of rebirth, but also something that is directed by intentional action.

What this means for the Buddhist is that not everything is the result of karma, rather there are coincidences, luck and the resultant consequences of circumstances. However, the intentional actions of a person will have karmic consequences immediately, later in this life or in future rebirths. It is, however, possible to change the consequences of karma through volitional action. In the aforementioned sutta the ability to change or remove the consequences of karma, meaning continued dukkha and rebirth, is to be found in the living of the Eightfold Path (see Chapter 3). Indeed, in exploring aspects of Vajrayana meditation Glenys Eddy (2012) highlights that kamma can be purified and its effects transformed.

Damien Keown (2013) suggests that the law of karma in Buddhism has 'transitive and intransitive effects' (40), meaning it affects the subject of the action and also shapes the agent. The imagery of a potter holding clay in their hands is often used to describe a person's relationship with their character. A person is the clay that they hold in their own hands, and through their own choices they shape their own character. Although a person may be subject to karmic consequences from previous lives, they are free to respond how they will, and as such can negate the negative consequence of such.

In seeking to develop positive karma a person may be subject to this craving of becoming; the purpose of existence is to seek freedom from the consequences of karma rather than a perpetuation of it. Karma keeps the cycle of rebirth turning, but as mentioned before is subject to change and ending through a living of the Eightfold Path.

An exception to the removal of karma as the driving force behind rebirth is shown in the example of bodhisattva (see Chapter 5). Peter Harvey (2000) suggests that 'the Bodhisattva goes beyond being reborn according to karma, and becomes a heavenly saviour being' (130). Indeed, in their role of bodhisattva in the different realms they are able to transfer their karma to answer the petitions of those who offer prayers.

3. Craving for non-becoming (sometimes translated as non-existence) (*vibhava-tanha*)

In this understanding for craving a person desires the removal of unpleasant situations. As outlined in the first form of craving for sensual pleasures, the two extremes of aversion and desire are rejected. A person's desire to remove the negative situations are evidence of craving, just as much as the desire for sensual pleasures. Merv Fowler (1999) suggests that people who crave non-becoming are ignorant of the true purpose of seeking to cease rebirth. He suggests that 'when we speak in terms of preventing "birth" on the Wheel of Becoming in order to break the cycle and thereby negate suffering, the birth to which we refer is not life itself but the birth of the ego. This is the key to end suffering' (46–7).

Each of the types of craving are a result of the corruption of the view of reality (which will be explored in the context of 'right view' in Chapter 4). Underpinning each of these cravings is the attachment to views (ditthi). Rupert Gethin (2004) outlines the importance of the recognition of this in suggesting that views should also be impermanent or they continue the existence of attachment and therefore dukkha:

> In certain contexts what seems to be significant about ditthi is not so much the cognitive content of a view, but the fact that we cling to it as a dogma, the fact that it becomes a fixed view: this alone is true, all else is foolishness. Thus, even so-called 'right views' can be 'views' (ditthi) in so far as they can become fixed and the objects of attachment. (20)

Linked with dependent origination, the emptiness of everything is an important aspect of the Second Noble Truth.

In the classroom there are many elements of samudaya and tanha that can be explored. Building on students' own experiences of desire and craving as a natural part of the human condition will form an important bridge to enable them to understand the problem of tanha within a Buddhist worldview. As an integral part of the nidanas, that continues to cause rebirth, there are different levels of exploration that can be undertaken, not least with the three types of tanha highlighted earlier on. In tandem with the First Noble Truth, the use of story will also bring alive the meaning and expansiveness of tanha and the need to let go of it. One of the most well-known stories of the Buddha with regard to tanha is that of the raft. In this story, the letting go of all attachments, including the dhamma, is taught as having built a raft, and travelled across the river, a person is determined to hold onto it:

> In the same way, monks, I have taught the Dhamma compared to a raft, for the purpose of crossing over, not for the purpose of holding onto. Understanding the Dhamma as taught compared to a raft, you should let go even of Dhammas, to say nothing of non-Dhammas. (*Alagaddupama Sutta*)

Even the dhamma one should let go. This does not mean that the monk ceases to follow the dhamma; rather, because of the character he has moulded he will continue to live the dhamma but not because it has been written or because it has been taught.

The Third Noble Truth: Nirodha/nirvana

Nirodha is the Third Noble Truth and is translated as 'cessation', 'extinction' or suppression. The Buddha taught in his First Sermon:

> And this, monks, is the noble truth of the cessation of stress: the remainderless fading and cessation, renunciation, relinquishment, release, and letting go of that very craving. (*Dhammacakkappavattana Sutta*)

This is the truth that dukkha can be ended by stopping desires and cravings. Buswell and Lopez (2013) describe two types of nirodha described in Buddhist literature:

1. The first is 'Apratisamkhyanirodha or "non-analytical cessation"' referring 'to a mere absence, such as the temporary absence of hunger after a meal, or to an uncompounded facto (asamskratadharma) that suppresses the production of all other dharmas, ensuring that they are restrained from ever arising again in the present'.

2. The second is 'Pratisamkhyanirodha, or "analytical cessation"', referring 'to a cessation that occurs as a result of meditative analysis of the real nature of phenomena; it is one of the uncompounded factors' (588).

In the sense of it being an Ennobling Truth it is the second type to which the Third Noble Truth mainly applies. The complete cessation of suffering is found within enlightenment, or in *nirvana* (Pali: nibbana). For this reason many writers prefer the term 'nirvana' to refer to the Third Noble Truth (see, e.g. Gethin, 1998). Although the word 'nirvana' is never found within the *Dhammacakkappavattana Sutta* (First Sermon) the state of perfect freedom and happiness that is described by the cessation of craving is the same as enlightenment or awakening. Walpole Rahula (1997) outlines elements of the Pali texts that suggest that cessation is best described as nirvana:

> '[Nirvana] is the complete cessation of that very thirst (tanha), giving it up, renouncing it, emancipation from it, detachment from it' ... 'The abandoning and destruction of craving for these Five Aggregates of Attachment: that is the cessation of dukkha'. 'The Cessation of Continuity and becoming (Bhavanirodha) is Nibbana'. (56–7)

Only upon awakening is a person free from desire and will not be subject to rebirth. Eve Mullen (2014) explains:

> The Third Noble Truth is nirvana. The Buddha tells us that an end to suffering is possible, and it is nirvana. Nirvana is a 'blowing out', just as a candle flame is extinguished in the wind, from our lives in samsara. It connotes an end to rebirth. (Mullen, 2014, 319)

This description is perhaps more satisfying than that which is sometimes expressed in the classroom. The First Noble Truth diagnoses the problem of dukkha, followed by an explanation of its cause samudaya or tanha. The Third Noble Truth is often described as a solution that exists to end suffering, which then quickly leads on to a discussion of the solution which is *magga* or the Noble Eightfold Path. A stage that only suggests a solution exists is perhaps slightly ethereal and may not seem to make sense as an aspect of a path; rather, the solution to both dukkha and tanha is nirvana, something to be worked towards through the living of the Middle Way. Nirvana is the 'end' point towards which everything else points.

A further exploration of nirvana as an end to rebirth can be found in Chapter 2; at this stage it is sufficient to note that it ends attachment, craving, dukkha. As will be shown by the life of the Buddha (Chapter 3), the nature of an arahant and the nature of a bodhisattva (Chapter 5), it is possible to attain this nirvana, awakening and enlightenment and then continue to exist. Rupert Gethin (1998) outlines this:

> Yet like the Buddha, any person who attains nirvana does not remain thereafter forever absorbed in some transcendental state of mind. On the contrary he or she continues to live in the world; he or she continues to think, speak, and act as other people do with the difference that all his or her thoughts, words, and deeds are completely free of the motivations of greed, aversion, and delusion, and motivated instead entirely by generosity, friendliness, and wisdom. This condition of having extinguished the defilements can be termed nirvana with the remainder (of life). (*sopadhisesa-nirvana*) (75–6)

Those who attain this level of cessation serve as an inspiration to all as they seek to attain the same. The story is told of a monk who once found a precious stone. One day he met a traveller with whom he shared his food. The traveller spotted the jewel and asked if he could have it. The monk happily handed it over. The traveller left the monk full of joy; the jewel would give him enough money to settle his security for the rest of his life. A few days later, however, the traveller returned begging the monk to give him something more precious than the jewel, 'that which made you able to give it to me'.

The Fourth Noble Truth: Magga

Magga (Skt: *marga*) is variously described as the Noble Eightfold Path, the Middle Way or the Way of Practice. It was outlined by the Buddha:

> Vision arose, insight arose, discernment arose, knowledge arose, illumination arose within me with regard to things never heard before: 'This is the noble truth

of the way of practice leading to the cessation of stress' ... 'This noble truth of the way of practice leading to the cessation of stress is to be developed' ... 'This noble truth of the way of practice leading to the cessation of stress has been developed. (*Dhammacakkappavattana Sutta*)

The importance of it as the Middle Way is shown in the Buddha's life when he had lived according to two extremes (see Chapter 3); it is also shown in an discussion with one of his disciples, Sona, in the *Sona Sutta*. The Buddha taught Sona that just as he was unable to attain the right pitch of music if the strings of his vina (lute) were too taut or too slack, so also a person's mind or effort could only be rightly attuned if it was not too taut or too slack. Extremes are to be avoided. This is shown as both desire and aversion are characteristics that keep the cycle of rebirth turning. Following this conversation with the Buddha, we read further:

> So after that, Ven. Sona determined the right pitch for his persistence, attuned the pitch of the (five) faculties (to that), and there picked up his theme ... And thus Ven. Sona became another one of the arahants. (*Sona Sutta*)

The living of the Eightfold Path enables a person to attain nirvana, and thus the cessation of craving, desire, attachment and rebirth. As a way of living, this Noble Truth will be explored in much more detail in Chapter 4 as each of the eight views (*dittha*) are explored separately.

Different views of the Four Noble Truths

Discussion in this chapter so far surrounding the Four Noble Truths has focussed on their centrality to the Buddhist way of life. It could be argued that they are most important in the Theravada tradition and that in other forms of Buddhism, while generally taught, they are less important. In Paul Williams's (2009) *Mahayana Buddhism: The Doctrinal Foundations Second Edition* it is interesting to note that there are only four references to the Four Noble Truths in the index. It is not that the teachings of the Four Noble Truths are not in evidence, particularly in their expression in sunyata and emptiness; it is that they are not discretely articulated. Could it, therefore, be argued that this book has spent a significant portion of its beginning in exploring concepts and beliefs that do not lie at the heart of Buddhism? Against this background we will briefly explore their importance in Buddhist traditions outside of Theravada.

For all Buddhists rather than a set of beliefs to be believed, it has been suggested that they are 'to treat them appropriately by respectively understanding, abandoning, realising, and developing them' (Keown and Prebish, 2010, 320). As such, they may not need articulating more than they need expressing and living. The realization of such is a step on the path to awakening. The ideal or goal of Mahayana schools tends to be the bodhisattva ideal (see Chapter 5), which puts of parinirvana (final and complete enlightenment or freedom from rebirth). As indicated earlier on a bodhisattva continues to experience rebirth but by choice and of their own volition. This is seen to be a higher goal, as it is selfless in the sense that the bodhisattva is seeking to help others in the realization of the truths of existence. In many Mahayana traditions the view of life and the goal of ultimate liberation is a preparatory or lesser step on the path. In the Tibetan text *A Lamp for the Path to Full Awakening*, Atisha suggests three levels of people:

1. Lowest scope: those who seek happiness in samsara through a providential and happy rebirth.

2. Mediocre scope: those who seek happiness or freedom from rebirth for themselves.

3. Supreme scope: those who attain awakening but go beyond seeking this peace for themselves, and therefore seeks the elimination of suffering for others. Anyone who, by whatever means, seeks to procure for himself happiness merely in cyclic existence is known as an individual of the lowest scope.

This would seem to be echoed by forms of Nichiren Buddhism (see Chapters 6 and 9); in discussing the Buddha Shakyamuni's preaching on Vulture Peak towards the end of his life recorded in the *Lotus Sutra*, Nichiren Buddhists would suggest that the teachings of the Four Noble Truths are evidence of skilful methods of teaching. In essence that they are evidence of teaching adapted to the understanding of his audience. As such they pale in comparison to the Buddha's final teaching, believed to have been recorded in the *Lotus Sutra*. Chapter 3 of the *Lotus Sutra* records this type of understanding:

> In the past,
> At Varanasi,
> You turned the Dharma wheel
> Of the four truths.
>
> Making distinctions,
> You taught that all things,
> Being made of the five constituent aggregates,
> Arise and become extinct.
>
> Now again you turn the most wonderful,
> Unexcelled, great wheel of the Dharma,
> The Dharma that is extremely profound
> And that few are able to believe.
>
> From a long time ago,
> We have often heard the World-Honoured One teach,
> But never before have we heard such a profound,
> Wonderful, and supreme Dharma.

Since the World-Honoured One teaches this Dharma,
We all respond with joy. (Reeves, 2008, 111)

The *Dhammacakkappavattana Sutta* was that which was taught in Varanasi, which contained the Four Noble Truths. This further turning of the Wheel of Dharma is now based on joy and supersedes that which came before. Although maybe not accepting the interpretation that Nichiren Buddhists place upon the *Lotus Sutra*, it is possible to see this as a reflection of wider Mahayana teaching. Williams (2009) suggests:

> The Four Noble Truths and so forth. This was a wonderful teaching, but it was not in itself the final teaching; it required interpreting and had to be understood correctly. (85)

The way for it to be interpreted and understood correctly is through the lens of Mahayana writings. The preparatory role that the Four Noble Truths serve is similarly reflected in an exploration of the stages of a Bodhisattva way, outlined by Williams:

> The Bodhisattva at this stage attains the five powers of deep faith, armour-like exertion and perseverance, recollection (of the Four Noble Truths and their ramifications), meditative absorption – the combination of calm abiding and insight – and wisdom, the 'ability to examine the void nature of the Four Noble Truths'. (2009, 201)

This will be explored in much greater depth in Chapter 5, but although they are viewed differently, the Truths of the nature of existence are perhaps more focussed upon concepts in Mahayana. Sunyata and dependent origination do exist and can be used to begin to understand the worldview of almost all Buddhists. Nagarjuna (living in the 1st–2nd centuries) wrote of the interrelatedness of the Noble Truths and sunyata:

> He who sees dependent origination sees this.
> Suffering, arising, cessation and the path. (2015, 373)

This is an important aspect of our teaching within the classroom; as discussed in both the Series Editors Foreword and the Introduction to this book, the teacher must recognize the diversity of approach within the wider religion. Teachers, and I have been guilty of this, in defaulting to the universal teaching of the Four Noble Truths, address the first stage, that they are accepted by most Buddhists. This is true, but it should be appended with an 'and', so that the range of interpretations based on interpretive lenses should be addressed. Consider this response of one Buddhist:

> One versed in the dhamma has realised that: The four noble truths: within life is the potential for suffering, There are general and unique causes to suffering – namely, attachment, ignorance, and aversion (three poisons) – the 5 hindrances (ill-will, sloth-torpor, restlessness/unhelpful remorsefulness, infatuation with sense desires, and doubt of one's own abilities and in the dhamma – the way things are), That there is a way to uproot these factors, And that there is a path that leads to the uprooting of suffering

which comprises of: reflection, thinking, critical thought, meditation (awareness of breath and loving kindness meditation), discipline, noble friendship and an openness to learning. The realisation of the four noble truths leads to the development of noble behaviour (ariya), a life where one moves away from suffering and towards loving-kindness – noble conduct.

The noting of the preparatory role of the Four Noble Truths is evident and should be developed further in classroom discussion.

One other group's approach to the Four Noble Truths that should be noted is the Navayana (New Vehicle) in India. The group is also known as the Buddhist Movement for Dalits, Ambedkarite Buddhist Movement, Dalit Buddhist Movement or Modern Buddhist Movement. The beliefs of the Dalit Buddhist Movement are based on the teachings of Bhimrao Ramji Ambedkar who is believed to be an incarnation of the bodhisattva Maitreya. He rejected Hinduism to embrace Buddhism, and subsequently announced his rejection of Theravada and Mahayana. Keown and Prebish (2010) outline the distinctiveness of Ambedkar's religious thought in establishing Navayana:

> The Buddhism upon which he settled and about which he wrote in The Buddha and His Dhamma was, in many respects, unlike any form of Buddhism that had hitherto arisen within the tradition. Gone, for instance, were the doctrines of karma and rebirth, the traditional emphasis on renunciation of the world, the practice of meditation, and the experience of enlightenment. Gone too were any teachings that implied the existence of a trans-empirical realm ... Most jarring, perhaps, especially among more traditional Buddhists, was the absence of the Four Noble Truths, which Ambedkar regarded as the invention of wrong-headed monks. (25)

Although the teachings can appear to be a modernist reinterpretation of the Buddha's teaching, and focused on social action, the growth of Navayana cannot be ignored in a discussion of Buddhism within the world. In the 2011 Indian Census Navayana Buddhists are seen to represent 87 per cent of India's Buddhist community of 8.4 million people (Moudgil, 2017); it should be noted that not all people who identify as Navayana would be part of the Dalit Buddhist Movement. Its success perhaps being related to its social action and the opportunities offered to Dalits. As an aside, in the Introduction it was noted that 66 per cent of Buddhists in India believe in a deity; with the belief in Ambedkar as a bodhisattva this may go somewhat to explaining this high number in a religion that is generally without a 'God'. Though, one area that is debated is Ambedkar's status being described by Indira Junghare (1988) as a deity. To support this assertion she draws on songs that were printed in a book to celebrate Ambedkar's birth. The words of these songs praise Ambedkar:

> Dr. Ambedkar is raised from a deity to a supreme deity. He is omnipresent, omnipotent, and omniscient. Dr. Ambedkar is present everywhere, as the singer expresses:

> Bhima is overhead, Bhima is beneath
> Bhima is in front, Bhima is behind.
> Oh my friend, nothing is here without him
> He is everywhere, he is everywhere.

The song also expresses a non-dualistic philosophy. That is oneness of God with the Universe. Ambedkar is the Supreme Soul, the Ultimate Reality, which resides in every thing and every being as in the following couplets:

> He is in the breath of the poor, he is in their tears,
> He is in their hearts, he is in the temples of their minds.
> He is in the light of lamps, he is in the rays of the sun,
> He is in the sorrow of the troubled, he is in the body and the soul of the Dalits. (101)

In a study of British Buddhism, the Triratna community (see Chapter 9) had links with Ambedkar through Sangharakshita, but its limited influence may mean that it has limited applicability to discuss within the classroom; however, in terms of teacher knowledge, this is a useful background to have. The place it may have is in a discussion of the boundaries of Buddhism; I have argued elsewhere (Holt, 2019) that teachers need to accept a person's self-identification in teaching big tent religions. Is this possible when some of, what are seen as, the deeply held beliefs are replaced and seem to go against tradition?

Thoughts for the classroom

Throughout this chapter we have paused at certain points to reflect on aspects of the Four Noble Truths that could find reflection in the classroom. The role of the Wheel of Life is particularly key in discussing elements of dependent origination, especially with the illustrations of the nidanas. These are rich for activities such as sequencing, or redesigning for the modern world. Similarly in exploring the nature of sunyata as empty yet full of everything at the same time could inspire some very interesting activities in the classroom. The example that was used earlier surrounds the emptiness of the piece of paper. If we were to use a page from a book as an example, what constituent parts and influences would form part of its dependent existence? Not just the wood, water, sun and earth but also the writer, the printer, the publisher, the paper maker, the logger and so on. In a world where students are exploring the various aspects of consumerism an understanding of the source of the things that are in their possession is a useful exercise when linked with a carbon footprint.

As also indicated the stories associated with the Buddha are a rich trove for exploring concepts important within Buddhism. Each of the Noble Truths have stories associated with them, beyond the ones suggested in this chapter. The use of stories will be explored in Chapter 3, but it would be remiss at this point not to acknowledge story's centrality in beginning to understand complex beliefs and concepts.

The final part of this chapter also highlights the significance of developing teacher and student contextual understanding for the things being studied. To focus solely on the Four Noble Truths as the beginning and end of Buddhism would be to present an understanding of Buddhism that is not universal and out of step with the experience of many Buddhists. The teacher needs to ensure that the Buddhism they have received in their teaching is not uncritically passed on. The world religions paradigm privileged the 'essential' aspects that fitted neatly; as teacher move towards a worldviews paradigm recognizing different views is an important part of classroom resources and discussion.

2

The nature of humanity

In some ways exploring the nature of humanity is tied up with the nature of existence, and we will build on aspects of the teachings that we discussed in Chapter 1, and in many ways this chapter is a continuation of what has come before. Within Buddhism the nature of humanity includes an exploration of anatta/anatman (no-self) and what this means; the nature of rebirth and what, if anything, continues after death; and the concept of Buddha-nature. As with every aspect of Buddhism that we have explored so far there is diversity of belief within Buddhist traditions, but also between individual Buddhists. This chapter will try and navigate the various nuances in belief and the varying impacts that these beliefs have on individuals.

Anicca and anatta

As one of the traditional 'Three Marks of Existence' within Buddhism, anatta or no-self is one of the central aspects of teaching within the classroom. Linked with the first of the Three Marks of Existence, *anicca* (impermanence), where it is said that nothing is permanent, and everything changes, this is extended to the person or to the self. The idea of the self is inextricably linked with the concept of dependent arising (see Chapter 1). This teaching is most clearly seen in the Buddhist understanding of the Five Aggregates (khandas/skandhas).

Five khandas/five skandhas

The belief in the five *khandas* (Skt: *skandhas*) is an integral part of anatta. A person is made up of five constituent parts. Nagasena is reported in the *Questions of King Milinda* to have taught that the constituent parts of a person is similar to a chariot:

> And Milinda the king replied to Nagasena, and said: 'I have spoken no untruth, reverend Sir. It is on account of its having all these things – the pole, and the axle, the wheels, and the framework, the ropes, the yoke, the spokes, and the goad – that it comes under the generally understood term, the designation in common use, of "chariot".'

Just as it is by the condition precedent
Of the co-existence of its various parts
That the word 'chariot' is used,
Just so is it that when the Skandhas
Are there we talk of a 'being'. (3.1.1. *Individuality and name; the chariot simile*)

The self is the name attached to the combined form (rupa) of these five parts:

- Form (or material image, impression) (rupa). This is the matter that is the physical body.
- Sensations (or feelings, received from form) (vedana). These are the sensations or feelings that are experienced in the physical world. They are of different kinds – pleasant, unpleasant or neither. There are seen to be six senses in Buddhism:
  - Sight
  - Hearing
  - Smell
  - Taste
  - Touch
  - Mind

  These have their own sphere of experience. For example, the ear hears but does not see or taste.
- Perceptions (sanjna/samjna). Perception enables a person to recognize, identify, classify and put sense experiences into words. For example a person can tell the difference between chocolate and lemon.
- Mental activity or formations (samskara/sankhara). This is the way that the mind forms impressions based on the former feelings and perceptions. It is not, however, purely based on logical thought; it also enables the formation of moral and emotional responses. Mental formation and a person's will determines responses to experience and helps people realize the moral consequences of them.
- Consciousness (vijnana), feeling (vedana), perception (sanjna), mental formation (samskara) and consciousness (vijnana). Consciousness is awareness of and sensitivity towards an object. People become aware of the objects around them that then needs to be built upon by the other khandas to provide personal experience

They work together to produce personal experience. For example, if a person were to take a walk in the garden, their eyes come into contact with an object. This would focus their attention on the object – the consciousness becomes aware of the visible object that is unidentified. Perception will then identify that visible object for what it is – a snake. Once that happens, a person will experience a feeling – the feeling of displeasure or fear. The person will then respond to the snake with mental formation – with the intentional action of running away.

The khandas are in a state of constant change. Something that causes great pleasure today may cause displeasure tomorrow. This belief in the impermanence of self and the khandas helps Buddhists realize that they should construct a worldview that is not dependent on the self. Through achieving this it is possible to remove aspects of dukkha. How? Let us go back to the example of the snake in the garden – if a person recognizes that their reaction to the snake of fear is the result of a changeable perception and feeling, then they are able to change that feeling and perception and not build their lives around it. Put simply, they may be able live a more balanced life, recognizing that fear and suffering are just the result of impermanent khandas.

Thich Nhat Hanh (1998a) suggests further that by understanding the Five Aggregates a person can be freed some suffering. He provides the example of 'Bodhisattva Avalokita' who 'looked deeply into the reality of the Five Aggregates' and in so doing 'saw the emptiness of self, and he was liberated from suffering' (183). This links inextricably with the discussion about dependent origination, sunyata and emptiness in Chapter 1.

The idea of no-self or anatta is prone to misunderstanding in studying and teaching about Buddhism. The common understanding is that there is no soul or aspect of a being that is permanent or integral to their identifty or existence. It would be better to phrase anatta as no permanent self; in this understanding there is a sense of self that a person thinks is who they are. Gaylon Ferguson (2022) suggests that what is being rejected is 'a self-contained, entirely independent individual', which results in the belief in a 'mistaken sense of self [which] arises as a solidified set of beliefs about who we are and how the world is'. Ferguson suggests that rather than this permanent identity, which rubs up against experience and change, it is possible to identify a fluid or 'non-solid self' where people are not wedded to an idea of themselves – 'dissolving of the seemingly solid walls of ego's fragile tower, our experience is porous and permeable, less cut off and isolated'. This suggests that there are aspects of the self, perhaps even the five khandas, that develop, but there is no aspect that is eternal and remains as the permanent self.

The concept or idea of the self leads to attachment or clinging. It creates an illusory self that a person becomes dependent on or clings to. Shantideva illustrates this point when he recognizes the concept of an unchanging self as the root of suffering:

> All the violence, fear and suffering
> That exists in the world
> Comes from grasping at 'self'.
> What use is this great evil monster to you?
> If you do not let go of the 'self',
> There will never be an end to your suffering.
> Just as, if you do not let go of a flame with your hand,
> You can't stop it from burning your hand. (Shantideva in Thondup, 1998, 3)

With nothing being permanent, there is nothing about an individual that is not subject to change, nor is anything independent. In seeking to cling to the idea of the self a person is subject to the suffering of change and impermanence, as they would like things to stay as they are, or that they are not satisfied with the way that they are. Thanissaro Bhikkhu (2014) suggests just this:

> In other words, [the Buddha] focused on the karma of selfing. Because clinging lies at the heart of suffering, and because there's clinging in each sense of self, he advised using the perception of not-self as a strategy to dismantle that clinging. Whenever you see yourself identifying with anything stressful and inconstant, you remind yourself that it's not-self: not worth clinging to, not worth calling your self.

Indeed, Bhikkhu suggests that the Buddha never taught that there was no self. Tenzin Wangyal Rinpoche expands on this further when he suggests:

> It is not true that there is no self. There is no inherently existing self. When you realize there is no inherent existence of the self you begin to connect with your conventional, relative existence. Usually we don't realize our relative existence because we experience ourselves as solidly existing. This seemingly solid self, or ego, is referred to as the karmic conceptual pain body. (Lion's Roar Staff, 2010)

The Buddha taught only that he refused to answer when faced with such a question. The Buddha warned that involvement in asking such questions would lead people to be entangled and dissatisfied. What was the Buddha, therefore, teaching? In tandem with anicca nothing is permanent and everything is subject to change. As such the idea of the atman or the self, the soul is not a permanent fixture. 'While the Buddha pointed to a lack of an abiding core, he did not deny an existential personality. In other words, things exist but they are not real' (Soeng, 2021). There is an 'I' but making the 'I' as part of a decision-making process means that a person is clinging to the idea of self and cannot be free of suffering and awakened.

Buddha-nature

The belief in anatta is common in almost all Buddhist traditions (the exception is the Dalit Buddhist Movement); it is, however further developed in Mahayana traditions when exploring the nature of a being. A central aspect of most Mahayana traditions is the concept of *buddha-nature* (Skt: *buddhadhatu*), which suggests that every person has the potential within themselves to become a Buddha. There are two understandings of what the buddha-nature is:

- In some traditions it is a potentiality that should be developed throughout life, maybe analogous to a seed.

- Others see it as always present but that it is veiled or hidden by delusions and attachments. The 'activation' or 'realization' of the buddha-nature occurs through practice.

Reference to buddha-nature is evident in many texts used in Mahayana Buddhism. It is not, however, a word that is found within the *Lotus Sutra* but it is implicit throughout. It is argued that when read properly the *Lotus Sutra* is 'an extended inner dialogue between multiple manifestations of awakened buddha-nature on the one hand and the sleeping or deluded self on the other hand' (Wawrytko, 2007, 65). The hiddenness of the buddha-nature is interpreted to be part of the parable of the Hidden Jewel in chapter 8 of the *Lotus Sutra*. In this parable the story is told of a man who when spending the evening at a friend's house fell asleep drunk. While he was asleep his friend took a precious jewel and sewed it into the lining of his cloak; the man remained asleep and oblivious throughout. Following this he spent many years working to earn a living, undergoing much hardship as he did so.

His friend met him years later and queried why he was undertaking such hardship to buy food and clothes. The friend who had sewn the jewel into the lining revealed that he had sewn such so that his friend would never be in need. He encouraged him to go and sell the jewel so that he would always have what he needed.

The interpretation is that the jewel is the buddha-nature within that is always there and waiting to be discovered. The monks listening to the Buddha respond:

> Now we understand that we are really bodhisattvas, assured of attaining supreme awakening. For this reason we are filled with joy, having gained something we never had before. (Reeves, 2008b, 215)

There might appear to be an incongruity between the existence of a buddha-nature and the rejection of a permanent self. To reconcile this 'many traditions interpreted buddha-nature in relationship to the nature of the mind itself; buddha-nature was something about the mind that is the same as a Buddha's mind ... Simply put, in this view buddha-nature is an essential nature of mind, but not a "self"' (Tricycle, 2019). The implications of this belief in buddha-nature will be explored in much greater detail in Chapter 5.

Nature of rebirth

One of the most difficult concepts for students to understand is the concept of rebirth within Buddhism. Linked with the idea of anatta, when compared to the concept of reincarnation, where the 'soul' or 'atman' transmigrates from one body to the next, understanding the nature of rebirth without an atman is difficult. At this point it is important to note the use of language within the classroom. Often the teacher and students speak about reincarnation and rebirth as synonymous. In discussing the two concepts it is often easier and clearer to maintain a distinction where rebirth is the terminology used for Buddhism. In using the different terms it is possible to highlight the differences between the two. It might also be a result of a Western mindset that 'gets hung up' on what continues to exist. Naryan Helen Lieberson has suggested: 'In countries where Buddhism is the predominant religion, rebirth is simply accepted as a fact of life, whereas from a Western perspective it requires a huge leap of faith' (Lion's Roar Staff, 2010).

The usual understanding that is taught about the nature of rebirth surrounds the metaphor of two candles. As one flame goes out another is lit. This is interesting and has been used by many different people, but it does not really show the link between the two; and while in a Theravada view the moment of death might be immediately followed by the moment of conception, within other traditions it is unclear as to the length of time between death marking the ending of the Five Aggregates and the next rebirth. Therefore the metaphor could be extended to one candle goes out and then months, years or aeons later another candle is lit. The fourth or fifth century text *Abhidharmakosa* by Vasubandhu describes it thus:

> What is an intermediate being, and an intermediate existence? ... This existence between two realms of rebirth (gati) is called intermediate existence. (Pruden, 1991, 383)

This intermediate state would be accepted across Buddhist traditions; within some traditions it is known as *bardo*. Within *The Tibetan Book of the Dead* (*Bardo Thodol*) the concept of bardo and its three types: *Chikhai Bardo* (moment of death), *Chonyid Bardo* (experiencing reality) and *Sidpa Bardo* (rebirth), are discussed at length (Dawa-Samdup and Baldock, 2013).

In exploring with Buddhists what they feel extends beyond death, there were a number of responses:

> The subtle mind that is a continuum that manifests in different life forms according to the being's karma, is reborn. The coarse mind, that is associated with the body, of course dies along with the body.
> The essence of our lives, that being refreshed reappears but with a new set of parents and circumstances, or as an animal ... either on this planet or elsewhere in the universe.
> The mind stream or mind of a being.
> The karmic consciousness.

In some ways, however, elements of the aforementioned suggestions of what is reborn would seem at odds with the teaching of anatta, that there is no permanent self. Would the 'subtle mind' or the 'essence of our lives' suggest an enduring element of a person? It may be that these terms are a best effort at articulating that which cannot clearly be expressed. It is also, perhaps, the result of a Western focus on the fixed self and the perpetuation of our lives that means that this is a question at all. Zenkei Hartman argues that asking the question of what continues after death is somewhat redundant:

> Before we become too concerned with what continues life after life, we need to ask, what is it that continues moment after moment? What is this 'self' that we think we are? Can you find it? Can you show it to me? What is it? Where is it? Is there anything apart from the five skandhas – form, feelings, perceptions, mental formations and consciousness – that can be pointed to? (Lion's Roar Staff, 2003)

The fruitlessness of such a question is perhaps why the Buddha refused to answer such questions. There are elements of an answer that can, however, be developed.

Referring back to the twelve nidanas of dependent origination the 'propelling' force of rebirth is karma, and it would appear that there is a consciousness that is part of the process of rebirth. Naryan Lierberson Grady suggests that: 'The process of rebirth is conditioned by mental factors that have been cultivated, either consciously or unconsciously. These qualities of mind, such as desire, generosity, anger and loving-kindness, then condition the energy and form of the next birth' (Lion's Roar Staff, 2003). A further metaphor may be of use in helping understand the nature of rebirth in Buddhism. There is an aphorism that suggests a person cannot step into the same river twice. This suggestion means that by the time a person re-enters the water, that water has moved on and the river is transformed. It is just so with the nature of existence; just as, each day, a person is changing and is not static so that they are different in this moment, than they were a moment ago, so it is with rebirth. Thich Nhat Hanh (2009) has suggested:

> Your body isn't a static thing – it changes all the time. It is very important to see our physical form as something impermanent, as a river that is constantly changing. Every cell in our body is a drop of water in that river. Birth and Death are happening continuously, in every moment of our daily lives. (27)

This is the same with the 'stream' of consciousness that is reborn:

> You see, something continues, but at the same time, nothing continues. In a sense we're like a running stream. You could say, such and such a river, such and such a stream. It has a name, but if you examine it carefully, that river you named three hundred years ago isn't there at all; it is completely different, changing, passing all the time. It is transforming from one aspect to another. (Chogyam Trungpa Rinpoche, in Lion's Roar Staff, 2018)

Throughout life the individual changes, just as an acorn changes and develops into an oak tree. As Peter Harvey (2021a) suggests:

> After death, a changing personality – flux flows on – a little like a river that has gone underground and then reappeared in a different place with a different name. Given long enough, a personality stream will become *very* different from how it is in the present life, yet how it is in that distant future life will have developed from its actions in this life. (97; emphasis in the original)

To suggest an immutable aspect of the individual that will continue from life to life is anathema to Buddhist teaching. The connection between the 'stream', however, explains how there are links to past lives that can sometimes be remembered through meditation. The being that exists 'now' is very different to the being in the past; there is no fixed self. Linking with the concept of sunyata and emptiness it is possible to see the person or the body that is reborn as full, both of life but mostly of everything.

The Buddha rejected the nihilism of his time, and this is evident within the teaching of anatta. At no point did the Buddha suggest that existence and life had no purpose. Quite the contrary; anatta and sunyata highlight the interconnectedness of all of existence, and the consciousness that continues to flow.

Exploring this concept within the classroom is key to help students understand what rebirth is not, but also what it is. One of the often asked questions, in my experience, about the nature of rebirth, in contrast to reincarnation, is the place of the Dalai Lama. Students recognize the Fourteenth Dalai Lama and often see him as the most recognizable Buddhist. The question is, if there is no 'atman', 'soul' or permanent self how can he be the fourteenth rebirth of Avalokitesvara, the Bodhisattva of Compassion. Within Tibetan Buddhism it is believed that Avalokitesvara promised the Buddha that he would take birth to protect the Tibetan people. Although the title, Dalai Lama, was not used until over a hundred years after the first Dalai Lamas death it is seen that the first 'incarnation' was Gendun Drup (1391–1474), a monk from the Kadampa tradition. Following Gendrun Drup's death, Sangyey Pel (later Gendun Gyatso Palzangpo [1475–1542]) at the age of three

> began to express the wish to go to Tashi Lhunpo Monastery. He would call out to birds and monkeys who came near him, 'Have you come to take me home to Tashi Lhunpo?' ... The father asked of him, 'And who are you? What is your name?' The boy replied in song, My name is Gendun Drubpa, the monkhood's great hope. (Mullin, 2001, 90–1)

It was with the third Dalai Lama, Sonam Gyatso (1543–88), in 1578, that the title of Dalai Lama was given and retrospectively applied. Throughout the subsequent years the various incarnations of the Dalai Lama are listed in Table 2.1.

This process does not deny the impermanence of the self, but it recognizes that though the stream of consciousness can be recalled, the fixed self has changed. The passing of the consciousness in Tibetan Buddhism is known as *phowa*, and immediately upon the death of the Dalai Lama the search begins for the next incarnation. An account of the search for a new Lama (not the Dalai Lama) is fictionalized in the 1993 film, *Little Buddha*.

Further exploration of the nature of a bodhisattva and the volitional rebirths that they undertake will be explored in Chapter 5.

Realms of rebirth

Having established the nature of what is reborn, it is helpful to explore Buddhist cosmology in terms of the possible rebirths that can be undertaken. There are commonalities within Theravada and Mahayana teaching but there are also differences. It seems sensible to explore each in turn before returning to a discussion of the common themes.

Mahayana cosmology

The most evident teaching or example of Mahayana descriptions of the realms of rebirth are shown within the Tibetan Wheel of Life (*Bhavachakra*) (see Figure 1.1).

Table 2.1 The Fourteen Dalai Lamas

Name	Birth/death	Recognized	Enthroned
Gendun Drup	1391–1474		
Gendun Gyatso	1475–1542	1483	1487
Sonam Gyatso	1543–1588	1546	1578
Yonten Gyatso	1589–1617	1601	1603
Ngawang Lobsang Gyatso	1617–1682	1618	1622
Tsangyang Gyatso	1683–1706	1688	1697
Kelzang Gyatso	1707–1757	1712	1720
Jamphel Gyatso	1758–1804	1760	1762
Lungtok Gyatso	1805–1815	1807	1808
Tsultrim Gyatso	1816–1837	1822	1822
Khendrup Gyatso	1838–1856	1841	1842
Trinley Gyatso	1857–1875	1858	1860
Thubten Gyatso	1876–1933	1878	1879
Tenzin Gyatso	1935	1939	1940

This illustrates the fact that there are six realms, which are described in the *Lankavatara Sutra*:

> There are six realms of transmigration where beings take birth.
> They are the realms of gods, demigods, humans, animals, hungry ghosts, and hell.
> You take birth in those realms because of superior, middling, and evil karmas. (in Rinpoche, 2006, 65)

In the centre, driving the Wheel, means that people continue to be reborn because of the three poisons – craving (desire), hatred (aversion) and ignorance, usually represented by a pig, a bird and a snake. Linked with the belief of karma explored in the discussion of dependent origination earlier on (see Chapter 1), it is possible to see karma as the driving force of the wheel, which is underpinned by ignorance. The wheel will stop turning and rebirth will end when actions are underpinned by wisdom rather than ignorance. The various realms will now be explored.

Gods

In the realm of the gods or the devas a person is reborn because of positive karma, and it is believed to be a blissful existence. There is the ability to enjoy all sensual pleasures, and as a result of the imbalance between pleasure and suffering in favour of pleasure, there is a lack of impetus to seek for awakening, and, for the most part, there is little regard or opportunity to listen to dharma. There are believed to be various heavens in the realms of the gods, numbers differ, but some think it is twenty-six, which is interesting when compared with Theravada cosmology explained further on. Perhaps, unsurprisingly, in some traditions with a bodhisattva ideal being outside of the possibility, or seeming so despite the buddha-nature within all, Kevin Trainor (2004) suggests that 'the prospect of a heavenly rebirth motivated the devotions of the vast majority of Buddhist lay people in history. A human or heavenly rebirth is the only desirable destiny in *samsara*' (62).

Demigods/demons

Although phrased as demigods, demons may be a more accurate description for those who dwell in this realm. They are focussed on the expression of, and quality of, anger, often fighting among themselves. They periodically launch assaults on the heavens, and are believed to cause problems for humans. Sometimes aspects of the human condition are attributed to the actions of demons, such as disease and natural disasters. They continue to accumulate karma in what is seen to be a 'bad' realm and will be reborn upon the end of their time in this realm.

Humans

The human realm is this realm of existence. Donald Lopez (2015a) offers an insight into the desirability of rebirth into this realm in the title of his article 'Of Buddhism's six alternately wretched and blissful realms, only ours offers a shot at complete ciberation'. This highlights the nature of this realm as an ideal place to live the Middle Way (see Chapter 4) in comparison to the first two and the last three realms. In this realm the balance between suffering and pleasure means that a human is able to listen to and practice the equanimity of the dharma. This is the ideal condition and the only place to become awakened.

Animals

The realm of the animals is an undesirable place to be reborn into as animals 'are governed by brute instinct and lack the intellectual capacity to understand the nature of their situation or do much to improve it' (Keown, 2013, 36).

Restless spirits/hungry ghosts

These are those beings whose senses can never be satisfied. They continue with cravings but have no capacity to eat or to act on any of the senses.

Hell (Pali: *naraka*, Sanskrit: *niraya*)

In identifying the final realm as 'hell' care should be taken to not allow students to draw too close a parallel to other interpretations of hell in other religions. Niraya is a realm in which evil karma has propelled a consciousness to rebirth. The evil karma is removed as a consequences through a variety of punishments 'such as eight extremely hot hellish realms and eight extremely cold, as well as realms in which beings are partially eaten alive, beaten or subjected to various other forms of torture – all this in proportion to the evil kamma accumulated' (Dhammasami, 2019, 88).

Once the evil karma is dissipated, a being in the hell realm dies, and the consciousness is reborn in another realm. There would appear to be no possibility of escaping the cycle of rebirth from this realm.

In exploring the potential rebirths of the stream of consciousness within Buddhism, the Wheel of Life is full of potential, and it will be good to engage students with how human life is viewed and the potential it offers. It is important to explore the Wheel of Life and Mahayana cosmology alongside the Theravadan view of the realms of existence, which are sometimes missed within the classroom.

Pure Lands

In addition to the six realms within the Wheel of Existence there are also infinite Pure Lands. Within Mahayana Buddhism there are many traditions that teach of Pure Lands. A Pure Land is sometimes referred to as a buddha-field (Skt: *buddhaksetra*). Although there are many Pure Lands within Mahayana traditions, the five main ones are associated with the *Five Tathagatas* or Great Buddhas who are seen to be emanations of the original Buddha within Vajrayana, and embodiments of the dharma. These five Pure Lands are distributed throughout the land:

- *Akanistha-Ghanavyuha*, the Pure Land of *Vairocana* situated in the centre.
- *Abhirati*, the Pure Land of *Aksobhya* situated in the east.
- *Srimat*, the Pure Land of *Ratnasambhava* situated in the south.
- *Sukhavati*, the Pure Land of *Amitabha* situated in the west.
- *Karmaprasiddhi* or *Prakuta*, the Pure Land of *Amoghasiddhi* situated in the north.

Within Buddhism today, the Pure Land tradition generally focuses on Buddha Amitabha (Japanese: Amida; the Buddha of Infinite Light) and his Pure Land of Sukhavati (land of bliss and happiness). During his life as the monk, Dharmakara, the future Buddha Amitabha, because of his compassion, promised in the presence of a Buddha that he would create a paradise, or a Pure Land, from which he would lead people to awakening. He promised that on attaining buddhahood that he would establish a buddhaland, and in *The Larger Sutra (Sutra on the Buddha of Infinite Life Delivered by Sakyamuni Buddha)* he vowed:

> Free of greed and with profound mindfulness
> And pure wisdom, I will perform the sacred practices;

I will seek to attain the unsurpassed Way
And become the teacher of devas and humans.

With my divine power I will display great light,
Illuminating the worlds without limit,
And dispel the darkness of the three defilements;
Thus I will deliver all beings from misery. (Inagaki and Stewart, 2003, 18)

This land of infinite bliss is available to all beings from the different realms, and by meditating on the Buddha Amitabha and reciting his name a being is able to attain rebirth in Sukhavati from where Amitabha will lead them to awakening. His infinite compassion and light means that karmic transference is available to all. This links closely with the belief in a buddha-nature within all that can be realized in a moment. The devotion required to Amitabha is seen to provide those without the capacity for the focus and learning of traditional methods to find a path to awakening.

In modern Pure Land Buddhism in Japan the recitation of the *nembutsu* (mantra of Amida) is an important aspect of devotion. The name nembutsu is a contraction of the mantra '*Namu Amida Butsu*' in Japanese, which is variously translated as 'Namo Buddha of Infinite Life' and 'I pay homage to the Enlightened One immeasurable'. For many devotion and meditation to the Buddha Amitabha will guarantee them rebirth in the Pure Land; whereas, for others, it is assured the moment a person expresses faith in Amitabha.

The concept of Pure Lands, and its expression in Pure Land Buddhism today, provides an opportunity in the classroom to explore an alternative path to awakening. This belief highlights the buddha-nature and the compassion of bodhisattvas, as well as the concept of karmic transference. It is interesting to compare elements of Pure Land practice with wider Buddhism, and as Wendy Dossett (2020) has done engage with the question *Is Pure Land Buddhism Buddhism?* The beliefs challenge the received structure of Buddhism that teachers and students are used to through a colonial lens, and for this reason alone it is a useful activity to engage with.

Theravada cosmology

In exploring the Mahayana interpretation of the realms of existence first, it is possible to use this as a reference point for the different realms of rebirth that are taught in Theravada cosmology (see Figure 2.1). At first glance, Theravada seems somewhat different in the sense that instead of six realms of rebirth, they teach that there are three realms (*loka*):

- *Arupaloka* is the immaterial or formless realm. In this loka there are four planes of existence (see Table 2.2). Once their karma has been exhausted they will be reborn into another world.
- *Rupaloka* – the fine material realm. There are sixteen planes of existence within this loka (see Table 2.2).

The Nature of Humanity

Figure 2.1 Nineteenth-century painting of Buddhist cosmology (Mandalay, Myanmar, 1886). 'The artist presents a liberally interpreted vision of the world, heavens and hells. The sun and moon are shown in their own pavilions, the sun being represented by a peacock on a red background, and the moon by a hare on a yellow background'.

Source: British Library, n.d.

Table 2.2 The Thirty-One Planes of Existence and Three Realms of Rebirth in Theravada Cosmology

Arupaloka

Plane of existence	Circumstances	Cause of rebirth
31. Neither perception nor non-perception (*nevasannanasannayatana*) 30. Plane of nothingness (*akincannayatana*) 29. Infinite consciousness/space (*vinnanancayatana*) 28. Infinite space (*akasanancayatana*)	These beings have no physical body, and have only a mind, but they can take on the form of a physical body if they wish others to see them. They still experience dukkha but less intensely. It is impossible to be enlightened in these realms as they are unable to hear the dhamma.	'Beings born in these realms due to having attained these states of meditative absorption when they were human beings stay in these states for aeons' (Dalai Lama and Chodron, 2014, 96). Respectively from 31 to 28 people in these planes have attained the fourth, third, second and first formless *jhanas* (see Chapter 7).

Rupaloka

Plane of existence	Circumstances	Cause of rebirth
27. Peerless devas (*akanitthabhum*) 26. Clear-sighted devas (*sudassibhum*) 25. Beautiful devas (*sudassabhum*) 24. Serene/untroubled devas (*atappabhum*) 23. Durable/not falling away devas (*avihabhum*)	There are five Suddhavasa (pure abodes) whose inhabitants are known as non-returners as they are on the path to becoming an arahant; as such they will attain nibbana in those worlds. These beings will not be bodhisattva in the sense that the Buddha was (see Chapter 3) as they will never take rebirth in another realm.	Someone who has entered the fourth jhana: 'There is the case where an individual, with the abandoning of pleasure and pain – as with the earlier disappearance of elation and distress – enters and remains in the fourth jhana: purity of equanimity and mindfulness, neither pleasure nor pain' (*Jhana Sutta*).
22. Mindless devas/unconscious beings (*asannasattabhum*)	Here only the body is present, and there is no 'mind'.	
21. Very fruitful devas (Vehapphalabhum) 20. Devas of refulgent/radiant glory (*subhakinna deva*) 19. Devas of unbounded glory (*appamanasubha deva*)	Those in this realm have bodies of very fine, refined light, and will enjoy lengthy lifespans. Once their karma has been exhausted they will be reborn into another world. Beings in these planes enjoy jhanic bliss in varying degrees.	Passing away in the third jhana is attained through *samatha bhavana* (concentration meditation).

The Nature of Humanity

18. Devas of limited glory (*parittasubha deva*)		
17. Devas of streaming radiance (*abhassara deva*)		Passing away in the second jhana is attained through *samatha bhavana* (concentration meditation).
16. Devas of unbounded radiance (*appamanabha deva*)		
15. Devas of limited radiance/ glory (*parittabha deva*)		
14. Great Brahmas (*maha brahma*)	The plane whose most well-known inhabitant is Brahma who believes himself to be a deity, and as such does not seek the truth of the dhamma: 'I, monk, am Brahma, the Great Brahma, the Conqueror, the Unconquered, the All-Seeing, All-Powerful, the Sovereign Lord, the Maker, Creator, Chief, Appointer and Ruler, Father of All That Have Been and Shall Be' (*Kevatta Sutta*).	First jhana
13. Brahma's minsters (*brahma-purohita deva*)	Beings in these planes enjoy jhanic bliss in varying degrees.	
12. Brahma's retinue (*brahma-parisajja deva*)		

Kamaloka

Plane of existence	Circumstances	Cause of rebirth
11. Devas who enjoy sensory pleasures/the creation of others (*paranimmitavassavati bhum*)	In this plane beings enjoy the sensuous pleasures designed by others. Mara exists in this realm.	As a result of positive kamma, particularly based on the Ten Wholesome Actions (see Chapter 8), the expression of *dana* (generosity) and the development of virtue and wisdom.
10. Devas who delight in creating (*nimmanarati bhum*)	In this plane beings enjoy acts of creation for themselves.	
9. Devas of happiness and contentment (*tusita bhum*)	A realm of pure bliss. Bodhisattva are said to dwell here before coming to earth. Maitreya dwells here.	'With the break-up of the body, after death, he reappears in the

8. Blissful existence (*yama bhum*)	Beings in this plane live in the air free of all difficulty.	company of devas. There he experiences the five strings of divine sensuality [delightful sights, sounds, smells, tastes, tactile sensations]. It's because he refrained from taking what is not given ... and had right views that he reappears in the company of devas. And it's because he gave food, drink, cloth, vehicles, garlands, scents, creams, bed, lodging, and lamps to contemplatives and brahmans that he experiences the five strings of divine sensuality' (*Janussonin Sutta*).
7. The thirty-three gods (*tavatimsa bhum*)	Many gods dwell in this realm, including Sakka, a devotee of Brahma who rules here.	
6. Heaven of four great kings (*catummaharajika bhum*)	In this plane dwell the celestial musicians (*gandhabbas*) and the tree spirits (*yakkhas*).	
5. Human beings (*manussa loka*)	Rebirth in this realm is seen to be most fortuitous as there is a balance of pleasure and pain, and the ability to hear the Buddha's dhamma and attain nibbana. The circumstances of life inspires people to develop morality (*sila*), mental development (*samadhi*) and wisdom (*panna*), which are part of the Eightfold Path (see Chapter 4).	Wholesome action and kamma can lead to rebirth into the human realm. Also, becoming a stream enterer (*sotapanna*) on the path to arahantship guarantees rebirth into this plane.
4. Demons (*asura loka*)	The demons or titans in this realm are always fighting.	Committing elements of the Ten Unwholesome Actions (see Chapter 8).
3. Spirits and hungry ghosts (*peta loka*)	Spirits, best represented by the hungry ghosts, wander in this realm seeking, but never finding, sensual pleasure.	Committing elements of the Ten Unwholesome Actions, holding wrong views and being unvirtuous.

2. Animals (*tiracchana loka*)	The inhabitants of this realm are animals.	Committing elements of the Ten Unwholesome Actions, holding wrong views, being unvirtuous and behaving like an animal. If a being has been generous to monks or nuns they can receive rebirth as a better animal: 'It's because he gave food, drink ... and lamps to contemplatives and brahmans ... he receives food, drink, flowers, and various ornaments' (*Janussonin Sutta*). The ornaments are often suggested to mean brightly coloured, such as peacocks.
1. Hell (*niraya*)	A place of unimaginable torment and suffering. The *Devaduta Sutta* describes red hot pokers, smiting with axes, boiling in copper pots and many more sufferings. Life in this realm continues until all negative kamma is used up.	Committing elements of the Ten Unwholesome Actions, holding wrong views, being unvirtuous, annoying others, murdering a parent, murdering an arahant or causing a split in the sangha.

- *Kamaloka* – also known as the planes of sensuous experience – is where beings can receive sensual experience within their lives. In this loka there are seven happy states and four states of deprivation (see Table 2.2).

Table 2.2 is fairly comprehensive in describing a Theravada cosmology. Despite the vast majority of teaching about Buddhism in classrooms being based on elements of a Theravada worldview, or a mixture of the two, it is interesting to note that when exploring the nature of the 'afterlife' that the main focus is on the Mahayana Wheel of Life. The learner may be left with the impression that Theravada Buddhists believe the same as Mahayana Buddhists, or that the belief is a focus on nibbana with rebirth on this earth and the multiple expressions of existence it contains.

It is important for the teacher, and for students, to recognize the harmony between the two cosmologies represented by the Wheel of Life and the various realms of Theravada belief. In comparing elements of belief it is always important to recognize the areas of convergence and divergence. The exploration of the realm of the gods in Mahayana is both similar and different to the twenty-six realms of devas and gods within Theravada.

Nirvana/nibbana

In the exploration of the Four Noble Truths nirvana was discussed as the Third Noble Truth; the recognition that there can be an end to dukkha and attachment and nirvana is that end. There were two elements of nirvana that were touched upon:

1. The nirvana that is attained upon awakening in this life. At this point in a person's life attachment and suffering are of no consequence, and they have overcome both. This person is said to live in a state of *sopadhisesa-nirvana*. It is not that they will not experience the vicissitudes of life. Rather that the sufferings and disappointments will be put in their proper perspective.

2. It is this *parinirvana* (*parinibbana*) that is the second element. This is the final cessation where rebirth is ended. It is this nirvana that will be explored here.

It is the ending or cessation of craving and dispassion. Following death the Five Aggregates cease to cling to one another. The traditional translation of nirvana is 'blowing out'; meaning that the fires associated with existence are extinguished. Richard Gombrich (2010) takes issue with the terminology of 'blowing' as it suggests that it is an outside action. Rather, he suggests the use of 'going out' to better reflect Buddhist teachings as it does not imply 'any agent who causes that going' (325).

While it may seem odd to a modern mind to ask the question 'Where has the flame gone?', 'the Buddha's audience in ancient India would generally have thought of an extinguished fire as going back into a non-manifested state as latent heat' (Harvey, 2013, 79). When considering the place and status of an arahant after death, it 'is beyond description' but 'early texts suggest that it is a radiant, radically transformed state of consciousness' (Ranatunga, 2021, 112). The phrase 'neither coming, nor going' is perhaps one of the most oft quoted descriptions of nibbana, but it is unclear as to the nature of existence and of nirvana following when nibbana is experienced. Indeed, in a further moment of explanation the Buddha used a number of descriptive terms that, in some ways, leave the reader no clearer. Nirvana is:

> far shore ... the subtle ... the very difficult to see ... the unaging ... the stable ... the undisintegrating ... the unmanifest ... the unproliferated ... the peaceful ... the deathless ... the sublime ... the auspicious ... the secure ... the destruction of craving ... the wonderful ... the amazing ... the unailing ... the unailing state ... Nibbana ... the unafflicted ... dispassion ... purity ... freedom ... the unadhesive ... the island ... the shelter ... the asylum ... the refuge. (*Anasavadi Sutta*)

Returning to the idea of a fire gone out, utilizing the way fire was viewed in the time of the Buddha can help to understand the nature of nibbana, not as a place, which it most certainly is not, but as a state of being. Thanissaro Bhikkhu (2018) outlines:

> What did an extinguished fire represent to the Indians of the Buddha's day? Anything but annihilation. However, when teaching his own disciples, the Buddha used nirvana more as an image of freedom. Apparently, all Indians at the time saw burning fire as agitated, dependent, and trapped, both clinging and being stuck to its fuel as it burned. To ignite a fire, one had to 'seize' it. When fire let go of its fuel, it was 'freed,' released from its agitation, dependence, and entrapment—calm and unconfined. This is why Pali poetry repeatedly uses the image of extinguished fire as a metaphor for freedom … The Buddha insists that this level is indescribable, even in terms of existence or nonexistence, because words work only for things that have limits. (63–4)

This description is important in beginning to explain to students the nature of nibbana after death. Viewed through a Western Christocentric mindset students will be more familiar with the ultimate goal of a heaven-like place. While it is important not to use Christianity, or any other religion, as a yardstick against which to judge others, it is important to recognize that something that may be taken for granted in a Buddhist worldview would be difficult to grasp for others. In some ways we are asking students from a particular context to unlearn their preconceived ideas about an afterlife. If the ultimate goal is neither existence nor non-existence then how a student can understand this may be problematic. The Buddha was clear that in certain situations there is no answer to the questions that people have. An adequate description of nibbana may be one of those, and teachers need to be clear in their teaching that nibbana is neither a place nor is it analogous to beliefs about life after death in other religions.

Thoughts for the classroom

The nature of humanity, and of existence more widely, is a central aspect of the exploration of any religion or worldview. Understanding this enables students to reflect upon how religious people respond to these questions. The comparison of the various approaches to the 'afterlife' in Buddhism can help understand the lenses through which beliefs are understood and put into practice. The image of the Wheel of Life, as suggested throughout the chapter, is central to the teaching of Buddhist cosmology, both in terms of expressing Mahayana philosophy and being an impetus to explore Theravada beliefs and practices. The visual arts lies at the heart of the teaching of religions and worldviews.

An important aspect of the use of art, and in this context the Wheel of Life, is that it is used for more than illustration. It should be used as a focus for learning. The Wheel of Life is more than a piece of art, or an expression of belief. For some Buddhists it is used in devotional activities as a mandala, to focus meditation. As such it should be treated with respect. There are questions that the teacher needs to ask themselves before using objects such as the Wheel of Life in teaching.

- Why are we using it?
- Do the students understand how it is viewed and used within the faith?
- How would an adherent of the faith feel about the way that we are using it?

This provides the teacher with safeguards in their mind about the purpose and treatment of the mandala. In planning an encounter with the Wheel of Life the teacher should recognize the importance of questioning. In using the art as a source of information and understanding for pupils it is important for appropriately structured questions be provided to point the discussion and discovery of learning in the right direction. The exercise could begin with pupils interrogating the Wheel of Life with minimal input:

- What do they notice?
- What questions would they like to ask?
- What do they think is happening in the picture?

The teacher could begin to introduce specific questions to focus and encourage discussion. This could then lead onto the purpose of the teaching, and as such could be referred back to throughout the learning. Reflection on the Wheel of Life, as with all art, can help 'incarnate our experience of mystery, wonder, and awe; they thereby aid us to encounter the holy or sacred' (Lealman and Robinson, 1983, xii). The focus could be the realms of rebirth, the nidanas, or the driving forces of the wheel.

3

The Buddha

It may appear to be odd that we are a number of pages and chapters into a book on Buddhism and it is only now that we are devoting our attention to the life of the Buddha, Siddhartha Gautama. If we look at many analyses of Buddhists since the nineteenth century they often begin with an exploration of his life. As already mentioned, the reason for this may well be that those first 'Western' commentators on Buddhism saw religion through a Christian lens, where the personality and life of the 'founder' was significant and provided the framework for understanding the wider religion. It could be suggested that the life of Shakyamuni Buddha provides an allegory for the truths that he taught. It is evident in conversation with Buddhists that his primary role is as a teacher and a role model. There are other elements within Buddhism, such as the lived experience of the dhamma, that might begin an exploration of Buddhism. Consider the following statements that Buddhists have made about the Buddha:

> He was the historical Buddha who founded Buddhism and showed the teachings by his behaviour and taught for many years. All Buddhist teachings refer back to his I believe some 80,000 teachings in total.
> The ultimate expression of the enlightened mind in all its aspects. A teacher, an aspiration and ultimate reality.
> He is the primary role model and teacher.

As the role model and teacher, and the person who rediscovered the path, he is worthy of study, both in terms of his life and his teaching. He left his teachings for people to follow, but the life he lived helps Buddhists today to live a life that will enable equanimity in this life and freedom from the cycle of samsara beyond.

Sources for his life

Who is Siddhartha Gautama, the Buddha? How do we know the events that happened to him? In many classrooms the received account of his life is presented as the accepted narrative, with sometimes little attempt to explore the sources of the accounts of his life, as well as the diversity of narrations that can sometimes tell us more about the author/narrator than it might well tell us about the Buddha himself.

At certain points within the 'Western' study of Buddhism there has been the question as to whether the Buddha actually existed in history. People would now reject this discussion and recognize that there was an historical figure, the Buddha, who was a renunciate teacher in the fourth to fifth centuries BCE. The earliest mention of the Buddha that are extant come in the reign of Emperor Ashoka (dates of reign: 269–232 BCE). Ashoka was emperor of the Mauryan Empire in South Asia; today there is evidence of Edicts of Ashoka that are found on pillars in modern countries such as Bangladesh, India, Nepal, Afghanistan and Pakistan. These pillars mention the Buddha and Buddhism. Ashoka was an emperor who followed Buddhism, and the evidence of these edicts are used by historians to recognize the inheritance of the life of the Buddha. The edicts are also early confirmations of aspects of the Buddha's teachings that can be found today; one such example from the Minor Edicts includes a recitation of the Three Jewels:

> The king of Magadha, Piyadassi, greets the Order and wishes it prosperity and freedom from care. You know Sirs, how deep is my respect for and faith in the Buddha, the Dhamma and the Samgha [i.e. the Buddhist creed]. Sirs, whatever was spoken by the Lord Buddha was well spoken. (Thapar, 1997, 261)

The Rummindei Edict of Ashoka in Lumbini recognized it as the birthplace of the Buddha:

> When King Devanampriya Priyadarsin had been anointed twenty years, he came himself and worshipped (this spot) because the Buddha Shakyamuni was born here. (He) both caused to be made a stone bearing a horse (?) and caused a stone pillar to be set up, (in order to show) that the Blessed One was born here. (He) made the village of Lumbini free of taxes, and paying (only) an eighth share (of the produce). (Hultzsch, 1925, 164–5)

These markers of events in the Buddha's life structured the writing of *Asokavadana* (*The Legend of King Ashoka*) written in the second century CE. This is an imagined account of a pilgrimage by Ashoka and a Buddhist monk, Upagupta. For many early Buddhists, however, the use of the pillars as stopping points in a pilgrimage reflected the assumption that the purpose of the Edicts was primarily to mark places of importance in the Buddha's life. John Strong (1983) suggests that 'they were [seen to be] ancient signposts piously erected by Asoka for the benefit of travellers and pilgrims' (8), recounting the events of the Buddha's life.

The importance of these sites and the events surrounding them seem to be established by the second century, and some may have been established as such by the time of Ashoka in the third century BCE. John Strong (2015) highlights the problem that the historian faces in using such an account of pilgrimage sites as an authoritative source for the events associated with them. He suggests it is a 'chicken and egg' dilemma, suggesting that it is not always clear what came first: the story or the place it happened. On the one hand, sites became established as the place where certain stories occurred and were visited by pilgrims. On the other, new stories came to be told to explain the existence (or bolster the popularity) of certain sites that were already being noticed. (59)

Whatever the veracity of *Asokavadana*, it is nonetheless reflective that an oral tradition had been passed down through the previous centuries that established a narrative of the Buddha's life.

There are earlier extant narrations of the Buddha's life that have been written and continue to be used today. These include aspects of his life events found in suttas:

- *Amazing and Astounding Qualities: Acchariy'abbhutadhamma Sutta* recounts aspects of the Buddha's birth.
- *The Noble Search: Ariyapariyesana Sutta* recounts his leaving the palace.
- *The Longer Discourse to Saccaka: Maha Saccaka Sutta* recounts elements of his life as an ascetic.
- *Padhana Sutta: Exertion* where the Buddha defeats Mara.
- *Mahavagga* (Great Division) *of the Pali Vinaya* (Book of Discipline) recounts the events immediately following his enlightenment.
- *The Discourse on the Fourfold Assembly: Catusparisat Sutra* tells the story of the Buddha from his enlightenment to the acceptance of his two chief disciples.
- *The Great Total Unbinding Discourse: Maha Parinibbana Sutta* recounts the last days of his life.

Although these are to be found within Pali canonical texts (see Chapter 7) they are subject to the same issues of memory and hagiography as other accounts of the Buddha's life. Some Buddhists may see these as more authoritative but not necessarily so. The early 'extra-canonical' accounts of the Buddha's life include:

- *Buddhaccarita*: *Acts of the Buddha* is believed to the oldest extant full version of the Buddha's life. It was written by Asvaghosa, a Buddhist monk of north Indian origin, in the first or possibly early second century. It was translated into Chinese by Dharmaksema in 420 and then later into Tibetan in the in the seventh or eighth century.
- *Abhiniskramana-sutra: On the Birth of the Buddha* translated into Chinese in the sixth century by Jnanagupta an Indian Buddhist monk who lived in China. The exact date of writing is unknown but Samuel Beal (2003) suggests that it was known in China towards the latter end of the first century. He posits that this suggests 'the original work was in circulation In India for some time previous to this date' (vi).
- *Lalitavistara Sutra: The Play in Full* records the story of the Buddha's life, and the Sanskrit play is traditionally dated to approximately the third century. There are elements of the narration that place it firmly in the Mahayana Tradition, not least the title (which will be

discussed in the next section about the Buddha's identity). Indeed, in the introduction to its translation, the Dharmachakra Translation Committee (2013) suggest that 'this scripture is an obvious compilation of various early sources, which have been strung together and elaborated on according to the Mahayana worldview. As such this text is a fascinating example of the ways in which the Mahayana rests firmly on the earlier tradition, yet reinterprets the very foundations of Buddhism in a way that fit its own vast perspective' (xii).

- *Mahavastu: Great Story* is believed to have been compiled between the second century BCE and fourth century. It would appear to be a collection from various sources; indeed, its original languages seem to be a mix of Pali, Sanskrit and Prakrit (see Jones, 1949). In addition to events from the life of the Buddha it does contain Jataka tales.
- *Nidanakatha: Introductory tale* is an introduction to the larger body of Jataka tales, Jatakatthavannana, which were collected together in the fifth century. The Nidanakatha has three sections: the first, narrates previous lives; the second, his birth up to his enlightenment; followed by the third section that narrates from his enlightenment to when the Jetavana monastery is donated by Anathapindika.

There are other narrations of the story of the Buddha's life, and many more that draw on these traditions and sources. For example Tenzin Chogyel's (2015) *The Life of the Buddha* is a Tibetan retelling from the eighteenth century that is seen to draw 'together the cosmic and the human'. In his retelling, 'we glimpse the majestic scale of the Buddha's epic journey toward enlightenment' (Schaeffer, 2015, xv).

This is the problem which we face when utilizing accounts of the Buddha's life in our teaching; there are no contemporaneous accounts of his life (though these would come with their own problems). The earliest written accounts that we do have were written by his followers and were more in the style of hagiography. These are important and frame the narrative, because they form the background to the received traditions that are told throughout the world today. Although I used the word 'problem' at the beginning of this paragraph, perhaps obstacle is better. The search for the authentic Buddha is something that is replicated with different figures throughout religion. In some ways, this search is 'academic' in the sense that Buddhists today respond to the stories in different ways, and we, as teachers, are not to make judgements on the veracity of events, but to help students understand how the different received traditions help provide a rich diversity of belief and practice within Buddhism.

However, this search for the 'authentic' narration of the story of the life of the Buddha is of importance to many Buddhists in seeking inspiration from his life, teachings and example. In defining Buddhism in the Introduction to this book we explored how modernism has led to some wishing to remove the 'mystical' from Buddhism and make it more rational in its presentation. Richard Hayes suggest that modern 'Western scholars (an many Western Buddhists)' have seen the Buddha to be 'a remarkably wise and thoughtful and kind-hearted man upon whom tradition has superimposed a bundle of superhuman attributes' (2018, 494). In addition to this approach being an attempt to discover the original figure of the Buddha, it can also be seen to meet the needs of the modern world. How this affects the aspects of the retelling of the story of the Buddha is shown by Glenn Wallis (2020); he suggests that he finds refuge and inspiration in the life of Siddhartha Gautama rather than the Buddha:

> I have given up on the Buddha. That is to say, I have given up on the Enlightened One, the Blessed One, the omniscient Lord of people and gods who works miracles, knows unknowable things, and continues to exert his power from beyond. (66)

I think the suggestion that he makes is that there is more to learn from the more human and mundane experiences of the Buddha. He is not rejecting the 'mystical', rather they are of no benefit to him in trying to follow the dharma. In interrogating the various narratives, we need to be careful not to go too far and unnecessarily delve into the lenses we bring, as well as the lenses of writers and believers. Peter Harvey (2020) makes just this observation:

> But trying to dig back to the 'bare facts' of the Buddha's life can be like stripping the patina off a fine antique—something many people would be wary of doing, since it might be disrespectful to the original. However, perhaps it is necessary, as the 'antique' Buddha needs restoring, and doing so may reveal the various decorations that have been added over the centuries. Still, we need to beware of being restricted by too narrow a view of what is possible; our modern perspectives and ideas may lead us to a rather thin and shallow way of seeing the world. (26–7)

This danger was realized in the nineteenth century when certain presentations of the Buddha presented him 'as a reformer of the 'evil' of the Hindu system, a spirit of Protestant opponent of Hindu papism … or he was viewed as a socialist, a radical revolutionary who sought an egalitarian society' (Strong, 2001, 3).

Recognizing the tendency to recreate the story of the Buddha in our own image and according to our needs, in the presentation of his life, I follow the approach of John Strong (2001) who suggested that we should 'try to respect the extraordinary supernatural elements in the tales told about him, to understand them without explaining them away', while trying 'at the same time to honour the ordinary down-to-earth elements that root him in humanity, in a given time and place' (3). Each aspect of his story illustrates aspects of Buddhist teaching that we can draw on as we teach both his life and how Buddhists live today.

His identity

Before narrating the events of his life, it is important to explain who the Buddha is seen to be. Sometimes in classroom the simple answer is that in exploring his life, he is 'simply' the Buddha and the differences between Mahayana, Theravada and other interpretations are inconsequential as we explore the events. However, there is a distinct difference between who the Buddha was prior to his life in the fifth century BCE, or thereabouts.

The Jataka tales, or stories about the Buddha's past lives, show many aspects of who he is during his life as Siddhartha Gautama and the preparation that he had undergone. One of the most famous stories of the Buddha's past life surrounds his encounter with a previous Buddha, Dipamkara. In the Pali retelling the future Siddhartha Gautama is called Sumedha, whereas in Sanskrit he is known variously as Megha or Sumati. Sumedha is a brahmin who has become an ascetic who, on seeing the Buddha Dipamkara approach, lays his hair across a muddy part of the path so that Dipamkara can walk across unsullied. It is at this point that Sumedha determines to become a Buddha like Dipamkara rather than attain liberation unknown and unbidden.

Dipamkara outlines the ten perfections that are required of a Buddha, and that in numerous aeons Sumedha would become Gautama Buddha. This marks his beginning as a bodhisattva (bodhisatta),[1] a Buddha in waiting. The timing of this lifetime is said to be four incalculable ages and 100,000 aeons ago. An aeon is thought to be 4.32×10^8, and an incalculable possible age of 10^{140} (Strong, 2015, 50). Since that time the bodhisattva went through innumerable lifetimes where he mastered the perfections required of a Buddha; the *Nidanakatha of the Jatakathakatha* (Jayawichrama, 2006) record tales of:

- The contributory conditions to enlightenment; the perfections of:
  - generosity
  - morality
  - renunciation
  - wisdom
  - effort
  - patience
  - truth
  - resolution
  - amity
  - equanimity

He is also said to have met the twenty-three Buddhas who came to earth between Buddha Dipamkara and Buddha Gautama (see Table 3.1).

Table 3.1 The Experience of the Bodhisattva (Future Buddha Gautama) with Previous Buddhas

Buddha	The bodhisattva's birth	Particular acts of the bodhisattva towards the Buddha
Dipamkara	Sumedha, a brahmin/ascetic	Determines to become a Buddha
Kondanna	Vijitavinl, a kshatriya	Gives food to the Buddha and to the wider community
Mangala	Surici, a brahmin	Gives gifts of food, perfumes and garland to the Buddha and the wider community
Sumana	Atula, a serpent king	Gives music, a meal and robes to the Buddha and the wider community
Revat	Atideva, a brahmin	Gives the Buddha a robe and takes refuge in him
Sobhitaa	Sujata, a brahmin	Gives food to the Buddha and to the wider community
Anomadassi	Yaaksa, a deity responsible for protection	Gives food to the Buddha and to the wider community
Padumma	A lion	Gave obeisance to the Buddha, roared three times and served him for a week
Narada	An ascetic with matted hair	Gives food and sandalwood to the Buddha and to the wider community
Padumuttara	Jatila, a district governor	Gives food and cloth to the Buddha and to the wider community
Sumedha	Uttara, a brahmin	Gives wealth to the Buddha and to the wider community
Sujata	A monarch	Gives kingdom and treasures to the Buddha
Piyadassi	Kassapa, a brahmin	Gives a monastic park to the Buddha and to the wider community
Atthadassi	Susima, an ascetic with matted hair	Gives flowers to the Buddha

Buddha	The bodhisattva's birth	Particular acts of the bodhisattva towards the Buddha
Dhammadassi	Lord of the gods, Indra	Gives perfumes, flowers and music to the Buddha and to the wider community
Siddhattha	Mangala, an ascetic	Gives fruit to the Buddha and to the wider community
Tissa	Sujata, a mendicant who had been a kshatriya	Held flowers above the Buddha's head
Phussa	Vijitavin, a kshatriya	Became a monk after giving up his kingdom
Vipassin	Atula, a serpent king	Gives music and a golden seat to the Buddha
Sikhin	Arindama, a kshatriya	Gives food and an elephant to the Buddha
Vessabhu	Sudassana, a kshatriya	Gives food, cloth and other gifts to the Buddha and to the wider community
Kakusandha	Kema, a kshatriya	Gives medicines, bowls and robes to the Buddha and to the wider community
Konagamanaa	Pabbata, a kshatriya	Gives cloth and sandals to the Buddha and to the wider community
Kassapa	Jotipala, a brahmin	Became a monk

Source: see Strong, 2015.

Many of the Jataka tales narrate lives of the bodhisattva that ranged from life as a monkey, a lion, a prince, nobleman, ascetic and many other beings. In the Theravada Jataka tales there are at least 547 past lives of the Buddha recorded. Each of these stories teaches important Buddhist principles as well as giving insights into the bodhisattva. The historicity of these stories is questioned by many, even whether they originate with the Buddha. There are commonalities with existing folk tales which may lead some to suggest that they were existing stories that were 'Buddhified' by the community of Buddhists. Naomi Appleton (2010) recognizes these commonalities but suggests that 'rather than dismiss the stories as common tales, we can ask how and why they were transformed into jatakas and established as Buddhist stories' (10).

The stories teach us many things, and are a rich resource for use in the classroom. Often, in the teaching of Buddhism, we focus on stories from the immediate life of the

Buddha, but there are many aspects of Buddhist life and teaching that can be harnessed and gleaned from the Jataka tales. Appleton (2010) highlights just this point:

> Stories do, of course, provide us with material quite different to explicitly philosophical and doctrinal texts, but the evidence they provide is no less important for a full understanding of Buddhism. (12)

We will return to the importance of storytelling later in this chapter, but it is important to note that we should include the Jataka tales in an exploration of the Buddha's life, and of Buddhism more widely.

The final rebirth of the bodhisattva, in line with all other Buddhas, was in the Tusita heaven (the heaven of the contented). Tenzin Chogyel (2015) gives an account of the events of the future Buddha Gautama's life in Tusita. When Kassapa, the Buddha prior to him, left Tusita heaven to teach the people of the world, he 'anointed [the bodhisattva, the future Siddhartha Gautama] as his replacement and he stayed in Tusita, teaching the Dharma to the gods' (10). After a time, through his compassion, he realized that 'the world has no one to guide it. It has no one to protect it, no place to go to refuge' (Chogyel, 2015, 10). It is at this point that the bodhisattva determined that the time to be born was upon him. He announced to gods in Tusita that he would be born, and removing his crown he placed it upon the head of Maitreya, who he anointed to teach the dharma in Tusita, until the time came for him to be born (see Chapter 5).

Before turning to his birth and the events of his life as Siddhartha Gautama it is important to note a difference in understanding between many Theravada and Mahayana Buddhists as to who and what the Buddha is at the moment of his birth, and throughout his life. The Dalai Lama and Thubten Chodron (2014) distinguish between the two main understandings of who the Buddha was:

1. In the Theravada tradition (the Dalai Lama and Chodron term it the Pali tradition) he lived many lives as a bodhisattva preparing for the time he would be born as Siddhartha Gautama. During his lifetime as Siddhartha Gautama he 'attained full awakening under the bodhi tree' and that he experienced 'physical pain due to having a body produced under the power of craving and kamma' (31). Upon his death he attained parinibbana and the cycle of rebirth ended for him.

2. The Mahayana tradition (the Dalai Lama and Chodron term it the Sanskrit tradition), in a similar manner, believed that the Buddha lived many lives as a bodhisattva, but he actually 'attained full awakening before his life as Siddhartha Gautama'. In this way when he lived as Siddhartha he was an emanation, 'appearing as an unawakened being who attained full awakening in that lifetime' (1); and in so doing provided an example of how to attain enlightenment in the living of an 'ordinary life'. This is a major theme of the *Lotus Sutra* which will be explored further in Chapters 5 and 6, but at the conclusion of his earthly life, just as it had no beginning it would have no end, indeed, 'the "fundamental teaching" of the *Lotus [Sutra]*, is that the

lifespan of the Buddha is immeasurable, revealing its true or "fundamental" nature as the primordial Buddha' (Lopez, 2016, 48).

The first interpretation of his life is by far the most common to be taught within the classroom. I am not suggesting that this ceases, rather recognizing that there is a diversity in understanding his life is an important part of our teaching. Again, this may be as simple as using 'many' or 'some'; but it might also include an exploration of the reasons why each view may be held, and the impact and importance that each has for Buddhists today will be an interesting aspect of the teaching of Buddhism in the classroom. There are writers such as Wallis (2020) who explore the place of 'the Buddha' versus 'Siddhartha Gautama' in striving to seek an exemplar as a way to live Buddhist principles. Wallis determines that he has more in common with Siddhartha than with the Buddha and can learn more. He offers no opinion on whether the 'human' Siddhartha was what he seemed or an emanation that made him more accessible for followers; but this is an area that it rich for discussion.

With this as a background, the life of the Buddha as a roadmap for the path to enlightenment, or as a way to understand the truths of existence, provides the context within which to explore the various stories of his life. It is to the events of his life that we now turn.

The birth of Siddhartha Gautama

Having determined the most opportune and appropriate time the bodhisattva entered the womb of his mother, Maya. At the moment of his entrance into her womb it is said that she was undertaking purification rituals and she dreamt of a white elephant with six golden tusks. The bodhisattva entered into her right side and stayed on that side throughout Maya's pregnancy. In the *Lalitavistara Sutra* it is recorded:

> He entered through his mother's right side in the form of a baby elephant, white in colour with six tusks. His head was the colour of a reddish insect, and the tusks were blazing gold. He had all his limbs intact and his full faculties. As he entered, he stayed only at the right side of the womb and never on the left. (Dharmachakra Translation Committee, 2013, 47)

With such an auspicious beginning to the pregnancy it is said that the brahmins told his father, Suddhodana, that there were two possible meanings and destinies for his son. On the one hand, he would be a great king and a universal monarch. On the other hand if he renounced all of his wealth and power, he would become a Buddha.

There are many traditions associated with the pregnancy of Maya. In Mahayana retellings the deities and bodhisattvas all played a part in ensuring that the pregnancy was as comfortable as possible, with one version suggesting that Queen Maya was provided with resting places in palaces of the gods. Such was the importance of the

Buddha who was to be born that he was worshipped by all of these attendants while in the womb. Even at this stage it is said that the Buddha had the thirty-two marks of a great being (*mahapurusa*) (see Table 3.2). These continued with him after birth and are re-emphasized when shortly after his birth, his father has him examined for these thirty-two marks.

As the time for the birth approached, after a period of between ten and twelve months, Maya retired to one of her gardens in Lumbini. Though accounts differ, some suggest she was returning from Kapilavastu to her parents' home in Devadaha, and Lumbini is halfway where she needed to stop to give birth. Others suggest that Lumbini makes no sense as a birth place for a heavily pregnant woman to travel to, and as such she would most likely have given birth in Kapilavastu.

The birth of Siddhartha Gautama

> It's normal that, as soon as he's born, the being intent on awakening stands firm with his own feet on the ground. Facing north, he takes seven strides with a white parasol held above him, surveys all quarters, and makes this dramatic proclamation: 'I am the foremost in the world! I am the eldest in the world! I am the first in the world! This is my last rebirth. Now there are no more future lives.' This is normal in such a case. (*Mahapadana Sutta*)

His proclamation is often known as the 'song of victory' or 'Lion's Roar'. *The Jataka Tales* holds that at the same time seven beings who were co-natal with the Buddha were born (Davids suggests in the footnotes that Ananda, his cousin, and chief disciple, should be added):

> Now at the very time when our Bodisat was born in the Lumbini grove, the lady mother of Rahula, Channa the attendant, Kaludayi the minister, Kanthaka the royal horse, the great Botree, and the four vases full of treasure, also came into being. Of these last, one was two miles, one four, one six, and one eight miles in size. These seven are called the Sahajata, the Connatal Ones. (Davids, 1878, 156)

The Jataka Tales further indicate that his birth and conception were further attended by thirty-two portents (see Tan, 2018, 51; Table 3.3).

For many Buddhists, it is most likely that these thirty-two portents, and the identification of the thirty-two marks of a great man, are seen as hyperbole, that highlight the importance of the birth of the Buddha. It further exemplifies the discussion at the beginning of the chapter about the hagiographical nature of the accounts of his birth and life. It is important to note that the accounts of his life indicate how he has been, and how he is, viewed by Buddhists. We have moved beyond the view that he was 'a mythological figure' that prevailed 'until about 1830'. His historicity is accepted as fact since the 1850s (Bluck, 2006, 5). This does not mean that every aspect of the narrative is factual, but his life is based on an historical figure and we can now understand how he is viewed by reading these accounts. For Buddhists his birth is an axiomatic moment in the

Table 3.2 The Thirty-Two Marks of a Great Being (Mahapurusa)

1. Feet are level
2. There is a thousand-spoked wheel marked on the feet
3. Heels are full and projecting
4. Long toes and fingers
5. Tender hands and feet
6. Webbed toes and fingers
7. Full-sized heels and ankles
8. Legs like a stag or antelope
9. Hands reach to the knees when stood up
10. Sheathed penis
11. Body is the colour of gold
12. Skin is soft and smooth
13. Each follicle has one hair and is dark coloured
14. Body hair curls to the right
15. Body stands straight
16. Body is perfectly proportioned
17. Legs, arms, shoulders and chest perfectly rounded
18. No hollow areas between his shoulders
19. His torso is lion-shaped
20. There is an aura around him
21. His shoulders are round
22. He has forty teeth
23. His teeth are white, evenly spaced and close
24. His canine teeth pure white
25. He has a jaw like a lion
26. An excellent sense of taste
27. He has a long and broad tongue
28. Has a deep voice like Brahma's
29. Blue eyes
30. Has eyelashes like a cow
31. Has a tuft of hair *urna* between his eyebrows
32. The crown of his head has a fleshy protuberance

Table 3.3 The Thirty-Two Portents of the Buddha's Birth

1. Radiance was throughout the universe
2. The blind were given sight
3. The deaf received their hearing
4. Those who could not speak were able to
5. Those with hunched backs could stand straight
6. Those unable to walk were able to walk
7. Beings in bondage were freed
8. Hell's fires were extinguished
9. Hunger was allayed in the realm of the hungry ghosts
10. Beasts were no longer afraid
11. Disease paused
12. All became friends, one towards another
13. Horses were gentle in the neighing
14. Elephants were gentle in their trumpeting
15. Musical instruments spontaneously played
16. Any ornaments on a human being plated a sound
17. All areas were clear
18. Everyone was refreshed by a cool breeze
19. Rain fell
20. Water flowed
21. Birds rested from flying
22. The flow of rivers were stopped
23. The seas' waters tasted sweet
24. Five colours of lotus covered the earth
25. Flowers bloomed everywhere
26. Lotus flowers bloomed in the cracks of rock
27. Lotus flowers appeared in the sky
28. It rained lotus flowers
29. Devas played music that could be heard everywhere
30. The 10,000 world systems rotated closer together
31. The world systems became fragrant
32. The world systems looked like streams of garlands

history of the universe. It was attended by great signs, and by the devotions of deities and bodhisattvas. So wide ranging was the impact that he and his teachings would have that each of the signs reinforce the importance of his life and every facet of such.

Siddhartha's childhood

Shortly after his birth, his mother passed away and was reborn in Tusita heaven. Siddhartha was raised by his mother's sister Mahapajapati Gotami (Skt: Mahaprajapati Gautami) who would later marry his father.

Other traditions hold that it was after his birth that his father was attended by a holy man, sometimes identified as Asita who had descended from his mountain hermitage, who declared that Siddhartha would be a great leader or a teacher. In response to this the narrative suggests that Siddhartha's father created an almost utopian existence where there was little or no evidence of suffering of any kind. Even the flowers were replaced before they had a chance to wilt, and that different palaces were used dependent on the season. Every whim of the young prince was catered for. The Buddha describes this part of his life:

> Monks, I lived in refinement, utmost refinement, total refinement. My father even had lotus ponds made in our palace: one where red lotuses bloomed, one where white lotuses bloomed, one where blue lotuses bloomed, all for my sake. I used no sandalwood that was not from Varanasi. My turban was from Varanasi, as were my tunic, my lower garments, and my outer cloak. A white sunshade was held over me day and night to protect me from cold, heat, dust, dirt, and dew. (*Sukhamala Sutta*)

The Buddha excelled in his schooling. It is reported that he studied all of the subjects that were taught at that time, including the arts, mathematics and other pursuits such as archery. In all of these Chogyel (2015) records that in each of these he 'was bale to teach his teachers more than they were able to teach him' (29).

Within this idyllic, yet ultimately unsatisfactory, childhood, the Buddha recalled an experience that was a portent of future events. He recalls:

> 'I recall sitting in the cool shade of the rose-apple tree while my father the Sakyan was off working. Quite secluded from sensual pleasures, secluded from unskillful qualities, I entered and remained in the first absorption, which has the rapture and bliss born of seclusion, while placing the mind and keeping it connected. Could that be the path to awakening?' Stemming from that memory came the realization: 'That is the path to awakening!' (*Sangarava Sutta*)

Further details surrounding this story suggest that Siddhartha became entranced by the furrowing of the soil and noticed that the plough had not just cut the earth, but also worms and insects, who were then eaten by birds. Sitting under the apple tree to reflect on what he had just observed it is reported that 'he sat for a long time, oblivious to all the singing, dancing, and picnicking taking place around him. Siddhartha continued to sit, absorbed by the images of the field and the many creatures'. His father and aunt discovered him in a serene pose and 'Gotami was moved to tears seeing how beautiful Siddhartha looked, like a small, still statue', while his father was worried that Asita's prophecy would come true (Hanh, 1992, 47).

At the age of sixteen Siddhartha was married to Yasodhara, daughter of King Suppabuddha and Amita. As indicated earlier it is taught that she was born on the same day as her husband. The wedding is described in the following terms:

> It was an occasion of great joy and celebration for the entire kingdom. The capital, Kapilavatthu, was decked with flags, lanterns, and flowers, and there was music everywhere. Wherever Siddhartha and Yasodhara went in their carriage, they were greeted with resounding cheers. They also visited outlying hamlets and villages, bringing gifts of food and clothing to many poor families. (Hanh, 1992, 62)

Although his father felt the marriage sealed his desire for his son to follow the path of a great leader, the marriage was to be happy but of a different kind to that envisaged by his father. They were not concerned with the trappings of wealth but 'they had their own dreams – to find answers concerning the spiritual quest and the renewal of society' (Hanh, 1992, 64). It is here that the traditional hagiography of the Buddha becomes a bit muddied; as the couple travelled the kingdom and the surrounding areas it is reported that he observed and encountered people who were living in less than ideal circumstances and were experiencing suffering. He also observed the trappings of courtly life and recognized the selfish ambition and actions of those who served on the court. In working with his father in the court he realized that the problem was not the consequences of people's actions, but that a person's heart needed to find freedom from negative feelings such as anger and jealousy.

At the age of twenty-nine Yasodhara gave birth to a son, Rahula. This was a happy time, but also the prelude to the leaving of Siddhartha from the palace. In contrast to the traditional story, that Siddhartha was solely motivated by the Four Sights (see further on) it is evident from the various biographies of the Buddha that this was a planned event, but that it was delayed so that Yasodhara and Siddhartha could have a child. Though it should be noted that in some traditions it is suggested that Rahula is not born until after Siddhartha leaves the palace.

The Four Sights

The traditional telling of the story of the Four Sights suggests that in desiring the palace, Siddhartha's father stage managed a route that would ensure that he would not see anything untoward. He was still concerned that his son would become a religious teacher, rather than the leader that he desired. Despite this stage management, Siddhartha encountered what are now termed the Four Sights:

- An old man
- A sick man
- A dead man
- An holy man

These sights are reported to have so moved Siddhartha that it was at that point that he realized the truth of dukkha and determined to leave the palace and his life of luxury to seek an answer to the problem of suffering.

Each story of the Four Sights is a variation on this theme. In some retellings, the Four Sights are four separate journeys outside of the palace, and he encountered one on each of the journeys. Still others report that he encountered these Four Sights on an excursion with Yasodhara, and on returning to the palace he realized that he could not live happily and needed to find a solution to this suffering, telling his wife that 'you are my partner, the one who can truly help me to truly fulfil my quest' and that 'I will never stop loving you' (Hanh, 1992, 81).

It is this aspect of the story that students tend to struggle with the most. How can he leave his wife and young child? From a Buddhist perspective it is important to note that these attachments would ultimately enable dukkha to arise, in the sense that their impermanence means that how could a person live happily, knowing things must end? The solution that he sought would enable all of these relationships to be more real when the nature of existence was realized and all could realize the freedom from dukkha. The Buddha in the *Ariyapariyesana Sutta* recorded that his leaving was motivated by these four conditions:

> What if I, being subject myself to aging ... illness ... death ... sorrow ... defilement, seeing the drawbacks of aging ... illness ... death ... sorrow ... defilement, were to seek the aging-less, illness-less, deathless, sorrow-less, unexcelled rest from the yoke: unbinding?' So, at a later time, while still young, a black-haired young man endowed with the blessings of youth in the first stage of life – and while my parents, unwilling, were crying with tears streaming down their faces – I shaved off my hair and beard, put on the ochre robe, and went forth from the home life into homelessness.

The story of the Four Sights is also almost identical to a retelling of a life of a previous Buddha, Vipassi. The *Mahapadana Sutta* tells of his encounter with the Four Sights in his lifetime when he had left his palace with his charioteer. It is not impossible that Siddhartha's life mirrored Vipassi's, and, indeed, the accounts of previous Buddhas are often seen to share similarities, and so such repetition may be expected.

A suggestion is often made that the Four Sights mark the beginning of Buddhism, in that it is the event where the Buddha realized the truth of suffering. It is apparent from other retellings of his life that he had encountered suffering earlier in his life. For some reason, however, the events of the Four Sights were particularly motivating in seeking for a solution to dukkha, and impelled Siddhartha to leave his home.

After speaking with his father, Siddhartha left the palace. When he was leaving the palace it is reported:

> Then four sons of the gods lifted Kantaka into the air. Indra opened the palace gate, and the four guardian kings and their troops protected the Bodhisattva. Brahma and the other gods prayed to him, and the Bodhisattva departed the palace. (Chogyel, 2015, 43)

Yet, within the classroom retellings of the story, we only read of Siddhartha and Channa (Skt. *Chandaka*) finding a way out of the palace. However he finds his way out of the palace (some traditions suggest that he and Channa fly), Channa and Siddhartha travel to the banks of the river Anomiya. It is here that he removes his jewels, cuts his hair and removes his clothes and exchanges them for the simple robes of a monk. In some traditions, the robes are provided by the gods; in others he exchanges his clothes with a passing hunter. In an echo of the future life of a bhikkhu, there are also stories which tell of Brahma providing him with a razor, a needle, a belt, a strainer and a bowl; all which are required items. Channa is then sent back to the palace with the worldly possessions of the future Buddha.

Life as an ascetic

Having thus embarked on the search for awakening, or freedom from dukkha, the Buddha went through various stages of life as a holy man, or as an ascetic. Sometimes, in the classroom teachers will go directly to the final stage of his asceticism, but it is also important to note that this stage of his life is a time of learning. As such there can be seen to be distinct phases that the Buddha recorded for himself.

Rajagaha (the mountain fortress of the Magadhans)

His first destination on leaving the palace was Rajagaha where he wandered seeking alms. While wandering through Rajagaha 'King Bimbisara, standing in his palace, saw him ... consummate in marks'(*Sutta Nipata*, 3.1). The King offered the renunciate wealth, power and status, which Siddhartha rejected recalling his place in the Shakya clan that he had given up:

> From that lineage I have gone forth, but not in hope of sensuality. Seeing the danger in sensuality – and renunciation as rest – I go to strive. That's where my heart delights. (*Sutta Nipata*, 3.1)

Study under Alara Kalama and Uddaka Ramaputta

In seeking the truth of existence and the answer to dukkha the Buddha then went to learn from Alara Kalama. He describes his motivation:

Having thus gone forth in search of what might be skilful, seeking the unexcelled state of sublime peace, I went to Aḷara Kalama and, on arrival, said to him: 'Friend Kalama, I want to practice in this Dhamma and discipline'. (*Ariyapariyesana Sutta*)

Siddhartha quickly learned what Alara Kalama knew and taught; this included 'conviction, persistence, mindfulness, concentration, and discernment' (*Ariyapariyesana Sutta*). He developed mastery of a meditation surrounding 'the realm of nothingness' (Narada, 1992, 19). After realizing that this was all that Alara Kalama knew, and that he was at the same stage of learning, having learned the dharma through direct knowledge, Siddhartha was ultimately dissatisfied and needed to leave to search for the truth of the dharma.

He then went to learn from Uddaka Ramaputta. In a similar way to his time with Alara Kalama, Siddhartha quickly learned from Uddaka Ramaputta and mastered the meditation of 'the sphere of neither perception nor non-perception' (Narada, 1992, 20), and in being invited to become a teacher of this dharma, he realized that he was dissatisfied:

> This Dhamma leads not to disenchantment, to dispassion, to cessation, to stilling, to direct knowledge, to self-awakening, nor to unbinding, but only to reappearance in the dimension of neither perception nor non-perception. So, dissatisfied with that Dhamma, I left. (*Ariyapariyesana Sutta*)

Extreme austerities

It was at this point that Siddhartha describes the next step in his search:

> I wandered by stages in the Magadhan country and came to the military town of Uruvela. There I saw some delightful countryside, with an inspiring forest grove, a clear-flowing river with fine, delightful banks, and villages for alms-going on all sides. (*Ariyapariyesana Sutta*)

He was joined by Annata-Kondanna, Bhaddiya, Vappa, Mahanama and Assaji in a life of extreme asceticism for the next six years. He describes some of the practices that he undertook:

- 'So, clenching my teeth and pressing my tongue against the roof of my mouth, I beat down, constrained and crushed my mind with my awareness' (*Maha Saccaka Sutta*).

- 'What if I were to become absorbed in the trance of non-breathing? So I stopped the in-breaths and out-breaths in my nose and mouth' (*Maha Saccaka Sutta*).

At this point the gods wondered if Siddhartha was dead, such were the extreme austerities that he had adopted.

- 'My body became extremely emaciated. Simply from my eating so little, my limbs became like the jointed segments of vine stems or bamboo stems ... My backside became like a camel's hoof ... My spine stood out like a string of beads ... My ribs jutted out like the jutting rafters of an old, run-down barn ... The gleam of my eyes appeared to be sunk deep in my eye sockets like the gleam of water deep in a well ... My scalp shrivelled and withered like a green bitter gourd, shrivelled and withered in the heat and the wind' (*Maha Saccaka Sutta*).

Siddhartha realized that these austerities accomplished nothing, and he decided to eat some food, offered to him by Sujata, to regain some nourishment. As he did so, his companions felt that he was giving up and left him 'thinking, "Gotama the contemplative is living luxuriously. He has abandoned his exertion and is backsliding into abundance"' (*Maha Saccaka Sutta*).

It is at this stage that we can see the parabolic message of the Buddha's narrated life. Just as he taught the Middle Way, his life is an example of how a life of extremes does not provide answers to life's questions. The Buddha had lived a 'hedonistic' life in the palace where every whim was catered for, and this was unsatisfactory. He had also lived a life of extreme asceticism and this, too, was unsatisfactory. It was at this point that Siddhartha realized the truth of the Middle Way and the way to awakening opened up for him.

Awakening

As a fulfilment of his previous lifetimes, and as a result of the preparation of this lifetime, it is said that Siddhartha Gautama, realizing that he was close to awakening, walked to Bodh Gaya and found a suitable place to meditate under a bodhi tree. It was on the full moon day of the fourth month of the lunar calendar that he sat down in meditation and vowed not to rise until he had attained enlightenment.

Having entered into meditation, Siddhartha was assailed by the demon Mara. Mara sought to distract him from his meditation with his battalions using arrows, stones, boulders and even mountains. Siddhartha refused to be distracted and turned these 'weapons' into flowers ad garlands that fell harmlessly to the ground. Realizing that these methods had failed to distract or deter the Siddhartha, Mara's daughters were sent to tempt or seduce him. Mara's daughters are *Tanha* (Thirst/Craving), *Arati* (Aversion) and *Raga* (Attachment/Greed). The *Maradhitu Sutta* records various attempts of them manifesting themselves:

- in the form of a hundred maidens.
- in the forms of a hundred women who have never given birth.
- in the forms of a hundred women who have given birth once.
- in the forms of a hundred women who have given birth twice.
- in the forms of a hundred women of middle age.
- in the forms of a hundred old women.

Had Siddhartha been engaged or repulsed by them, he would have been distracted from his goal and would not have been enlightened. He sat devoid of response, in perfect equanimity. Some traditions record Siddhartha turning the young maidens into ugly hags, and then back again, when they failed in their task. During his encounters with Mara and his daughters Siddhartha touched the earth, and in so doing invited the earth goddess to be a witness to his awakening and that he is able to attain such, having defeated Mara. The Buddha said:

> The earth is witness for all living beings,
> It is impartial to all existence.
> The earth shall be my witness, I do not lie.
> You, Earth, I call you as my witness here!
>
> The ground trembled, and Sthavara, goddess of the earth, emerged halfway out the soil. She folded her hands in reverence to the bodhisattva. (Chogyel, 2015, 58–9)

The daughters of Mara are understood in different ways by Buddhists. For some, they are real demons, while, for others, they are temptations within one's own mind. The opposites of desire and aversion. Any of these temptations would distract a person from their search for enlightenment; there needs to be an equanimity and a detachment from all influences.

Following his encounters with Mara and his daughters, Siddhartha was able to progress towards awakening, and became the Buddha. The stages related to the different watches of the night:

1. In the first watch of the night, he recalls his former existences. Siddhartha develops a realization of karma and the truth of no fixed self.

2. In the second watch of the night, he sees the comings and goings of all other beings in the different realms. He realizes with compassion the reality of rebirth and death throughout the different realms.

3. In the third watch of the night, he realized the Four Noble Truths and the truth of the asravas which are the negative attachments that bind a person to this life. In some recitations it is here that he realized the truth of dependent origination. 'With release, there was the knowledge, "Released." I discerned that "birth is ended, the holy life fulfilled, the task done. There is nothing further for this world"' (*Maha Saccaka Sutta*).

Thus awakened, he contemplated to whom he should teach the dharma. His initial thought was that people were too enmeshed in attachment, passions, desires and aversions that they would not be receptive and 'cloaked in the mass of darkness, [they] won't see' (*Ariyapariyesana Sutta*). It was only with the intervention of Brahma that the Buddha decided to teach the dharma to others: 'O Teacher, wander without debt in the world. Teach the Dhamma, O Blessed One: There will be those who will understand' (*Ariyapariyesana Sutta*).

Motivated by compassion to teach the dharma, he went to teach his old teachers, Alara Kalama and Uddaka Ramaputta, but they had died. He then made his way to meet with his companion ascetics who had abandoned him.

The founding of the sangha

Following his experience of the Bodhi tree the Buddha travelled to the Deer Park near Varanasi in northern India. Here he delivered his first sermon to a group of five companions with whom he had previously sought enlightenment. Buddhists also believe that many devas and brahmas (angels and gods) were also in attendance. He taught them the Four Noble Truths and the Middle Way (the Eightfold Path). The six of them together formed the first sangha (community of Buddhist monks). All five become arahants (in Theravada this means those who have achieved enlightenment); soon a man called Yasa and fifty-four of his friends followed the Buddha; the number of arahants swelled to sixty within the first two months. This was soon followed by the three Kassapa brothers and their 200, 300 and 500 disciples which helped the sangha grow to over 1,000. They were then sent out to explain the dharma to the wider populace.

At first the sangha was limited to monks (bhikkhu) but after five years it was extended to include nuns at the request of Maha Pajapati Gotami (the Buddha's aunt). The Buddha had initially refused her request for ordination three times. She cut her hair, put on yellow clothes and walked 150 miles to Vesali. On this walk her feet became swollen; she waited outside where the Buddha was staying in tears hoping for ordination.

Ananda (one of the companions of the Buddha) saw her like this and offered to ask the Buddha on her behalf. Ananda asked three times and the Buddha refused each time. Ananda rephrased the request asking if women could attain the stages of an arahant (see Chapter 5). When the Buddha answered in the affirmative Ananda asked if women could be ordained as nuns. The Buddha replied that only if she was willing to live the Middle Way. Maha Pajapati Gotami agreed and became a nun (bhikkhuni) and not long after an arahant.

The Buddha's death and parinibbana

When he was eighty the Buddha announced that he would soon achieve parinibbana (final and complete nibbana at the passing away of a Buddha). Interestingly, he spoke of there being no need of a successor to his disciple Ananda:

> So, Ananda, you should all live with yourselves as your island, yourselves as your refuge, with no other as your refuge; with the Dhamma as your island, the Dhamma as

your refuge, with no other as your refuge. And how does a monk live with himself as his island, himself as his refuge, with no other as his refuge; with the Dhamma as his island, the Dhamma as his refuge, with no other as his refuge? (*Maha Parinibbana Sutta*)

Soon after this the Buddha ate his last meal provided by Cunda, the blacksmith. He soon became rather ill (though he was at pains to reassure Cunda that it had nothing to do with the meal he provided) – what was in the meal is an area of debate (Theravada's believe that it may have been some kind of pork; Mahayana believe it was mushroom). In Mahayana belief the Buddha was not really ill but was merely presenting an ill countenance to teach people about the suffering and impermanence of this life. Before he died Buddha asked his companions to ask any questions they had. They had none.

At this point he died and entered parinibbana. His final words were:

Now, then, monks, I exhort you: All fabrications are subject to ending and decay. Reach consummation through heedfulness. (*Maha Parinibbana Sutta*)

Buddhists believe that he did not die in the normal sense of the word but achieved nibbana, which is deathless. He died lying on his right side with his right hand under his head (some rupas of the Buddha can be seen in this position). The death was the final teaching on impermanence.

The Buddha was cremated; elements of his body (teeth and bones) did not burn and were placed into eight stupas which have since become places of pilgrimage to Buddhists.

The stupas locations include:

- Sri Dalada Maligawa or the Temple of the Sacred Tooth Relic in Kandy in Sri Lanka
- Sarnath
- Sanchi

Whether these stupas were of the original eight is a matter of debate but they are places of pilgrimage with relics associated with the Buddha.

Thoughts for the classroom

Within an exploration of the sources for the narratives surrounding the events of the life of Buddha, there are a range of possibilities that arise for their use in the classroom. The stories of the Buddha are normally narrated in the classroom with little discussion, but in a similar way to the Christian Gospels, the narrations of the lives of the Gurus, along with texts from many religions, are opportunities for critical reading of such. At no point does this mean that the teacher or pupils seek to criticize the person or role of the Buddha.

It is possible in analysing the writing of the text to explore the texts in terms of understanding both the life of the Buddha and the communities which produced these texts.

Within the classroom there has been an development in the use of hermeneutics in terms of reading sacred texts. As historical texts that are used within the Buddhist community, it is possible to see that the Jataka Tales can be used in the same way. As we understand a hermeneutic approach to be about 'the art or science of interpretation, concerned with meaning and significance' (Bowie et al., 2020, 3), it is possible to move beyond sacred text to read the stories of the Buddha to see how the narratives are imbued with meaning and significance.

This type of approach should include the reading of the text (most likely in English) to explore the things we learn about the Buddha from the narrative; what we learn about the community that produced it; what links there are to wider Buddhism; the possible historicity claims that can be made; and how the text links with, and is used, by Buddhists today. Pupils in schools are used to having narrative curated or mediated for them, and engagement with the source material helps pupils engage with the narrative in a much more effective and authentic way.

There are many stories told of the life of the Buddha. There have been volumes filled with stories from throughout his life, and there is only the opportunity to draw on brief examples. It should also be noted that throughout this book there have been, and will be, examples from the Buddha's life that are used to underpin or illustrate teachings as given expression in Buddhism. The narrative undertaken earlier has, necessarily, only touch on brief aspects of his life.

For each of the lifetimes of the Buddha there are a multitude of stories that could form the basis of an exploration of Buddhist beliefs and values in the classroom at all stages of education. Storytelling lies at the heart of understanding Buddhism. It has to be utilized correctly and enthusiastically by the teacher.

To an extent, stories lie at the heart of religion, and especially of Buddhism. The stories of the bodhisattva and Buddha can be used to frame morality, teachings and also the boundaries of Buddhism. Trevor Cooling suggests that stories are 'big ideas sometimes referred to as a metanarrative, which express our whole understanding of the whole world and help people to make sense of their lives' (2002, 45). This is just so with Buddhism. As we reflect on some of the stories, whether it is his enlightenment, the decision to seek rebirth as a Buddha or the story of the founding of the sangha, they can help us understand the important aspects of Buddhism. We can understand the nature of existence, a Buddha, of dukkha, through a utilization of stories of the Buddha in the classroom.

Robin Mello (2001) explains that learning can be deepened with the use of story. Stories also have many levels of understanding that need to be analysed and studied for academic understanding. The stories that are told help us understand what is important for Buddhists then, and today. Miller Mair suggests that this is so: 'All our stories are expressions of ourselves even when they purport to be accounts of aspects of the world. We are deeply implicated in the very grounds of our story telling' (1989, 257). Buddhism can thus be experienced through its stories. Whatever age of student we are working with, using the stories of the Buddha can help them understand more deeply not just the life of the Buddha but also the teachings of Buddhism and their importance to Buddhists today.

There is also a caveat to the exploration of the life of the Buddha in that he is not an end in himself. He is an exemplar, or a guide, rather than an object of devotion. One Buddhist has suggested how he should be viewed:

> He is just one, an ordinary man, gone before me who realised the Dhamma (the way things are in regards to suffering) and developed a life that moves away from suffering and towards loving-kindness, clarity and understanding. He transmitted what he had learned to others interested and they benefitted.

However, there are also many other ways that he is seen within Buddhism.

4

The Middle Way and the Threefold Path

As explored in Chapter 1, the Fourth Noble Truth is magga (Skt: marga), which is variously referred to as the Noble Eightfold Path or the Middle Way. This chapter will build on the brief summary developed earlier in the chapter on the Four Noble Truths. Having explored the life of the Buddha in Chapter 3 it is evident that his life, as taught, is a parable for the Middle Way. This does not mean that it is not true, but that in its shaping the important truth of the Middle Way for Buddhists is able to be taught. Reflecting on the story told earlier about the string of a lute not being too taut or too slack, and it being just so, with the mind it is possible to extend this to other examples. One such is the bow of an archer/hunter who does not keep his bow string too tight for it would lose its elasticity. In the Buddha's life that he lived, what appears to be a hedonistic life, where every sensuous pleasure was catered for, he also lived the life of an ascetic where tradition holds that he lived on a grain of rice a day. Awakening was not to be found in either of these extremes, only in the living of the Middle Way.

Reflecting on Buddhist cosmology explored in Chapter 2 it is also possible to reflect on the perfect or beneficial circumstances of life as a human. In some ways this could link with the concept in philosophy of the Goldilocks theory. This was suggested by Aristotle (though not by its name) (Aristotle and Ross, 2009, 31). This is a reflection of the Buddha's teaching on the Middle Way, and the idea within the story of Goldilocks who was searching for porridge that was not too hot, and not too cold, but just right. This is an approach to the living of life, but also the place of the human world. The realms of the devas (either within Theravada or Mahayana cosmology) have 'too much' bliss and 'not enough' dukkha for the beings to have any impetus to seek the dharma, equanimity and awakening. Whereas in the lower realms the suffering and instincts are generally base and it is not possible to realize the truth of the dharma and seek awakening, in the human realm, it is a Middle Way that provides the 'just right' for awakening. It can be argued that throughout Buddhist teaching the Middle Way between opposites find balance between opposites. It is important for the teacher and students to recognize that the Middle Way is fundamental to an understanding of Buddhist practice, and also of Buddhist belief.

The aspects of the Noble Eightfold Path as taught by the Buddha are:

> In the same way I saw an ancient path, an ancient road, travelled by the Rightly Self-awakened Ones of former times. And what is that ancient path, that ancient road, travelled by the Rightly Self-awakened Ones of former times? Just this noble eightfold path: right view, right resolve, right speech, right action, right livelihood, right effort, right mindfulness, right concentration. That is the ancient path, the ancient road, travelled by the Rightly Self-awakened Ones of former times. I followed that path. (*Nagara Sutta*)

Summarized as follows:

1. Right view/understanding (Skt: *samyak-drsti*, Pali: *samma-ditthi*)
2. Right resolve/intention/attitude (Skt: *samyak-samkalpa*, Pali: *samma-sankappa*)
3. Right speech (Skt: *samyag-vac*, Pali: *samma-vaca*)
4. Right conduct/action (Skt: *samyak-karmanta*, Pali: *samma-kammanta*)
5. Right livelihood (Skt: *samyag-ajiva*, Pali: *samma-ajiva*)
6. Right effort (Skt: *samyag-vyayama*, Pali: *samma-vayama*)
7. Right mindfulness/awareness (Skt *samyak-smrti*, Pali: *samma-sati*)
8. Right concentration (Skt: *samyak*-samadhi, Pali: *samma-samadhi*)

It is these eight views (*ditthi*) that are reflected in a symbol of Buddhism (Figure 4.1).

Each aspect of the Eightfold Path is summarized as part of the Threefold Way: the way of morality/moral virtue (*sila*), the way of meditation (*samadhi*) and the way of wisdom/insight (Skt: *prajna*, Pali: *panna*). As an aside, Vetter (1988) sees the division into three as a later development, when insight and wisdom became more focussed upon. It is important to note that this Threefold Way is fairly well ingrained into Buddhist teaching and it is usual to find each of the aspects of the Eightfold Path to be found as part of the different ways (see Table 4.1).

While most Buddhist would see each aspect of the Eightfold Path as contiguous with one another, meaning that each are able to be followed at the same time, and that they are not linear steps to awakening, the Buddha suggested that a living or development of the other seven aspects of the path provides suitable conditions for the flourishing of right concentration (*Maha Cattarisaka Sutta*).

All aspects are linked. Buddhists would see that it is impossible to acquire wisdom without being moral; everything goes hand in hand. It is impossible for the wise person to be immoral or for the moral person to lack wisdom. Bhikkhu Bodhi (1994) suggests that, while they all feed into one another, the Threefold Way are structured in such a way to enable awakening to be attained following the development of wisdom:

> Thus the path evolves through its three stages, with moral discipline as the foundation for concentration, concentration the foundation for wisdom, and wisdom the direct instrument for reaching liberation. (13)

Figure 4.1 The Noble Eightfold Path.
Source: Creative commons: Shazz / pl.wiki: Shazz☼, GFDL <http://www.gnu.org/copyleft/fdl.html>, via Wikimedia Commons.

Each needs to be achieved to attain awakening. Recognizing the contiguous, rather than consecutive nature, of each aspect of the Noble Eightfold Path, this chapter will explore them in the context of the Threefold Way.

Way of morality/moral virtue (sila)

The way of morality incorporates right speech, right action and right livelihood from the Noble Eightfold Path. Often times the way of morality is called ethical conduct because it reflects how a person should behave towards others. The others it refers to is summarized in a teaching of *karuna* (compassion) where it is to be expressed to all. The Buddha

Table 4.1 The Threefold Way and the Eightfold Path

Way	View
Morality	Right speech
	Right action
	Right livelihood
Meditation	Right effort
	Right mindfulness
	Right concentration
Wisdom	Right view
	Right resolve

taught that his disciples should exercise compassion and goodwill in every situation and direction (*Kalama Sutta*).

Buddhist ethics are sometimes expressed in teachings or rules, and some of these will be explored in Chapter 8 when the ethical dimension of Buddhism will be explored (these may include the various precepts and paramitas). However, Buddhist ethical conduct or morality is a way for a Buddhist to try and develop compassion, which is the ultimate goal in both the arahant and bodhisattva ideals (see Chapter 5). The morality that Buddhists adhere to should be based around what is the best way of developing a harmonious relationship with themselves, others and the world around them.

Although these elements of the Eightfold Path may appear to be about the maintenance of harmonious relationships, and potentially the accumulation of good karma, their overwhelming purpose is to purify the mind of the Buddhist, so that they are prepared to be awakened. As a person lives the way of morality it brings the '"public" benefit of inhibiting socially detrimental actions' but it also 'entails the personal benefit of mental purification' (Bodhi, 1994, 41).

Right speech

> And what is right speech? Abstaining from lying, from divisive speech, from abusive speech, and from idle chatter: This is called right speech. (*Sacca-vibhanga Sutta*)

If Buddhists are to be governed by compassion this means that they will speak kindly to people. The Buddha outlined four types of speech to avoid:

- Lying
- Divisive speech
- Abusive speech

- Idle chatter or gossip

The intention behind a person's speech must be compassion. A person will never speak to another with a desire to hurt or humiliate. If none of this is possible then it is necessary to maintain a silence. This aspect of the Middle Way will be explored further in the context of the Five Precepts (see Chapter 7). That which people speak should be uplifting and ennobling, rather than being used to tear down and cause division. False, or wrong, speech is often driven by the Three Poisons: greed, hatred and aversion/delusion.

In today's world this approach to speech may seem to be counter-cultural. Society has become full of partisan and hateful language; as such it will be useful for students to explore how easy it is to live, and to avoid the various aspects of wrong speech, and to practice right speech meaning to 'speak truthfully, gently, kindly, and at the appropriate time' (Dalai Lama and Chodron, 2014, 56). Indeed, an exploration of news sites and newspapers would be indicative of whether the world is more focussed on right or wrong speech.

Right action

> And what is right action? Abstaining from taking life, from stealing, and from sexual misconduct: This is called right action. (*Sacca-vibhanga Sutta*)

Just as right speech is about ensuring that nobody is harmed through a person's speech, right action is about not harming others through actions. The aforementioned examples from the Buddha's life form part of the Five Precepts and will be explored further in Chapter 7. Although this aspect of the Eightfold Path is focussed on 'action', it can be seen that this is also a mental abstinence through the training of the mind to not desire to carry out these acts, and to carry out compassionate acts in their place. If one considers the positive aspect of each of the acts, as part of a right action a person should develop compassion, honesty, and fidelity or celibacy dependent on whether a person is lay or ordained.

Right livelihood

> And what is right livelihood? There is the case where a disciple of the noble ones, having abandoned dishonest livelihood, keeps his life going with right livelihood: This is called right livelihood. (*Sacca-vibhanga Sutta*)

In exploring a livelihood without lying, the Buddha further develops what is meant by right livelihood:

> And what is right livelihood? Right livelihood, I tell you, is of two sorts: There is right livelihood with effluents, siding with merit, resulting in acquisitions; there is right

livelihood that is noble, without effluents, transcendent, a factor of the path. (*Maha Cattarisaka Sutta*)

Those livelihood concerned with effluents are those focussed on satisfying the sense and those that go against the desire to practice compassion for all. The Buddha signified examples of work that Buddhists should not participate in:

Monks, a lay follower should not engage in five types of business. Which five? Business in weapons, business in living beings, business in meat, business in intoxicants, and business in poison. (*Vanijja Sutta*)

Developed further in the *Maha Cattarisaka Sutta*, where 'Scheming, persuading, hinting, belittling, and pursuing gain with gain'. It is, therefore, not just specific careers or jobs that are against right livelihood, but also the way that one pursues or carries out a career that could be considered 'right'. For example a lawyer who seeks to protect others or the rights of others may be considered to be following a right livelihood; but a lawyer could also pursue a career where dishonesty may be justified, or the desire to make more money or attain accolades are the driving force. As such, the same job is evidence of both right and wrong livelihood, and therefore reveals the importance of intention in the way that a person lives.

In a world where everything is interconnected, this may provide a springboard for a discussion about whether any livelihood in modern society can ever be 'right'. There are groups in the UK, such as the Triratna Buddhist Community, who establish co-operatives that ensure that things that are made, sold and consumed are ethically sourced. The extension of such a discussion surrounding the place of Buddhists in positions such as soldiers and police officers raise interesting questions. For example, Thich Nhat Hanh has suggested:

If you see someone who is trying to shoot, to destroy, you have to do your best in order to prevent him or her from doing so. You must. But you must do it out of your compassion, your willingness to protect, and not out of anger. That is the key point. If you need to use force, you have to use it, but you have to make sure that you act out of compassion and a willingness to protect, not out of anger. (WRN Editorial Staff, 2015)

This seems to sit well with the intention of an act, but it is far from settled and as such ensures a rich debate within the classroom as various imperatives in Buddhism seem to clash.

Way of meditation (samadhi)

Samadhi is the way of right mindfulness, concentration and effort. As such meditative practices are a way to attain equanimity of mind as a prelude to awakening. The exploration of the practice of meditation will be developed further in Chapter 7, but in the focussing of the mind the purpose should be to understand the truth of the dharma. In actuality it is essential to the expression of Buddhism in every aspect of the Eightfold Path:

> The benefits of concentration (samadhi) and serenity (samatha, samatha) are many. Serenity united with insight (vipassana, vipasyana) into selflessness uproots the causes of samsara. It enables us to develop virtuous qualities, integrate Dharma understanding with our minds, and attain the superknowledges, which are essential to benefit others most effectively. If we are serious about actualizing the paths, the practice of samadhi is a must. (Dalai Lama and Chodron, 2014, 83)

This mindfulness forms the beginnings of Buddhist meditation and is expressed in right effort, right mindfulness and right concentration.

Right effort

> And what is right effort? There is the case where a monk generates desire, endeavours, arouses persistence, upholds and exerts his intent for the sake of the non-arising of evil, unskillful qualities that have not yet arisen ... for the sake of the abandoning of evil, unskillful qualities that have arisen ... for the sake of the arising of skilful qualities that have not yet arisen ... (and) for the maintenance, non-confusion, increase, plenitude, development, and culmination of skilful qualities that have arisen: This is called right effort. (*Sacca-vibhanga Sutta*)

In light of samadhi this suggests the effort necessary to avoid unwelcome states of mind and maintain the concentration necessary to attain awakening. In essence, keeping the mind clear of anything that might draw a person away from meditation on the Four Noble Truths and the path to enlightenment. This is, perhaps, best exemplified by the Buddha's struggle with the four daughters of Mara: during his meditation during the first part of the night many evil thoughts (daughters of Mara sent to dance for him) came into his mind. Thoughts of desire, craving, fear and attachment arose, yet he did not allow these thoughts to disturb his concentration. He sat more firm than ever. It is noticeable that this effort is in contrast to the easy focus of the evil thoughts or alternatives to concentration offered to the world.

Right mindfulness

> And what is right mindfulness? There is the case where a monk remains focused on the body in and of itself – ardent, alert, and mindful – putting aside greed and distress with reference to the world. He remains focused on feelings in and of themselves ... the mind in and of itself ... mental qualities in and of themselves – ardent, alert, and mindful – putting aside greed and distress with reference to the world. This is called right mindfulness. (*Sacca-vibhanga Sutta*)

This aspect is linked with right effort as the effort is employed to maintain right mindfulness. This is the ability to focus on the here and now rather than the future which is uncontrollable. It, similarly, impacts on right action. The only way that a person can hope to have compassion towards other living things is to have the right mindset and an idea of how everybody and everything fits into the universe. Without right mindfulness right effort would be disorganized and ineffectual – only with this goal constantly in mind can the effort be properly focused.

Right concentration

> And what is right concentration? There is the case where a monk – quite secluded from sensuality, secluded from unskillful qualities – enters and remains in the first jhana: rapture and pleasure born of seclusion, accompanied by directed thought and evaluation. With the stilling of directed thoughts and evaluations, he enters and remains in the second jhana: rapture and pleasure born of concentration, unification of awareness free from directed thought and evaluation – internal assurance. With the fading of rapture he remains equanimous, mindful, and alert, and senses pleasure with the body. He enters and remains in the third jhana, of which the noble ones declare, 'Equanimous and mindful, he has a pleasant abiding.' With the abandoning of pleasure and pain – as with the earlier disappearance of elation and distress – he enters and remains in the fourth jhana: purity of equanimity and mindfulness, neither pleasure nor pain. This is called right concentration. (*Sacca-vibhanga Sutta*)

The ability to concentrate and maintain attentiveness is fundamental within Buddhism. It is what makes right mindfulness possible. The purpose of concentration is to obtain a focussed mind that cannot be distracted by the inclinations that arise in daily lives. Buddhists concentrate on meditation while other things vie for our attention; Buddhists concentrate and follow the Eightfold Path while other things seek to divert them from it. It is the ability to concentrate on dhamma at the expense of short-term pleasure. The way that this concentration is maintained through meditation is different according to the person and tradition of Buddhism, which will be explored further in Chapter 7.

Way of wisdom/insight (prajna/panna)

The wisdom that is developed as part of the Threefold Way is based around the Four Noble Truths and the resultant behaviour. The Buddha taught:

> It's through not awakening to or penetrating four noble truths, monks, that we have transmigrated and wandered on for such a long time, you and I. (*Maha Parinibbana Sutta*)

Through developing wisdom a person is able to see the truths of dependent origination and existence. Damien Keown (2003) suggests that while prajna is 'often translated as "wisdom"' it is actually 'closer in meaning to insight, discriminating knowledge, or intuitive apprehension. It is the faculty which apprehends the truth of Buddhist teachings' (218). All beings are possessed of it, but it lies undeveloped in most.

It is interesting to note that prajna includes right view and right resolve; wisdom is far more than the accumulation of knowledge; it is the application of such and knowledge and its accumulation by itself can be a hindrance to enlightenment. The only way for a person to achieve enlightenment is to decide for themselves to act according to the Four Noble Truths. In this way people are able to recognize that attachments are temporary and therefore behave accordingly. Similarly, through wisdom people gain an understanding of how to behave – this is an act of wisdom in deciding and applying the knowledge gained.

There are many examples from the life of Buddha where an application of wisdom enabled him to go further along the path to awakening. For example, when living as an ascetic, all the knowledge of the time suggested that this was the way to attain liberation. It was his wisdom that allowed him to see the futility of such efforts and that it was as ineffective as his life of hedonism.

The way of wisdom is linked with right view and right resolve.

Right view

> And what is right view? Knowledge in terms of stress, knowledge in terms of the origination of stress, knowledge in terms of the cessation of stress, knowledge in terms of the way of practice leading to the cessation of stress: This is called right view. (*Sacca-vibhanga Sutta*)

Although right view is the last of the Threefold Way, placing it at the beginning of the Eightfold Path indicates its importance for the living of the rest of the path. Every other aspect of the Eightfold Path can only be practised fully if built on right view. This enables people to have a true understanding of the nature of existence. Framed within the knowledge of the Four Noble Truths, sunyata and dependent origination everything is able to be placed into their proper perspective.

Right view includes, and perhaps it does not just include but is everything, the truth of the dharma. With this view a person is able to act and respond in a correct way. There are seen to be a mundane view of right view (of this world) and a supramundane view (outside the concrete world). The mundane view focuses on the importance of karma (see Chapter 1) as a driver for a positive rebirth. The supramundane view recognizes that this is not sufficient for awakening, rather the peace that comes from a full understanding of the Noble Truths. Both of these approaches will fully underpin the actions that a person performs in this life.

Care should be taken, however, not to make the views an end in themselves. Paul Fuller (2005) has suggested, drawing on Gethin, that:

> 'even so-called 'right-views' can be 'views'(ditthi) in so far as they can become fixed and the objects of attachment'. The Buddhist view, samma-di hi, is not meant to express a position because, as Gethin suggests, 'right-view should not be understood as a view itself, but as freedom from all views'. (13)

Right resolve

> And what is right resolve? The resolve for renunciation, for freedom from ill will, for harmlessness: This is called right resolve. (*Sacca-vibhanga Sutta*)

Right resolve, or intention, is inextricably linked with right view, and to try and separate the two may be to go too far. The Buddha taught earlier on that there is a threefold approach to right resolve, and conversely to wrong action resolve as their opposite:

- The right resolve of renunciation compared with the wrong resolve of desire.
- The right resolve of good will compared with the wrong resolve of ill will.
- The right resolve of harmlessness compared with the wrong resolve of harmfulness.

A person's resolve or intentions are the drivers of action and so need to be harnessed to ensure that actions are positive and compassionate.

Mahayana

In a similar way to the presentation of the Four Noble Truths mentioned earlier on (Chapter 1), the discussion of the Noble Eightfold Path has been explored in a way that builds on the Buddha's teaching, but this may be seen as more of a Theravada approach. With regard to the Four Noble Truths, including the Noble Eightfold Path, it is possible to recognize the importance of these within all traditions, but in Mahayana they are particularly seen as a preparatory step to the bodhisattva ideal (see Chapter 5). In some ways it can be seen that Buddhists tread the same path, but it is the end of that path, or the ultimate goal, that differs. Within the Theravada tradition the aim of becoming an arahant and parinibbana is the driving force behind the Four Noble Truths and the Noble Eightfold Path. In Mahayana, this 'aim' is transcended. Paul Williams (2009) has explained how this is so:

> When developed fully and properly these can lead to the nirvana of an Arhat. But in doing so the Bodhisattva is also inspired by pity for those who suffer, and also by another set of meditations familiar from mainstream Buddhism, the four *brahmaviharas* ('divine

abidings') of immeasurable friendliness, compassion, sympathetic joy, and equanimity (or 'impartiality'). He combines the Perfection of Wisdom with his use of clever means and stratagems (*upaya*) to prevent himself from becoming an Arhat. He practises not to destroy but actually to keep (albeit under his own control) those factors that would lead to further rebirths. Through such clever means and stratagems he fires and projects his spiritual career onwards to Buddhahood. (61)

As suggested extra steps are added that enable a bodhisattva, through their infinite compassion, to control a further rebirth. As a preparatory step that was superseded, the elements of the Eightfold Path are important but are not all that are needed.

In addition to the aim of a Mahayana worldview being the bodhisattva ideal, the motivating factor and driving factor of the path can be seen to differ. While the Theravadan understanding of the Noble Eightfold Path is driven by wisdom or insight, and as such it places everything in its proper perspective, in Mahayana Buddhism it might be suggested that compassion is more of the driving force.

The Noble Eightfold Path of 'disciples' (Skt *sravakas*) of a perfect Buddha, directed at Arahatship, was still respected, but was seen to be in need of supplementing by the *Bodhisattva*-path to perfect Buddhahood, now exalted into the state of a heavenly saviour being. While wisdom was a key part of the Eightfold Path, and itself encompassed compassion, the Mahayana developed a more philosophically sophisticated account of it, and made compassion an equal complementary virtue which was the motivation of the whole path. (Harvey, 2000, 123)

This is expressed most clearly in Shantideva's (2015) *Bodhisattvacharyavatara* (A Guide to the Bodhisattva's Way of Life:

Thus by the virtue collected
Through all that I have done,
May the pain of every living creature
Be completely cleared away.

May I be the doctor, the medicine
And may I be the nurse
For all sick beings in the world,
Until everyone is healed. (III, 7–9)

This will be further explored in Chapter 5; but it is of utmost importance to note that the goal of the two traditions, drastically alter the emphasis that is placed on certain aspects. It will be important to explore and emphasize this in any exploration of the Eightfold Path in the classroom. As the basis for Buddhist practice the Eightfold Path is central but needs to be expanded to include a Mahayana view.

Thoughts for the classroom

In exploring the Eightfold Path in the classroom there are two aspects that are important to consider. The first is how the Eightfold Path links to the daily living of a Buddhist. How does it affect the way that Buddhists live? Although the beliefs are important, for most Buddhists they serve little purpose if they are only words on a page, or ideas in the mind. They need to be put into the context of life in the modern world. Perhaps the easiest to engage with in this kind of task, as already explored, is right livelihood, but each have an important application. Sometimes rather than asking pupils to imagine how people could put them into practice, it is useful to use a video or story of a Buddhist and ask students to look for evidence of the Eightfold Path. In this way it may prompt discussion and help students realize how interrelated each of the aspects are. To consider whether something is right view or right intention, means that it might be both. The concern with this type of task is whether teachers are suggesting that practices are a checklist that can be ticked off, and that interpretation of Buddhism could not be further from the truth.

It is important to not use just 'religious' tasks but also, for example, people who are engaged in the moment. A mindful person would be engaged in conversation noticing what is being said and how best to respond through right speech. Maybe, someone who is not mindful or concentrating is distracted by their phone and is not fully engaged with life. The everyday nature of living should be emphasized and the fact that a living of the Eightfold Path cannot be separated from ordinariness.

The second aspect that is important to consider is how students themselves respond to the Eightfold Path. This does not mean that teachers are asking students to pick and choose aspects of the Eightfold Path to follow; rather that in recognizing similarities and differences between the Eightfold Path and their own practices, whether Buddhist or not, will help break down the illusory and dangerous barriers of 'them' and 'us'. In utilizing an activity such as that found in Table 4.2 enables comparisons to be drawn. The reasons for these differences and similarities would be very interesting to explore.

There may be a temptation for teachers, in exploring the lived reality of Buddhism with students, to have experiential activities designed. McGuire (2021) suggests that students might be encouraged 'to experientially engage with Buddhism in their everyday lives include trying to live according to the five precepts for several days ... and engaging in 'analogous activities' that resemble Buddhist practices' (9). For me, these activities are problematic, as although they may be attempts to use 'secular activities that are simple, accessible, and analogous to religious practice in order to facilitate comparative religious study' (McGuire, 2019, 114). While there is much literature on the use of experiential learning in religious education (see Holt, 2022), the use of activities that engage the student in experiences may be fine if they are not pseudo-religious. A further exploration of this 'experiential' learning and its suitability can be found in Chapter 7 and the discussion around the application of mindfulness in schools and teaching.

Table 4.2 Comparison of the Eightfold Path and Student Views

What do Buddhists think?	Similarities/differences	What do I think?
Right view/understanding		What is something that I believe about life?
Right resolve/intention/attitude		What do I want to do?
Right speech		What do I think is good to say?
Right conduct/action		What are good things to do?
Right livelihood		What job do I want to do? Why?
Right effort		What am I trying my best to do?
Right mindfulness/awareness		How do I live in the moment?
Right concentration		How do I concentrate on what I need to?

As already indicated, an area that must not be ignored is the applicability of the Noble Eightfold Path to all Buddhists. The way that teachers phrase their teaching is key. Mahayana should not be an afterthought; the compelling force of compassion leading to the bodhisattva ideal should be recognized. In younger age-group classes it may be that this recognition is limited to the use of 'many', 'most' or 'some'; when describing practices, beliefs or aims one recognizes that Buddhism is not a monolith and there is diversity that will be encountered as students delve deeper into the religion.

5

The bodhisattva and arahant ideals

In delineating beliefs between the different traditions of Buddhism, especially between Mahayana and Theravada expressions, there are many different elements that could be explored. One of the key aspects of difference is found in the exploration of the identity of the Buddha and its associated beliefs, some of which were developed in Chapter 3. There will, also, inevitably be a merging of traditions and beliefs as was discussed in the Introduction and also, to some extent, in Chapters 1 and 2. In this chapter the concept of the Buddha, and also of the aims of life within the different traditions, will be explored. The two concepts, and ideals, that will be at the heart of this exploration will be the *bodhisattva* and *arahant* (Skt: arhat) ideals. Each of these, and their attendant beliefs, will be explored in turn, to be followed by a discussion of their similarities and differences.

The bodhisattva ideal

The bodhisattva ideal has been referred to throughout this book, and, as established in Chapter 3, there are two understandings of the term. The first is accepted in both Theravada and Mahayana, in that it is a Buddha in waiting; someone who has made the vow to become a Buddha and help others escape the cycle of samsara. Through numerous aeons and lifetimes Shakyamuni Buddha was such a bodhisattva, and since his life on earth, Maitreya has been a bodhisattva waiting in Tusita heaven. As explored in greater depth in Chapter 3 there are ten qualities of a bodhisattva in Theravada thought: generosity, morality, renunciation, insight, energy, patience, truthfulness, resolution, loving kindness and equanimity.

The second understanding is the one that is the concern of this chapter. The bodhisattva ideal is seen to be a higher goal than that of purely attaining nirvana as an arahant. *The Lotus Sutra* describes it this way:

> For those who sought to be *shravakas* he taught the Dharma of the four truths for overcoming birth, old age, disease, and death and for attaining nirvana. For those who sought to be *pratyekabuddhas* he taught the Dharma of the twelve causes and conditions. And for the *bodhisattvas* he taught the six transcendental practices to lead them to attain supreme awakening and all-inclusive wisdom. (Reeves, 2008a, 65)

The concept is that if a being is truly devoid of the sense of self, full of wisdom and compassion, then they are not satisfied with only their own awakening. As was seen in Chapter 4 the view of a bodhisattva is that they are able to delay parinirvana and control their rebirth to assist others in this path. In Chapter 2 the example of Amitabha/Amida Buddha was shown as a being who created a Pure Land to enable all who venerate him to attain awakening in their next rebirth into the Pure Land.

In this sense the bodhisattva path is open to anyone and refers to anyone who has begun this path. James Apple (2014) outlines the four stages of becoming a bodhisattva. The first stage highlights when a person determines to attain buddhahood and has 'the thought of awakening (*bodhicittotpada*)' (62). *The Lotus Sutra* speaks of itself as a possible spark to this awakening desire:

> The Buddha said: 'Good sons, first, this sutra leads a not-yet-awakened bodhisattva to aspire to awakening, leads one without human kindness to aspire to kindness, leads one with a murderous heart to aspire to great compassion. (Reeves, 2008a, 42)

When the vow (pranidhana) is taken to attain buddhahood, from that point on a person is a bodhisattva. This may be a formal declaration such as 'I will attain the immortal, undecaying, pain-free *bodhi*, and free the world from all pain', and 'by this Thought of Enlightenment, the Root of Good, and by my renunciation of everything that can be given away, may I become a Buddha in this blind world, which is without a guide and a leader' (Dayal, 1970, 65). Khenchen Appey Rinpoche outlines the Seven Branch Practice that may precede the making of the vow:

1. Paying homage to the Buddha, the dharma and the sangha
2. Making offerings, usually garlands of flowers but maybe of jewels. Showing that attachment and desire mean nothing.
3. Confession as an expression of humility, and the opposite of aggression.
4. Rejoicing in the deeds of others, rejecting jealousy.
5. Request to turn the Wheel of Dharma.
6. Requesting the Buddhas to remain and not pass into nirvana.
7. Dedication. Dedicating virtues to attain buddhahood and extend compassion to all beings. (Bernert, 2018)

Although open to anyone, it is a decision not to be taken lightly. The Dalai Lama highlighted the importance of the vow and the seriousness with which it should be taken:

> In order to take this vow, we should imagine that in front of us are the Buddha and his eight close disciples; the six ornaments, and the two supreme teachers, including Shantideva; and all the realized masters of the Buddhist tradition, in particular the holders of the Sakya, Gelug, Kagyu, and Nyingma schools of Tibet – in fact, all the Buddhas and Bodhisattvas. Consider also that we are surrounded by all the beings in the universe. With this visualization, we shall now read the Seven Branch Prayer …

> Consider that we are surrounded by all the beings in the universe and generate compassion for them. Think of the Buddha and feel great devotion to him. Now, with compassion and devotion, pray, 'May I attain Buddhahood!' ...
> When we recite these lines for the third time, at the words, 'I will generate this self-same attitude,' think that you have generated this bodhichitta in the depth of your hearts, in the very marrow of your bones, and that you will never go back on this promise. Traditionally we now recite the last nine verses of the chapter as a conclusion to taking the vow. (2009, 32–4)

Once this vow is taken it is important that, as a reminder, they are repeated each day (Gyato, 1995). Ngulchu Gyalas Thogmed Zangpo (1297–1371) outlined *Thirty Seven Practices of a Bodhisattva* that are the basis of a bodhisattva path for many Tibetan Buddhists. Examples of such include:

> One ... It is the practice of Bodhisattvas to listen,
> Contemplate and meditate day and night to free
> Themselves and others from the ocean of samsara
>
> Four: It is the practice of Bodhisattvas to renounce this life
>
> Six: It is the practice of Bodhisattvas to hold excellent
> Spiritual friends as even more than their own bodies
>
> Twenty three: It is the practice of Bodhisattvas to renounce
> Clinging attachment when meeting with pleasant objects. (Dalai Lama, 1995, 19, 26, 28, 90)

Space does not allow for a listing of all thirty seven, but each highlights how a bodhisattva should live.

The second stage of becoming a bodhisattva is recognition that things are not created (*anutpattikadharma ksanti*). The third stage is the 'attainment of the status of irreversibility or nonretrogression (*avaivartika*) from Buddhahood' (Apple, 2014, 62). These stages involve the attaining of stages (bhumis) of awakening:

> All bodhisattvas will (1) enter the bhumis of the wisdom of the radiance of the Buddha's inconceivable Dharma, (2) completely accumulate all roots of goodness, (3) become skilled in examining the entire Dharma of the Buddha, (4) possess a vast wisdom of the entire Dharma, (5) teach the perfectly preserved Dharma, (6) have the purified wisdom of indivisibility, (7) be unstained by all worldly qualities, (8) purify the transcendent roots of goodness, (9) realize the scope of inconceivable wisdom, and (10) ultimately attain the scope of omniscient wisdom. (*Mahavaipulya Sutra* 1:6)

These bhumis or stages are explained further in the *Dasabhumikasutra* as the stages/planes bodhisattvas go through as they progress to buddhahood:

- *Great joy* – in this stage all the paramitas (perfections) are practised with an emphasis on dana (generosity).
- *Stainless* – in this stage the bodhisattva is free from immorality, and the paramita emphasized is sila (morality).
- *Luminous* – in this stage the bodhisattva radiates the light of the dharma, and the paramita emphasized is khanti (patience).
- *Radiant* – the bodhisattva radiates light against anything that opposes them, and the paramita emphasized is virya (vigour).
- *Very difficult to train* – the bodhisattvas try and help other beings and do not become frustrated when they fail to respond, and the paramita emphasized is dhyana (meditative concentration).
- *Obviously transcendent* – the bodhisattva does not exist in samsara or nirvana, and the paramita emphasized is prajna (wisdom).
- *Gone afar* – the paramita emphasized is of (upaya) skilful means in an attempt to help others.
- *Immovable* – in this stage the bodhisattva is able to choose their own rebirth, and the paramita emphasized is aspiration.
- *Good discriminating wisdom* – the paramita emphasized is understanding self and non-self.
- *Cloud of dharma* – following this stage a being attains buddhahood, and the paramita emphasized is primordial wisdom.

The fourth stage of becoming a bodhisattva is the occasion of a Buddha predicting when and where a bodhisattva's awakening will take place. This does not fit neatly after the bhumis, as this stage is possibly reflected around the time of the immovable bhumi.

Six paramitas

The path of the bodhisattva, in this life, is followed in different ways. The two main ways are those of the six paramitas and the tantric path. A paramita is a 'transcendent action' or one that 'transcends ego' (Ray, 2004, 128). This is central to a bodhisattva's path; all actions are not performed for the go, rather for out of compassion for others. The six paramitas generally found in Mahayana Buddhism are:

- *Dana* (generosity)
- *Sila* (morality)
- *Ksanti* (patience)
- *Virya* (effort or vigour)

- *Dhyana* (concentration)
- *Prajna* (wisdom or insight)

In a similar way to how the Buddha developed the perfections through many lifetimes, this will be an effort for all who enter the bodhisattva path. In the living of the paramitas there will be 'a tendency to impress a "thought of enlightenment" upon all acts and choice' as 'taken together [the paramitas] provide concrete guidance for the construction of character' (Wright, 2009, 8). It is to be noticed that sila, virya, dhyana or wisdom can be seen to be related to aspects of the Eightfold Path and Threefold Way (see Chapter 4), and the paramitas of ksanti and dana will be explored in Chapter 8 as the ethical dimension of Buddhism is discussed. Each of these paramitas enable a person to overcome the Three Poisons and to develop the wisdom and insight necessary to realize the truth of existence and sunyata. Those who attain buddhahood will be full of these perfections.

Of note is that gradually a further four paramitas were added to reflect the bhumis outlined earlier on. The last four are:

- *Upaya-kausalya* (skilful means)
- *Pranidhana* (vow)
- *Bala* (power)
- *Jnana* (knowledge).

The significance of prajna cannot be overstated within Mahayana Buddhist expressions of compassion and the realization of buddhahood. The *Prajna-paramita* (Perfection of Insight) texts express some of the most central aspects of Mahayana teachings. Edward Conze (2001) notes that there are 'thirty-eight different books, composed in India between 100 BC and AD 600' (xxviii); examples of these sutras include *Asta-sahasrika-prajna-paramita Sutra* (The Perfection of Insight in Eight Thousand Lines), the *Heart Sutra* and the *Diamond Sutra*. Without being too simplistic, Conze summarizes the message of the wisdom sutras:

> The thousands of lines of the Prajna-paramita can be summed up in the following two sentences. 1) One should become a Bodhisattva (or Buddha-to-be), i.e. one who is content with nothing less than all-knowledge attained through the perfection of insight for the sake of all beings. 2) There is no such thing as a Bodhisattva or as all-knowledge or as a being or as the Perfection of Insight or as an attainment. To accept both these contradictory facts is to be perfect. (Conze, 1978, 7–8)

It is slightly more full than that, especially as Keown (2013) notes that the concepts of skilful means and merit transference, central to understanding the bodhisattva path, particularly in relation to the arahant ideal, are developed within the wisdom sutras. Throughout this book many of the teachings explored have drawn on the Pali Canon (see Chapter 6); and these are important as they are the teachings of Shakyamuni Buddha;

but in the bodhisattva path these are seen to be 'skilful' means to encourage people onto the path, or to be content with an individual awakening, but the wisdom sutras provide the truth of the overall message and goal. Only through understanding the wisdom of these sutras with regards to sunyata, dependent origination and the bodhisattva can a person truly understand the message of the Buddha.

Tantra

Tantric Buddhism is often identified with Vajrayana Buddhism, but it is far more diverse than that one group. Lewis and Angelis (2016) emphasize this:

> The Tantric Buddhist traditions have been given several labels, but there is no single label that is accepted by all of these traditions ... It is important to note the use of this term in a plural form. Tantric or esoteric Buddhist traditions are multiple and also originated as multiple, distinct traditions of both text and practice. (73, 77)

Although sometimes seen as separate to Mahayana, Vajrayana (and its associated traditions) can be seen to be a part of the Mahayana tradition, as it accepts the boodhisattva ideal as its goal, indeed, 'the difference between Mahayana is primarily one of approach' (Jones, 2021b, 197). Defining tantric Buddhism is seen to be difficult but is seen to be based on the tantric literature between the third and twelfth centuries, but the range of literature is vast and unexplored. Mainly translated from sanskrit there appear to be over two thousand such texts in Tibetan, Chinese and Japanese (Williams et al., 2012). Although difficult to define, Williams et al. (2012) suggest some shared chracteristics:

- *Esotericism:* there is an initiation and elements of practice are seen to be secret. Tantras and their meanings are taught to the initiated but may have different levels of interpretation.
- *Importance of the teacher:* the vajra-master (*vajracarya*) or guru is central in passing on the practices and interpretations.
- *Transgressive and controversial practices:* it is suggested that so controversial were the teachings that early Buddhists destroyed tantric texts. In early modern history tantric Buddhism was seen to not be Buddhism: 'Tantric Buddhism was seen as degenerate – typified by disgusting practices and a welter of gods – and far removed from the conception of (early and 'true') Buddhism' (Williams et al., 2012, 143).
- *Revaluation of the body:* the place of the material bodily form is re-evaluated and seen to be positive. It is seen to be a channel of energy. The *Hevajra Tantra* II: ii, 36–7 teaches: 'Likewise without form and so on, bliss would not be perceived' (Snellgrove, 1959).
- *Revaluation of the status and role of women:* female deities are highly regarded.

- *Analogical thinking:* there are many correlations and connections between actions and meanings within tantric Buddhism. One example is that of the five cosmic ('directional') Buddhas from the *Vajradhatu mandala* of the *Tattvasamgraha*, where each Buddha is seen to have a corresponding hand gesture, knowledge, colour, aggregates and so on.
- *Revaluation of negative mental states:* passions and sensual pleasures can be a means to overcome them, and in certain situations can be positive, reflecting the belief that 'one knowing the nature of poison may dispel poison with poison – by using the very poison that a little of would kill other beings' (*Hevajra Tantra* II: ii, 46)

The path of tantric, and more specifically of Vajrayana, Buddhism, is that as the Diamond Vehicle, it offers a path to buddhahood that is described as a 'thunderbolt' or a way that is much quicker. It offers this path through various practices:

- The recitation of mantras.
- The visualizing of and seeing one's self in the deity.
- The use of mandalas, usually with a king or an awakened one in the centre.
- *Sadhana* – framework of practice: 'Mantras, visualization and mandalas are brought together in texts called sadhanas (literally, 'means of accomplishment'), works specifically designed to guide the tantric practitioner through a sequence of practice focused on a particular deity' (Williams et al., 2012, 173).

This may seem to be a 'different' kind of Buddhism then so far explored, but as discussed in the Introduction there are many different types of Buddhism, and the goal of buddhahood and the bodhisattva path is a central aspect of tantric Buddhism.

Heavenly beings

Thus far in this chapter, the bodhisattva as a path on which all people may commence has been discussed. The 'completion' of such is evidenced in the lives of bodhisattvas who, having attained awakening, influence and help people today. These beings are the object of devotion (see Chapter 7) as Buddhists strive to emulate them, and to either be awakened or gain positive rebirth. These are signified in the Wheel of Life (Figure 2.1), as in each of the realms there is a figure of a bodhisattva helping people to escape that realm, and in some cases become awakened (dependent on the realm). Examples of these bodhisattvas include the Eight Great Bodhisattva of Tibetan Buddhism (Dalai Lama, 2009):

- Manjusri (Gentle Glory) a bodhisattva of wisdom
- Avalokitesvara (Lord Who Looks Down at the World) a bodhisattva of compassion
- Vajrapani (Vajra in Hand) a bodhisattva of protection
- Maitreya (Friendly One) the future Buddha

- Ksitigarbha (Earth Source)
- Akasagarbha (Space Source)
- Sarvanivaranaviskambhin (Blocker of Hindrances)
- Samantabhadra (All Good)

Further bodhisattva include Amitabha/Amida (see Chapter 2). The *Lotus Sutra* speaks of thousands of bodhisattva who came out of the earth to listen to the Buddha at Vulture Peak but it is more likely that these are beings destined for buddhahood, rather than those who attained such already, though the four leaders of the bodhisattva of the earth are sometimes considered to be such beings. There is also the female bodhisattva Prajnaparamita (Bodhisattva of Wisdom). The Dalai Lama (see Chapter 2) is perhaps the most well-known bodhisattva outside of Buddhism.

These figures are able to transfer merit and help people along the path to awakening. They are beings of such compassion that parinirvana has been put off so that others can be helped to awakening. This was exemplified in the example of Amitabha discussed at length in terms of the Pure Land in Chapter 2.

The arahant ideal

Within Theravada Buddhism (see Introduction) an arahant (Skt: arhat) is someone who attains enlightenment by following the teachings of the Buddha, rather than the Buddha who discovers the path for himself. The arahant is seen to be the ultimate aim or destiny for people within Theravada Buddhism. Damien Keown and Charles Prebish (2010) suggest:

> When the great Theravada commentator, Buddhaghosa, wrote the *Visuddhimagga* delineating the nature of the gradual path to enlightenment, he placed the arahant at the completion of that path. (36)

With it established as an ideal, it is possible to describe four possible paths to attain such. Ananda, the disciple of the Buddha, outlined these four ways in the *Yuganaddha Sutta*:

> There is the case where *a monk has developed insight preceded by tranquillity*. As he develops insight preceded by tranquillity, the path is born...
> Then there is the case where *a monk has developed tranquillity preceded by insight*. As he develops tranquillity preceded by insight, the path is born...
> Then there is the case where *a monk has developed tranquillity in tandem with insight*. As he develops tranquillity in tandem with insight, the path is born...
> Then there is the case where *a monk's mind has its restlessness concerning the Dhamma [Comm: the corruptions of insight] well under control*. There comes a time when his mind grows steady inwardly, settles down, and becomes unified and concentrated. In him the path is born. (emphasis added)

Within the context of each of these paths, 'the fetters that are abandoned' are those things that keep a person chained to the cycle of rebirth, and the unsatisfactoriness of existence. In the discussion further on about the stages to become an arahant, the fetters that are abandoned are explained.

It is often suggested that the arahant ideal is about personal liberation and, as such, lacks compassion for those who are around them. In a sense, it is argued that a religion that teaches that there is no permanent self, and that ego should be removed, can be fairly egotistical and self-centred as a person seeks for their own liberation. Bhikkhu Bodhi (2010) suggests that such a position in relation to the arahant ideal is misguided and mischaracterizes the nature of the path:

> The quest for liberation as an arahant is not a purely private, personal undertaking, but has a far-reaching influence and can have an impact upon a whole society. In the traditional Theravada countries, before the corrupting influence of the West set in, the whole life of the community revolved around the Dhamma. The monks who meditated in the forests and mountains were the inspiration and model for the society; those who preached and taught in the villages helped to transmit the Dhamma to the people.

In this essay, Bodhi seems to be trying to defend the arahant ideal in light of the Bodhisattva ideal in suggesting they are two sides of the same coin. In some ways, the argument he is making is similar to the idea that a person on an aeroplane should affix their own oxygen mask before attempting to help anyone else. A person cannot be in a position to help others if they have not first attained enlightenment and become an arahant. In the same way the Buddha may be viewed as the first arahant who, once enlightened, spent the remainder of his days teaching the dhamma and helping others attain arahantship. This compassionate approach to arahantship is perhaps the best way to understand the ideal within Theravada Buddhism, where once an arahant has attained 'nirvana in this present life' (Bodhi, 2010) they are then able to help others in the time between attainment and the final passing into nirvana at death.

There are four stages to awakening as an arahant (with arahant being the fourth stage) that are known as *ariya puggala*. These are according to the *Silavant Sutta*:

- *Sotapanna* (a stream-enterer)
- *Sakadagamin* (a once-returner)
- *Anagami* (a non-returner)
- An *Arahant*

Each of these stages are characterized by the development of freedom from the fetters of existence. For the Arahant:

there is nothing further to do, and nothing to add to what has been done, still these things – when developed and pursued – lead both to a pleasant abiding in the here and now and to mindfulness and alertness. (*Silavant Sutta*)

Although these four stages are laid out, it could be suggested that it is not as simple as simply deciding to 'enter the stream'; rather there will have been some preparatory work. Buddhaghosa in chapters 18–22 of *Visuddhimagga* describes 'seven purifications' (*satta-visuddhi*) that prepares a puthujjana (ordinary person) encumbered by the deceit of existence to become a stream-enterer. These stages described by Buddhaghosa are:

1. Purification of moral conduct (*sila-visuddhi*)
2. Purification of mind by developing calm (*citta-visuddhi*)
3. Purification of view through an awareness of the five khandas (*ditthi-visuddhi*)
4. Purification by overcoming doubt by recognizing the interdependence of all (*kankha-vitarana-visuddhi*)
5. Purification by knowledge and vision of what is the way (path) and not the way. Here a person recognizes the impermanence of everything (*maggamagga-nanadassana-visuddhi*). The person at this stage is at risk of attachment here as the ten imperfections may cause distraction. The ten imperfections are:

    (1) illumination, (2) knowledge, (3) rapturous happiness, (4) tranquillity, (5) bliss (pleasure), (6) resolution, (7) exertion, (8) assurance, (9) equanimity and (10) attachment (Buddhaghosa & Nanamoli, 2010, 661).

6. Purification by knowledge and vision of the course of practice (*patipada-nanadassana-visuddhi*). The eight knowledges in this purification are elucidated by Buddhaghosa and Nanamoli:

    (1) knowledge of contemplation of rise and fall, which is insight free from imperfections and steady on its course, (2) knowledge of contemplation of dissolution, (3) knowledge of appearance as terror, (4) knowledge of contemplation of danger, (5) knowledge of contemplation of dispassion, (6) knowledge of desire for deliverance, (7) knowledge of contemplation of reflection and (8) knowledge of equanimity about formations (2010, 666).

7. Purification by knowledge and vision (nanadassana-visuddhi). This involves a change of lineage, from that of puthujjana to that of stream-enterer:

    Change-of-lineage knowledge comes next. Its position is to advert to the path, and so it belongs neither to purification by knowledge and vision of the way nor to purification by knowledge and vision, but being intermediate, it is unassignable. Still it is reckoned as insight because it falls in line with insight (Buddhaghosa & Nanamoli, 2010, 701).

Elements of these purifications will be explored in Chapter 7. We will now briefly explore the three stages prior to that of arahant:

Sotapanna

The 'stream-enterer' is one who has entered into the stream by beginning to live the Eightfold Path:

> 'Sariputta, "The stream, the stream": Thus it is said. And what, Sariputta, is the stream?' 'This noble eightfold path, lord, is the stream: right view, right resolve, right speech, right action, right livelihood, right effort, right mindfulness, right concentration'. (*Sariputta Sutta*)

The *Sariputta Sutta* describes further the characteristics of one who has entered the stream:

> Association with people of integrity, lord, is a factor for stream entry. Listening to the True Dhamma is a factor for stream entry. Appropriate attention is a factor for stream entry. Practice in accordance with the Dhamma is a factor for stream entry.

Stream enterers stand distinct from puthujjana who are 'ordinary' people encumbered by the deceit of existence. By entering the stream a person on the path of an arahant is able to be free from the fetters or 'effluents' of 'self-identification view, doubt, and grasping at habits and practices' (*Sabbasava Sutta*). In casting off these fetters, those with a self-identification view have recognized the truth of anatta, that there is no permanent self. As such they will begin to view existence in a way this is not self-centred. A stream-enterer has experienced insight into the true nature of existence, and as such has no doubt about the Buddha and the dhamma. Further, the stream-enterer no longer clings to habits (sometimes translated as rituals) and practices that are used by those who are seeking freedom from suffering. They recognize that there is ultimately no benefit to such actions.

The result of becoming a stream-enterer, or as sometimes described a 'stream-winner', is that there will be a maximum of seven more rebirths, and none of these will be in the lower realms of existence (see Chapter 2) but will be in the higher realms (Bodhi, 1995).

Sakadagamin

As is perhaps evident from their appellation as 'once-returner' those in this stage will be subject to one more rebirth before the attainment of enlightenment and becoming an arahant. In this stage, the first three fetters remain detached, and further a once-returner 'permanently weakening the next two fetters, sensual desire and aversion' (Williams et al., 2012, 62).

Anagami

An anagami (non-returner) is freed from the first five (lower) fetters of self-identification view, doubt, grasping at habits and practices, sensuality and ill will. As such an anagami will be not be reborn into a sensual world, but will be reborn into one of the five suddhavasa (pure abodes) realms (see Chapter 2) where only those who are free of the first five fetters exist. These realms are:

- Akanistha
- Sudarsana
- Sudrsa
- Atapa
- Avrha

At the end of their time in this realm, a person will transition into arahantship and nibbana.

Arahant

In addition to being free from the five lower fetters, an arahant is also free from the five higher fetters:

- Form/material rebirth desire
- Formless/immaterial rebirth desire
- Conceit
- Restlessness
- Ignorance

An arahant is awakened, and being free from all attachment, at death, will never be reborn and pass into nibbana (see Chapter 2). For Theravada Buddhists this is the ultimate goal, and is attained through wisdom and a living of the Eightfold Path.

Gethin (1998) highlights two interpretations of the way that these stages of an arahant ideal function. On the one hand it may be independent, and not sequential; indeed, 'one may attain any one of the first steps immediately' (194). The alternative is a sequential development over many lives; a slight concern with the consecutive nature of the stages surrounds the 'never-returner' and the arahant in this world seeming to be independent of one another. If it is sequential, then an arahant would never take rebirth in a lower realm. It could, therefore, have both approaches. Some go through the process sequentially, passing into arahantship after anagami, while others, at least, skip the step of anagami.

Thoughts for the classroom

There are perhaps many outward differences between Mahayana and Theravada Buddhism. Some of these surround the focus on beings from other realms (see Chapter 2), but when one peels away the layers it can be seen that there are elements of these in both traditions to varying degrees. The major difference is discussed in this chapter; it is the focus of the goal towards which Buddhists are working. The use of the pejorative term 'Hinayana' to describe 'older' traditions of Buddhism, of which Theravada is seen to be the surviving school, is indicative of the difference. One thing that must be done in the classroom is to ensure that both goals are recognized and taught. One student was heard to ask: 'If a Buddhist wants to get rid of desire, how can they desire nibbana?' This is the question that Mahayana seems to go beyond. In Chapter 2 the capability of a bodhisattva to put off nirvana to choose their future rebirth was explored and ensured that compassion enabled them to seek the awakening of all living things.

One of the most interesting concepts that might be engaging for students to discuss in light of the relationship between Mahayana traditions and Theravada is the idea of skilful means. Essentially, for many Mahayana Buddhists, this means that the Buddha taught people most of his life according to their ability to understand, and as such the arahant ideal is a lesser (and for some, false) path. It inspired people to begin the path, but it was preparatory to the higher path of the bodhisattva. How, then, could the Buddha be justified in sharing a view that ultimately paled in comparison? Is skilful means different from deceit? In a Mahayana view, it is very different, as this teaching was given out of compassion, but it does raise questions that students may want to engage with. A further explanation might be suggested by the XIV Dalai Lama:

> After his parinirvana, the Mahayana teachings degenerated until they remained only in name and this state of affairs lasted for a long time. According to the Buddha's prediction, Nagarjuna and Asanga laid the foundations for the resurgence of Mahayana, and the Mahayana teachings flourished for many centuries after that. (1995, 13)

As explored in this chapter, the categorization of the arahant ideal as intrinsically selfish is a caricature and not indicative of the compassion that arahants develop and express in the interregnum between attaining awakening and parinibbana. Bodhisattvas, however, extend this beyond the time period experienced by arahants. There are many aspects of the paths that are similar, but the emphasis placed on wisdom and compassion leads to the explanation of different 'end' points.

The universal potential of each path also leads to questions about the accessibility, and the actions, which people on each path perform. Is there a significant difference or are they just different ways to package expectations and practices?

In light of these questions I think it is imperative that our classroom practice at all ages changes. Unless we are suggesting that the teaching of the goal of nibbana is a skilful means in earlier years, we should recognize the difference in goal for each tradition. This may be with small adaptations to our language or a more nuanced explanation of nirvana as the Third Noble Truth.

The bodhisattva ideal and the arahant ideal and the methods used to attain them can also lead to a discussion of what constitutes Buddhism. While Theravada is often seen as the 'original' tradition, while others see 'Mahayana' as unfettered by colonial lenses and influences, the whole range of differences can lead to interesting lessons. What is it about Vajrayana and Pure Land Buddhisms that make them different, yet also the same? Ajahn Brahm suggests:

> I am often asked what the difference is between the major strands of Buddhism – Mahayana, Theravada, Vajrayana and Zen. The answer is that they are like identical cakes with four different icings: on the outside the traditions may look and taste different, but when you go deeply into them, you find the same taste – the taste of freedom. (Brahm, 2015, xv)

Although in many schools the comparison of the two ideals does not occur until older teenage years, it could be suggested that it must begin much earlier if students are to have any chance to understand the various Buddhisms in the world. Teachers already do this with reference to the Dalai Lama and the Wheel of Life; it is to add context to these teachings that will enable the comparisons to begin and further exploration of concepts such as nirvana.

6

The dhamma/dharma and the sangha

In the Introduction to this book the importance of the Three Jewels (*triratna*) or Refuges was explained. The mantra of:

I take (go for) refuge in the Buddha.
I take (go for) refuge in the Dharma.
I take (go for) refuge in the Sangha.

is repeated in devotional activities and in other areas of a Buddhist's life. The Refuges are key to understand and find safety in this life:

> But when, having gone for refuge to the Buddha, Dhamma, and Sangha, you see with right discernment the four noble truths ... That's the secure refuge, that, the supreme refuge, that is the refuge, having gone to which, you gain release from all suffering and stress. (*Dhammapada* 188–92)

The declaration of taking refuge at the time of the Buddha denoted 'a formal act of allegiance, submitting to the pre-eminence and claiming the protection of a powerful patron' (Robinson et al., 2005, 43); thus, taking refuge in the Buddha, the dharma and the sangha associated oneself with the Buddhist community and placed oneself under its protection. What this means in terms of the dharma and the sangha will be developed in this chapter. The importance of the Buddha was explored in Chapter 3. It is for this reason that the dhamma (Skt: dharma) and samgha (Skt: sangha) will be explored in this chapter, along with any differences of understanding between Buddhist traditions.

The dharma

The second of the Three Jewels or Refuges is the dharma (Pali: dhamma). It is an embracive term that is difficult to contain and define. Rahula (1997) suggests:

> The term dhamma is much wider than samkhara. There is no term in Buddhist terminology wider than dhamma. It includes not only the conditioned things and states, but also the non-conditioned, the Absolute, Nirvana. There is nothing in the universe or outside, good or bad, conditioned or non-conditioned, relative or absolute, which is not included in this term. (58)

Most commonly, within Buddhism, the dharma is equated with the teachings of the Buddha. In the *Vakkali Sutta*, the monk Vakkali is lamenting that he has not been able to visit with the Buddha because he has been too weak. The Buddha replies:

> Enough, Vakkali! Why would you want to see this rotten body? One who sees the teaching sees me. One who sees me sees the teaching. Seeing the teaching, you see me. Seeing me, you see the teaching.

There seems to be no distinction between the person of the Buddha and his teachings. In some ways, that is the aim of Buddhism; it is the dhamma that is most important:

> So, Ananda, you should all live with yourselves as your island, yourselves as your refuge, with no other as your refuge; with the Dhamma as your island, the Dhamma as your refuge, with no other as your refuge. (*Maha Parinibbana Sutta*)

For a person to discover and live according to the reality of existence is what should be sought. The intricacies of the dharma are tied up with the living of the Buddhist way of life; the two cannot be separated. When a person goes for refuge in the dharma, it is through the living of the teachings that a person can find safety and protection. The words by themselves are not able to provide refuge unless they are lived.

Dhammadharo (1994) continues this unity of the teachings and living when he suggests that there are three stages in which the dharma is expressed. Firstly he suggests *pariyatti-dhamma*, which is the study of the words of the Buddha, particularly those in the Pali canon (see further on). Secondly is *paipatti-dhamma*, which refers to the living of the words of the Buddha, and then, finally, is *paivedha-dhamma*, which is the attainment of nibbana. Therefore, the description of the dharma as synonymous with the teachings of the Buddha is only partially correct; it is the totality of his teaching but is also its living, and ultimately its realization in nibbana. The teachings cannot be separated from its wider context; as indicated by Rahula's definition mentioned earlier, there is no place where dharma is not – indeed, having the same root as the Sanskrit word dhri, which can be translated as that which is integral to something. It lies at the heart of what something is. Dharma could be seen to lie at the heart of everything, and it describes the true nature of all things.

One 'problem' with the identification of dharma as the teachings of the Buddha, and the attendant living of such, is the interpretation of what constitutes the teaching of the Buddha. One Buddhist has suggested:

> The principle at the heart of all schools of Buddhism is Dhamma (identifying the way things are). I associate with a Theravadan sect related to the Ajahn Chah forest lineage but I also work with a secular Buddhist project also. My own work is making the ideas associated with Buddhism palatable and highlighting how it isn't about identifying as 'a Buddhist' but more about practising and working to realise the core principles as these principles are not owned by any institution. The differences only arise because of people of different cultures interpreting the dhamma differently.

This Buddhist highlights the problem of 'people of different cultures interpreting the dhamma differently'. What does this mean? In some ways, this links to the transmission of the teachings of the Buddha, but also the context in which they were written and used. In wider teaching about religion this may be described as hermeneutics. Within the classroom there has been a development in the use of hermeneutics in terms of reading sacred texts. As texts that are used within Buddhist communities it is possible to see that the recorded dharma can be used in the same way. As we understand a hermeneutic approach to be about 'the art or science of interpretation, concerned with meaning and significance' (Bowie et al., 2020, 3), it is possible to see how the choice of teachings are established and imbued with meaning and significance. The texts that are used within Theravada and Mahayana will now be discussed in terms of their authority and use within Buddhism as a basis for the expression, and living, of the dharma.

The Tipitaka

The *Tipitaka* (Skt: *Tripitaka*) is the three collections of the Buddha's teachings. Buddhists tend to have a different view of scriptures than most of the other world religions. They are not the revealed word of God but the teachings of the Buddha. These are important because he gained enlightenment and could teach others the way to achieve this. For about 400 years the Buddha's teachings were passed on by word of mouth. The first scriptures were written down by monks in Pali. There is a legend that they were written on palm leaves and stored in three baskets; the writing of them is reported to have begun in the first century BCE at the time of the Fourth Buddhist Council. The dating of this writing has been described by Drewes (2015) as little 'more than a guess' and that it does not refer to 'the first time writing was ever used for Buddhist texts, but the first creation of a complete set of written scriptures in Sri Lanka' (131). This collection became known as the Pali Canon, or Tipitaka (literally means three baskets). The Tipitaka consists of three sections or baskets.

Vinaya Pitaka

This contains 227 rules that monks and nuns have to follow and is reported to have been recited by Ananda at the First Buddhist Council, not long after the Buddha's parinibbana..

These rules are usually accompanied by a story, which prompted the Buddha to create the rule. These rules aim to achieve a cohesive community.

Sutta Pitaka

This contains the teachings of the Buddha and is reported to have been recited by Upali at the First Buddhist Council, not long after the Buddha's parinibbana. The suttas are conversations between the Buddha and a follower. It is split into five *nikayas* (collections):

- *Digha Nikaya*: long discourses.
- *Majjhima Nikaya*: middle-length discourses.
- *Samyutta Nikaya*: connected discourses.
- *Anguttara Nikaya*: numerical discourses.
- *Khuddaka Nikaya:* small or minor discourses. The number of suttas within this collection varies according to country; Thailand and Sri Lanka have fifteen, whereas Myanmar has eighteen.

The Sutta Pitaka also contains the Four Noble Truths, the Noble Eightfold Path, a collection of the Buddha's sayings known as the Dhammapada and the Jataka tales (stories about the Buddha's previous lives). The Jataka tales show how the Buddha lived out the ten qualities or perfections which lead to enlightenment: generosity, virtue, renunciation, wisdom, energy, patience, truthfulness, resolution, loving kindness and an even temper. They encourage people to live out these qualities.

Within the Khuddaka Nikaya is the *Dhammapada*, which has been described as 'one of the most popular texts with Buddhist monks and laypersons' (Buswell & Lopez, 2013, 627). There are different versions of the Dhammapada but the Theravada version is the one that is most well-known and used. The Dhammapada is essentially a collection of the sayings of the Buddha in a way that they form 'a perfect compendium of the Buddha's teachings, comprising between its covers all the essential principles elaborated at length in the forty-odd volumes of the Pali Canon' (Buddhharakkhita, 1985, 2).

Abhidhamma Pitaka

This contains discussions on how to interpret and understand the Buddha's teachings. Some Buddhists feel that this is the work of the Buddha himself, while others believe it is the work of later Buddhists. Narada Maha Thera (1979) suggests its relationship to the Sutta Pitaka:

> Abhidhamma, as the term implies, is the Higher Teaching of the Buddha. It expounds the quintessence of His profound doctrine. The Dhamma, embodied in the Sutta Pitaka, is the conventional teaching (vohara desana), and the Abhi-dhamma is the ultimate teaching (paramattha desana). (ix)

This 'higher teaching' is seen to be the 'crown jewel of the Buddhist scriptures' (Bodhi, 2003). In contrast to the Sutta Pitaka, while it is a collection of the sayings of the Buddha, they are brought together in a way to teach the truths of existence such as the Four Noble Truths and dependent origination. They are 'full-blown treatises in which the principles of the doctrine have been methodically organised, minutely defined, and meticulously tabulated and classified' (Bodhi, 2003, 2). The beauty of the Abhidhamma Pitaka for Theravada Buddhists lies in its explicit codification of the truths that the Buddha taught and therefore of the dhamma. It has been described as 'the most perfect expression possible of the Buddha's unimpeded omniscient knowledge (*subbannuta-nana*). It is his statement of the way things appear to the mind of a Fully Enlightened One' (Bodhi, 2003, 3). This is more fully brought together in later commentaries on the Abhidhamma such as Buddhaghosa's *Visuddhimagga* (The Path of Purification, fifth century); Buddhadatta's *Abhidhammavatara* (Introduction to Abhidhamma, fifth century) and Anuruddha's *Abhidhammatthasangaha* (Compendium of the Topics of Abhidhamma, twelfth century).

The Abhidhamma has been studied for centuries and the complexity of its teachings has led to different interpretations. The two types of writing within the Abhidhamma Pitaka have been described as falling into one of two categories:

1. A summary and analysis of the Buddha's teachings.
2. Explaining and analysing the teachings through an example of dispute or questioning (Gethin, 2022).

The Abhidhamma Pitaka follows a similar structure of attempting 'to give a systematic and exhaustive account of the world by breaking it down into its constituent physical and mental events (dharma/dhamma)' and then it addresses 'various points of dispute that arise out of the preceding exercise' (Gethin, 1998, 204). It is split into seven sections (although the focus in this chapter is the seven sections of the Theravada Abidhamma Pitaka, whereas in early Buddhism there was the Abhidharma of the Sarvastivada [an early school] which differs from the Theravada version, it survives in a Chinese translation but is unavailable in European languages). The seven sections are:

- *Dhammasangani* (Summary of Dhamma) is essentially a discussion of ethics for monastic Buddhists. It contains a list of dhammas (sometimes translated as factors, or phenomena). There are two threefold classifications which include categories such as wholesome, unwholesome or unclassified. A further 100 twofold classifications and a final 42 twofold classifications are found within the *Dhammasangani*.
- *Vibhanga* (Division/Classification/Analysis) has eighteen chapters, each of which addresses a different topic. It has been described as a commentary on the vinaya which 'typically describes the incident that gave rise to each of the rules, the conditions under which they must be applied, or in light of which an infraction of the rule does not actually constitute an offense' (Buswell & Lopez, 2013, 888).

- *Dhatukatha* (Discussion of Elements) is a discussion of the classifications and elements found in the previous section, the Vibhanga.
- *Puggalapannatti* (Designation of Persons) is the section where the classification of people is discussed. Drawing on the Sutta Pitaka there are many classifications which range from groups of one to ten.
- *Kathavatthu* (Points of Discussion/Controversy) contains over two hundred discussions on points of doctrine. They are usually stated in ways that are wrong, and then expositions are given as to why they are wrong, and what is right. Its compilation is often attributed to Moggaliputtatissa, a monk who lived in the time of Ashoka.
- *Yamaka* (Pairs) is a series of ten chapters. Throughout pairs of questions are asked and listed alongside their answers. Some questions are straightforward, others are more complex.
- *Patthana* (Foundational Conditions) explores the law of cause and effect, in the context of twenty-four types of conditional relations (paccaya) related to the Dhammasangani.

Although the aforementioned breakdown of the Abhidhamma Pitaka seems complex, and leans heavily onto the idea of it as a higher teaching, it is summarized by Gethin (1998) as the flip side to meditation: 'Abhidharma represents the theoretical counterpart to what the meditator actually experiences in meditation. It can be summed up as the attempt to give a systematic and exhaustive account of the world in terms of its constituent physical and mental events' (209).

The view of the Tipitaka (Skt: Tripitaka) within Mahayana Buddhism will be explored in greater detail in the next section, in the context of wider developments in the Buddhist community. Here, it should be noted that the Tripitaka and its teachings are seen to be a prelude to the higher teachings of the Buddha found in the distinctly Mahayana sutras. Thus the Theravadan hermeneutic lens is very different to the Mahayana lens. For Theravada this is the final teaching of the Buddha, whereas for Mahayana Buddhists while being important they are evidence of skilful means in teaching employed by the Buddha, and that if viewed correctly, the teachings about the bodhisattva can be inferred or found in them. When we are teaching in the classroom we need to be careful not to establish the primacy of the Tipitaka, unless it is caveated with reference to it being so in Theravadan understandings. There is further comment to be made if we are talking about the breadth of Buddhist belief. It is important, however, to also recognize the value and use of different elements of Mahayana Buddhism, for example, Thich Nhat Hanh (2012a) in his *Awakening of the Heart. Essential Buddhist Sutras and Commentaries* lists six sutras from the Pali Canon out of the nine he includes in total. The ones he includes as essential, though this should be recognized as a selection rather than the complete list of sutras focused on, are:

- *Anapanasati Sutta*
- *Bhadekaratta Sutta*

- *Satipatthana Sutta*
- *Alaggaddupama Sutta*
- *Mangala Sutta*

Mahayana and the decline of the dharma

In line with the impermanence and ebb and flow of existence that is at the heart of Buddhist teaching, there is also a tradition within Buddhism that the teachings of the Buddha and the living of the dharma will decline throughout the years. Indeed, in the story of the life of the Buddha (see Chapter 3) it was noted that the decline would be expedited because of the acceptance of women into the ordained sangha. Jan Nattier suggests that 'Within a century or two after the death of the Buddha, detailed accounts began to emerge predicting ... the eventual "death of the dharma"' (1995, 249). Indeed, in the Mahayana text *Inquiry of the Bodhisattva Candragarbha to the Buddha Sakyamuni* various stages of the decline are outlined.

After the Buddha's parinibbana 'during the first five hundred years there will be many living beings who will practice my teachings and attain liberation'. There will then be a decline in the next five hundred years where 'there will be many who will practice meditation (samadhi). But even though kings and ordinary people will believe in and practice the true dharma, eventually such people will become few'. The next five hundred years will be characterized by

> many teachers who instruct people in the true dharma, serve as leaders for living beings, and cause them to attain liberation. But sravakas and arhats will become few. Kings, ministers, and ordinary people will be reduced to merely listening to the teaching; they will not take it to heart and practice it, nor will they exert themselves, and their faith will decrease. (Nattier, 1995, 252)

During the fourth five hundred years the unseen protectors of the dharma 'will go elsewhere to spread the true dharma. And even those beings who do practice the dharma will not do so according to the basic dharma texts.' In the two hundred years following 'even monks will not practice in accordance with the true dharma. They will seek worldly profit and fame; their compassion will be meagre, and they will not live according to the law of the land. They will put down and malign those who do practice in accordance with the true dharma' (Nattier, 1995, 252).

It is against this background, and with reference to prophecies about Maitreya, that Mahayana Buddhism in particular do not expect the teachings of the Buddha to be practised forever. Rather, they will decline, and it is important that this is guarded against. This 'decline' can be seen to influence certain views within Buddhism. The development and recording of Mahayana sutras could be seen to be linked with the idea of a moving away from the original ideas of the Buddha and thus needing to be reclaimed. One of the issues identified in this interpretation of the development of Mahayana and the attendant sutras is that it may be applying a Western Protestant or Reformation lens onto the religion of Buddhism. For many Buddhists this would be a mischaracterization of the history of Buddhism. The development of Mahayana teaching is variously seen as disagreement over the rules for the monastic vinaya, or possibly a development of sutras that reflected different emphases or, as many Mahayana Buddhists would suggest, the idea that the 'higher' teaching was taught by the Buddha before his death and carried on through different lineages or disciples. What can be observed is that over the centuries, while Theravada Buddhists would generally see the Pali Canon as closed, there was an ever-expanding collection of sutras that are used by different Mahayana traditions. Shantideva (1961) suggested that these new sutras that were attributed to the Buddha had certain criteria which they had to meet to be considered authentic:

> Through four factors is an inspired utterance [pratibhana] the word of the Buddhas. What four? (i) ... the inspired utterance is connected with truth, not untruth; (ii) it is connected with the Dharma, not that which is not the Dharma; (iii) it brings about the renunciation of moral taints [klesa] not their increase; and (iv) it shows the laudable qualities of nirvana, not those of the cycle of rebirth. (12)

The sutras themselves also adopted the general structure of beginning with *Evam me sutam* (Skt: *Evam maya srutam*) based on the tradition that Ananda was reciting many of the suttas and as such began with 'Thus I have heard ...' This added to the authenticity of the writings, though they would still be rejected by Theravada Buddhists. Even within Mahayana traditions there are various understandings of what makes them authentic:

- They are directly traceable to the Buddha through his disciples.
- They lead directly to awakening and as such are teachings that can be considered the word of the Buddha.
- It is in the 'same spirit' as that of the Buddha while not being directly traceable to him. Suzuki (1907) suggests:

> Its spirit and central ideas are all those of its founder. The question whether or not it is genuine, entirely depends on our interpretation of the term 'genuine.' If we take it to mean the lifeless preservation of the original, we should say that Mahayanism is not the genuine teaching of the Buddha, and we may add that Mahayanists would be proud of the fact, because being a living religious force it would never condescend to be the corpse of a by gone faith. The fossils, however faithfully preserved, are nothing but rigid inorganic substances from which life is forever departed. (15)

Each of these interpretations can also coexist alongside one another. Mahayana Buddhists would see the Tripitaka as authentic but laying the basis for the higher teachings of the

Buddha of the bodhisattva ideal. There are many Mahayana sutras that focus the Buddhist on distinctive teachings and emphases such as the bodhisattva, and also shared beliefs such as dependent origination and sunyata. To try and attempt to list all of the Mahayana sutras across the various traditions would be a large task. At this point we will outline a few that are seen to be expressions of the dharma:

The Lotus Sutra

The *Lotus Sutra* is a text that has significant meaning within different traditions of Mahayana Buddhism. It tells of the teaching of Shakyamuni Buddha's teaching on Vulture's Peak. In this sutra the teaching prior to the Vulture's Peak Sermon is revealed to be an example of skilful means, and that the true or higher teaching of the Buddha is taught by the Buddha to the assembled bodhisattva. The major themes of the *Lotus Sutra* surround sunyata and the bodhisattva ideal as well as skilful means. Each of these have a specific importance within Mahayana Buddhism. It holds a particular place within Nichiren Buddhism (see further on and in Chapter 9). Little more will be said of the sutra at this point as elements have been explored at different points earlier (aspects of the *Lotus Sutra* were explored earlier in the Introduction, Chapter 1, Chapter 3 and Chapter 5).

The *Heart Sutra* (*Prajnaparamita Sutra*)

To give the *Heart Sutra* its full title, it is 'The Heart of the Perfection of Wisdom'. Karl Brunnhozl (2012) describes it as 'the most frequently used and recited text in the entire Mahayana Buddhist tradition'. (1). It focuses on the central concept of sunyata and the emptiness of all things. Aspects of the sutra reinforce this:

> Listen Sariputra,
> this Body itself is Emptiness
> and Emptiness itself is this Body …
> Listen Sariputra,
> all phenomena bear the mark of Emptiness. (*The Heart Sutra*, Hanh, 2014)

It has been described as a meditation manual; rather than something to be read and understood, it is to be meditated upon. Indeed, Brunnhozl (2012) has described it as one 'big koan' (9). It is challenging in the sense that it breaks down a person's perceptions, but not only this, along with others of the wisdom sutras, it rejects certain elements that a Buddhist may hold true such as the Four Noble Truths:

> Ill-being, the Causes of Ill-being, the End of Ill-being, the Path, insight and attainment,
> are also not separate self-entities.
> Whoever can see this
> no longer needs anything to attain. (*The Heart Sutra*, Hanh, 2014)

It is seen to combine the central aspects of a Mahayana worldview, that of compassion and emptiness. It is the only wisdom sutra that has Avalokisvara speaking, and as the bodhisattva of compassion he is able to combine wisdom and compassion, 'In fact, the heart essence of the prajnaparamita teachings and the Mahayana is the union of emptiness and compassion' (Brunnhozl, 2012, 10).

The *Diamond Sutra* (*Vajracchedika Sutra*)

A further translation of its title is 'The Perfection of Wisdom Text That Cuts Like a Thunderbolt.' One of the perfection of wisdom sutras, this sutra is believed to have been written between the second and fifth centuries; its Chinese translation emerged in the fifth century. The *Diamond Sutra* is a conversation between the Buddha and his disciple, Subhuti. Hsing Yun (2012) outlines that there are four main teachings of the sutra:

1. To give without notion
2. To become liberated without a notion of self
3. To live without abiding
4. To cultivate without attainment (xi).

Although the word 'sunyata' is not found, it is a key theme of the sutra. It highlights how a bodhisattva can become awakened, reinforcing the emptiness of everything.

Pratyutpanna Samadhi Sutra

Believed to have been written in the first century BCE, its full title of *Pratyutpannabuddha Sammukhavasthita Samadhi Sutra* can be translated to 'Sutra on the Samadhi for Encountering Face-to-Face the Buddhas of the Present'. The sutra focuses on, as the name suggests, a focus on meditation. Compassion and insight are brought together in a discussion of the Buddha fields, and this meditation is one 'in which one is brought face to face with the Buddhas of the present' (Harrison, 1998, 2). One notable element of this sutra is the earliest mention of the Buddha Amitabha. In requesting rebirth in his Pure Land, Amitabha replies to the various bodhisattva:

> If you wish to come and be born in my realm, you must always call me to mind again and again, you must always keep this thought in mind without letting up, and thus you will succeed in coming to be born in my realm. (*Pratyutpanna Samadhi Sutra*, Harrison, 1998, 19)

It is, thus seen to be evidence of, or inspiration for, the development of Pure Land Buddhism, which maintains a focus on the other central aspects of Mahayana such as sunyata, compassion and the bodhisattva.

The *Longer Sukhavativyuha Sutra* (*Infinite Life Sutra*), *Amitayurdhyana Sutra* (*Contemplation Sutra*), and the *Shorter Sukhavativyuha Sutra* (*Amitabha Sutra*)

These sutras are all important in Pure Land Buddhism as they talk about Amitabha (Amida) and his Pure Land of Sukhavati. The *Longer Sutra* describes the Pure Land of Sukhavati in detail and explains the thirty-two vows of a bodhisattva seeking rebirth in the Pure Land. The promise of remembering or reciting Amitabha's name for rebirth in the Pure Land is found in the *Longer Sutra*:

> And again, O Ananda, those beings who meditate on the Tathagata by giving him the ten thoughts, and who will direct their desire towards that Buddha country, and who will feel satisfaction when the profound doctrines are being preached, and who will not fall off, nor despair, nor fail, but will meditate on that Tathagata, if it were by one thought only, and will direct their desire toward that Buddha country, they also will see the Tathagata Amitabha, while they are in a dream, they will be born in the world Sukhavati, and will never turn away from the highest perfect knowledge. (Mueller, 1894, 46)

The *Shorter Sukhavativyuha Sutra* is mainly a discourse between Shakyamuni Buddha and his disciple Sariputra, wherein he describes the beauty and decoration of Sukhavati.

In the *Amitayurdhyana Sutra* Shakyamuni Buddha teaches Vaidehi the importance of, and how to visualize, the Pure Land of Amitabha. He takes him through a series of visualizations such as the setting sun (see Chapter 7).

Sandhinirmocana Sutra (*Explanation of the Profound Secrets*)

Paul Williams (2009) has suggested that the *Sandhinirmocana Sutra*, as part of the Yogacara school, is a 'completely definitive, absolutely marvellous and it cannot be surpassed. It is not a basis for disagreement and there is no higher teaching' (86). Within the Ygacara tradition it is identified as the third and final turning of the wheel of dharma. The sutra highlights the Three Natures (*trisvabhava*) that form part of the Yogacara tradition:

1. *Parikalpitasvabhava* (constructed nature). The *Sandhinirmocana Sutra* indicates that language suggests that things exist intrinsically of themselves, whereas in fact their existence is only a perception and they are not as they seem.

   'The pattern of clinging to what is entirely imagined refers to the establishing of names and symbols for all things and the distinguishing of their essences, whereby they come to be expressed in language' (*Sandhinirmocana Sutra*, Keenan, 2000, 31).

2. *Paratantrascabhava* (dependent nature). This is the idea that the flow of consciousness is not split into entities, but are all interrelated.

   'The pattern of other-dependency refers to the pattern whereby all things arise co-dependently: for if this exists, then that exists, and if this arises, then that arises.

This refers to [the twelvefold conditions, starting with] "conditioned by ignorance are karmic formations," [and ending with] "conditioned by origination is this grand mass of suffering," [the last of the twelve conditions]' (*Sandhinirmocana Sutra*, Keenan, 2000, 31).

3. *Paripannavabhava* (consummated nature). This is the true nature of things discovered through meditation.

'The pattern of full perfection refers to the universally equal suchness of all things. Bodhisattvas penetrate to this suchness because of their resolute zeal, intelligent focusing, and true reflection. By gradually cultivating this penetration, they reach unsurpassed true awakening and actually realize perfection' (*Sandhinirmocana Sutra*, Keenan, 2000, 32).

It is believed to have been written as early as the first or second centuries.

Vimalakirti Sutra

The *Vimalakirti Sutra* contains the words of a lay disciple called Vimalakirti. It explains his search for, and near attainment of, awakening. There are sometimes seen to be seven themes that highlight important Mahayana teachings:

- The removal of the Buddha from a historic context. Rather he is seen to have presented himself as mortal, and that in reality, he is a 'spiritual' figure who taught through mundane means.
- Skilful means.
- The use of magic or the appearance of magic. For example, the turning of 500 hundred parasols into one canopy in the first section.
- Buddha lands.
- The admonishing of the Buddha's disciples because of attachments, whether they be sensuous, views, practices or the self.
- Non-duality. This is particularly highlighted when bodhisattvas begin to discuss what non-duality is. Vimalakirti remains silent suggesting that in discussing non-duality the bodhisattva have fallen into its trap, something noted by one of the bodhisattva. This text is important for many Zen Buddhists in the power of silence to explain teachings.
- The importance of silence, at the end of the example outlined earlier on:

Then the crown prince Manjusri said to the Licchavi Vimalakirti, 'We have all given our own teachings, noble sir. Now, may you elucidate the teaching of the entrance into the principle of nonduality!' Thereupon, the Licchavi Vimalakirti kept his silence, saying nothing at all. The crown prince Manjusri applauded the Licchavi Vimalakirti: 'Excellent! Excellent, noble sir! This is indeed the entrance into the nonduality of the bodhisattvas.

Here there is no use for syllables, sounds, and ideas.' When these teachings had been declared, five thousand bodhisattvas entered the door of the Dharma of nonduality and attained tolerance of the birthlessness of things. (*Vimalakirti Sutra*, Thurman, 1976, 77)

Emptiness is also a theme that permeates the sutra. Each of these reflect that the central differences between Mahayana and Theravada are in evidence. It is not a sutra that is designed to be used against the foil of Theravada; rather it stands on its own as a summary of many Mahayana themes. It would be wrong within the classroom to use sutras in a way that may suggest they were written as refutations, rather than as texts in their own right to teach and aid devotion. The example of a lay Buddhist in his search for awakening is a very powerful message. The chapters are often used as stories to illustrate the teachings, such as Martin Goodson (2022) who has published retellings of this 'dream like sutra for the modern reader' to aid the teaching of Zen.

Lankavatara Sutra (Entering into Sri Lanka)

The *Lanavatara Sutra* is mostly a conversation between Shakyamuni Buddha and the bodhisattva Mahamati (Great Wisdom) in the form of 108 questions. The conversation takes place in Sri Lanka and is mainly focussed around emptiness and consciousness. There is also the suggestion within that words are not needed to teach the dharma, which lies at the heart of Zen Buddhism. It is believed to have been written in the fourth century and then translated from Sanskrit into Chinese in the fifth century.

Shurangama Sutra (Heroic Gate Sutra)

The *Heroic Gate Sutra* focuses on the importance of meditation and explores different methods used to discover the truth about the five skandhas. As part of this it describes many different methods to discover the true nature of existence and the buddha-nature within. It is an eighth-century translation from Pali into Chinese, brought into China by the monk Zhisheng. There has been some dispute about its origin, but it is used widely in Chinese and Tibetan Buddhism.

Avatamsaka Sutra (Flower Garland Sutra)

Cleary (1993) describes the *Avatamsaka Sutra* in magniloquent terms:

> Also referred to as the major Scripture of Inconceivable Liberation, it is perhaps the richest and most grandiose of all Buddhist scriptures, held in high esteem by all schools of Buddhism that are concerned with universal liberation. Its incredible wealth of sensual imagery staggers the imagination and exercises an almost mesmeric effect on the mind as it conveys a wide range of teachings through its complex structure, its colourful symbolism, and its mnemonic concentration formulae. (1)

The *Avatamsaka Sutra* contains descriptions of the cosmos, and has a focus in distinctly Mahayana beliefs. It is believed to have been written in India in the first two centuries, with Chinese translations emerging in the second century. Within the forty chapters of the Avatamsaka sutra there are sutras that are focussed on in their own right, including:

- *Gandavyuha Sutra (Entering the Dharma Realm)*, where Sudhana visits fifty-two masters to receive a teaching from each one.
- *Dashabhumika Sutra (Ten Stages Sutra)*, which focuses on the bodhisattva ideal.
- *Amitayurdyhana Sutra (Amitayus Conetmplation Sutra)* see above with regard to the Pure Land Sutras (The Longer Sukhavativyuha Sutra (Infinite Life Sutra), Amitayurdhyana Sutra (Contemplation Sutra), and the Shorter Sukhavativyuha Sutra (Amitabha Sutra)).
- The Vows of Bodhisattva Universal Worthy which explores the vows of the bodhisattva.

These sutras outlined here have necessarily only been a selection, but they are indicative of the teachings of Mahayana, and the lens through which the Tripitaka must be viewed. It is also necessary to realize that for Buddhists, that although 'these sutras are thousands of years old … it is only by relating them to your own real-life experiences that they come alive' (Hanh, 2012a, 3).

The Decline?

The reclamation of the higher teaching, or the continuation of it, is central to Mahayana teachings, and different forms of Buddhism such as Nichiren (see Chapter 9) would see themselves within this history. Nichiren is believed to be the figure who helped Buddhism reclaim the true dharma, slow its decline and ensure that it continued as originally taught. This view of decline may also be reflected in the attitude towards forms of Tibetan Mahayana Buddhism as the authentic form of Buddhism that survived unencumbered by the colonial influences that, some would argue, Theravada Buddhism had been affected by (see Chapter 10).

The final impact of this decline is the place and role of Maitreya (Pali: *Metteya* also known as *Ajita*) in Buddhist teaching. As observed earlier (see Chapter 3) Maitreya is in Tusita heaven where he was appointed successor to the Buddha Shakyamuni when he came to earth. He was left to teach the gods and goddesses there until the time that he would come to earth as a future Buddha. He is thus seen to be the successor to the Buddha Shakyamuni in Tusita heaven as well as on the earth in the teaching of the dharma. When the Buddha's teachings have been forgotten and the world is at its lowest point Maitreya will be born.

In light of the exploration of the identity of the Buddha in Chapter 3, it is noticeable that the dhamma that is to be taught by Maitreya is identical to that of the Buddha Shakyamuni. The Four Noble Truths are the truths realized by the noble ones, and as such both Buddhas have and will realize the truth for themselves. This belief in Maitreya is common across Theravada and Mahayana traditions, and the beliefs about his identity is similar to the debate surrounding the identity of Shakyamuni Buddha. For Theravada Buddhists he is a bodhisattva, meaning a Buddha in waiting; while in Mahayana he is a bodhisattva meaning an awakened one who has put off parinirvana to teach the dharma and help others realize such.

There have been claimants to being Maitreya throughout history, either as the incarnation of the future Buddha or the future Buddha himself. Many of these can be found in China, but there are also examples in Ahmadiyya Muslim and Baha'i traditions. Examples include Wu Zhao (Wu Zetian), the ruler of China from 665 to 705, who proclaimed herself as an incarnation of Maitreya. Gung Ye the ruler of the Korean kingdom of Taebong (901–918) similarly proclaimed himself an incarnation of Maitreya. Among Navayana Buddhists, Babasaheb Ambedkar (1891–1956) is regarded as a Maitreya. The most commonly identified expression of Maitreya is the tenth-century Chinese Buddhist monk, Budai, within Chan Buddhism. He is often known as the 'Laughing Buddha' or the 'Fat Buddha' (see Figure 6.1). He is, perhaps, the most recognized image of Buddhism in the Western world outside of the Buddha Siddhartha Gautama.

Figure 6.1 Budai.
Source: G41rn8, CC BY-SA 4.0 <https://creativecommons.org/licenses/by-sa/4.0>, via Wikimedia Commons.

Budai, is again, viewed as an incarnation of the future Buddha, rather than being identified as the incarnation prophesied by the Buddha Shakyamuni. Shi Daoyuan, a tenth-/eleventh-century monk records in the *Ching-te ch'uan-teng-lu* (the *Transmission of the Lamp*) Budai's identification as Maitreya in the following way:

> Maitreya, truly Maitreya/Divides his body into ten thousand million parts/From time to time appearing to that time/But recognized by none. (Edwards, 1984, 12)

These incarnations and their associated stories would only be applicable to the different traditions within Mahayana.

It would be interesting in the classroom to explore this view of the decline of the dharma against the history of Buddhism. In defining Buddhism in the Introduction to this book, the concept of a modern Buddhism was explored. In this view of Buddhism it is possible to see people trying to reclaim the 'original' Buddhism that is rational and unencumbered by what may be seen to be cultural or mystical accretions. It might also be possible to suggest that in the terms of the development of 'Western' Buddhism that, in the words of one Buddhist, these efforts at modernizing are an evidence of a 'diluted, westernised teaching' and the decline of Buddhism (Holt, 2022, 223). The idea of a 'religion' or way of life with an inbuilt expiry date is perhaps a realistic view based on the nature of humanity, or a pessimistic description that was more a reflection of the various reformations within Buddhism that have taken place throughout the years.

The sangha

The sangha is the third of the Three Jewels/Refuges and is commonly translated as 'community'. It has been suggested that the sangha is the pre-eminent refuge:

> The Sangha is the most important of the three treasures. I cannot emphasize the importance of the Sangha too much ... if we are not connected with the Sangha, we cannot understand the true Buddha and the true Dharma. It is only within the context of the Sangha, our teachers and Dharma friends, that we can understand the true Buddha and the true Dharma. (Haneda, 2012, 1)

Although, to outside commentators on Buddhism, it can often be taken to refer to the whole community of Buddhists, in Theravada and Mahayana expressions of Buddhism it is not as simple as that, and there are seen to be nuances that would help explain the importance of taking refuge in the sangha.

Theravada

Within Theravada Buddhism, the term 'sangha' can be used to refer to two different communities:

- The ordained sangha, or the community of monks and nuns (*bhikkhu-sangha and bhikkhuni-sangha*). It can also be applied to a smaller community where a minimum of four fully ordained bhikkhus or bhikkhunis are.

- The community of disciples who have at least entered the stream-entry stage (sotapanna), that may include members of the laity. This interpretation of the sangha may be termed the fourfold sangha of monks, nuns, laymen and laywomen (who have taken refuge and are sotapanna).

There is not an understanding where all of the laity are included within the sangha; in *parisa* (Skt. *parisad*) it is used when referring to the whole Buddhist community. The vast majority of times that the sangha is referred to, it is to the ordained sangha. The Buddha is reported to have taught:

> Where you recollect the Sangha: 'The Sangha of the Blessed One's disciples who have practiced well ... who have practiced straight-forwardly ... who have practiced methodically ... who have practiced masterfully – in other words, the four types (of noble disciples) when taken as pairs, the eight when taken as individual types – they are the Sangha of the Blessed One's disciples: deserving of gifts, deserving of hospitality, deserving of offerings, deserving of respect, the incomparable field of merit for the world. (*Mahanama Sutta*)

The laity are to provide material goods to the ordained sangha, so that bhikkhus and bhikkhunis are able to live apart from the 'world' where their concentration would necessarily be on running a household and all of its attendant attachments. In the monastic life, a Buddhist bhikkhu or bhikkhuni would not beg, but rely on donations.

The bhikkhus and bhikkhunis would teach the laity, as an act of generosity and compassion. Thus there is a symbiotic relationship between the ordained sangha and the laity. One cannot function effectively without the other. In receiving the teachings of the Buddha from the sangha, a lay Buddhist is able to take refuge in, and receive the protection, of the sangha, but also of the Buddha and the dhamma. The blessings are described by the Buddha:

> At any time when a disciple of the noble ones is recollecting the Sangha, his mind is not overcome with passion, not overcome with aversion, not overcome with delusion. His mind heads straight, based on the Sangha. And when the mind is headed straight, the disciple of the noble ones gains a sense of the goal, gains a sense of the Dhamma, gains joy connected with the Dhamma. (*Mahanama Sutta*)

The ordained sangha, throughout history, have been seen to safeguard and promulgate the Buddha's teachings. They are able to devote themselves to this because they are free of the responsibilities of a householder. Monasteries are places that house bhikkhus and bhikkhunis as places of study, meditation on and passing on of the stories of the Buddha.

Ordination as a bhikkhu or bhikkhuni is a significant step and one that should be taken with a determination to live a monastic life. This is attended by the vow to live the ten precepts (pansils):

1. Avoid from harming living things.
2. Avoid from taking that which is not given.
3. Avoid from misuse of the senses and sexual misconduct.
4. Avoid lying.
5. Avoid taking intoxicants.
6. Avoid eating food after midday.
7. Avoid singing, dancing or playing music.
8. Avoid wearing adornments such as perfume, cosmetics and garland jewellery.
9. Avoid sitting on high chairs and sleeping on soft beds.
10. Avoid from accepting money.

It is in the living of these with precision that an ordained member of the sangha is seen to be in a position to teach and safeguard the dhamma. In Theravada ordinations, lineage is important, and they should be 'legally valid'.

> Among other things 'legally valid' refers to adherence to the relevant rules. According to these rules a monk's ordination must be performed by at least ten (in border districts, (in border districts, five) monks. For the ordination of women a functioning bhiksunis' order with ten to twelve members is required. If a local community (sangha) does not consist of a sufficient number of bhiksus or bhiksunis, no legally valid ordination can be performed. (Hüsken and Kieffer-Pülz, 2011, 259)

This ensures an authority that links to the Buddha. This does mean, however, that in some areas of the world there are no orders of bhikkhunis. In many Theravada countries women live as bhikkhunis but are not ordained because there are insufficient women of a lineage to ordain them. This is not insurmountable as ordinations that establish new lineages, based on the ordination by bhikkhus, have been carried out in Sri Lanka. However, 'in Burma and Thailand the new bhikkhuni ordination is not generally accepted, and in Sri Lanka not all of the diverse Buddhist schools (nikaya) accept the bhiksuni ordination unanimously. Here too the performative efficacy of the ordination rituals is challenged' (Hüsken and Kieffer-Pülz, 2011, 257). In some ways, this is reminscent of the struggle that Mahapajapati Gotami faced in trying to receive ordination from the Buddha (see Chapter 3). The place of women will be discussed further in Chapter 8.

Mahayana

There are different attitudes towards the sangha throughout Mahayana Buddhism. An important aspect generally of the Mahayana traditions is the belief that everyone has a buddha-nature (see Chapter 5) and as such have the potential for awakening. This may lead some traditions to have a sangha that is without division. Even in these, though, in general, there is a delineation between the ordained and lay members of the sangha. The most common definition of the sangha within Mahayana refers to the traditional definitions of Theravada Buddhism, though it is possible to extend the definition of the sangha as Refuge to include the bodhisattva who have been awakened. The Dalai Lama has taught:

> The Sangha Jewel has inner wisdom that correctly knows reality and knows some portion of the diversity of phenomena. The arya sangha is free from some portion of afflictive obscurations – ignorance, afflictions, their seeds, and polluted karma. Some aryas are also free from some portion of the wish for only personal nirvana that prevents generating bodhicitta. Some arya bodhisattvas are free from a portion of the cognitive obscurations – the latencies of ignorance and the appearance of inherent existence. The representation of the Sangha Jewel is a community of four or more fully ordained monastics. (Dalai Lama and Chodron, 2014, 30)

Rinpoche suggests that understanding the nature of sangha means that Mahayana Buddhists view the sangha as a community of people who:

> are lovers of virtue who undertake and uphold positive actions, who try to transform their bad habits, purify their negativity and increase their virtuous acts mentally, verbally, and physically in order to benefit others ... and to engage in that path one pointedly until we reach the shared goal of enlightenment. (Rinpoche, 2005)

Those in the ordained sangha include *bhiksus* or *bhiksunis*, and Lamas. Indeed, so important are teachers in the Mahayana tradition that some have suggested that the *guru* be added as a fourth jewel. A Zen/Chan text *Daily Life in the Assembly* written in the early thirteenth century by Wuliang Zongshou highlights the delineation of the sangha:

> Having left the dust [of the world] and separated from the vulgar, we shaven-headed and square-robed [Buddhist] monks, for the most part, spend our lives in monasteries. (Foulk, 1995, 461)

In a similar way to Theravada, Mahayana bhiksus or bhiksunis are supported by lay Buddhists in a reciprocal relationship. However, Tibetan Buddhism, in a similar way to Theravada, is without an order of bhiksunis, though movements are being made and female ordinations have taken place in the United States.

Within the Japanese Nichiren tradition, the different aspects of the sangha have been maintained, while for Soka Gakkai (see Chapter 9) there has been a breaking down of barriers where all are members of the sangha. The *Soka Gakkai Dictionary of Buddhism* recognizes the traditional definition but has expanded it:

> Samgha refers specifically to the group of monks and nuns who renounced secular life and dedicated themselves to Buddhist practice night and day, but in a broad sense

includes all Buddhist practitioners: monks, nuns, laymen, and laywomen. The Sanskrit term originally meant a collective body or assembly and later came to refer to the body of Buddhist practitioners ... With the rise of Mahayana Buddhism, the samgha came to refer to the body of Mahayana practitioners, or bodhisattvas, including monks, nuns, or laypersons. (Soka Gakkai, n.d.)

This may be because it was a lay-inspired movement and their relationship with ordained Nichiren priests has not been positive.

Thoughts for the classroom

This chapter has necessarily covered an immense amount of content with regards to the dharma and the sangha. When we begin to explore both of these concepts within the classroom it is essential, as we have noted in every other chapter, that the diversity of belief within Buddhism should mean that we qualify or expand the content that we teach. The temptation, and perhaps reality, within the classroom is to present the dharma as the teachings of the Buddha, and if further explanation is required it focuses around the Tipitaka. As with other aspects of Buddhism, this is only part of the story. Although a large number of British Buddhists originally came from places that were previously colonies of the Empire, meaning that Theravada Buddhism was the largest group, this is changing and in a globalized world an exploration of Theravada interpretations of dharma is insufficient. Mention of hermeneutics was made within this chapter, and this is an engaging activity for students, as they begin to look at how both Theravada and Mahayana Buddhists would interpret certain sayings of the Buddha. The Mahayana Sutras open up a wealth of opportunity that may not be evident within the classroom.

This also has important implications for the issue of authority in the Buddhist community (see Chapter 9). Although there are figures who have authority, and texts that can be seen to have influence, the reconciling of a teaching that encourages people to internalize and sift what is received is at odds with some of the other religions of the world. In a post-truth world of the twenty-first century it is important to equip students of all ages with the critical thinking skills to recognize the validity and applicability of the sayings and sources that they read. This seems especially true with regards to the Buddha. It is almost impossible to flick on a social media feed without seeing an unreferenced quote from the Buddha. In today's world it is always easier to trust the received knowledge and the hive mind of our community to confirm the authenticity of a source, than perhaps to take time to find the original source. Why is this important? Maybe we think it's not, after all what harm is done? There may be little or none, but any paraphrase slightly skews the message or the authenticity of the message being delivered. To some extent the internet can make people lazy – the teacher needs to be much more secure in their use of quotes. We are teaching people to be robust in the points that they are making. They are also being asked to question the veracity of arguments being made. How can they trust me if they can't trust my sources. The use of reliable evidence and sources is crucial to an exploration of news stories and political opinions. This is an important aspect of teaching religion as the interrogation of truth provides skills in exploring religion and worldviews:

> What distinguishes this concern for truth from forms of confessional religious education is that it approaches the question of truth with an open rather than a closed horizon ... where confessionalism seeks to transmit one particular answer to the question of ultimate truth, the critical approach is concerned to equip pupils to engage intelligently in the quest for themselves. (Easton et al., 2019, 286)

Returning to the criteria of Shantideva for the authentication of the sayings of the Buddha maybe there is a bit more flexibility:

1. It is connected with truth.
2. It is connected with the dharma.
3. It brings about good morality.
4. It shows the qualities of nirvana.

Maybe this is a task that teachers could have students complete. In trying to authenticate the sayings of the Buddha, they could explore authentic and fabricated sayings of the Buddha and try and justify them according to the four categories, and being able to justify them.

Linking with the discussion of storytelling mentioned earlier (see Chapter 3) each of the aspects of the writings associated with the dharma have opportunities for the inclusion and teaching of Buddhist concepts through story.

The 'decline' of the dharma, or the inbuilt expiration date, is an intriguing aspect of Buddhism that similarly might create opportunities for discussion.

An important aspect of religions more generally is the community aspect, and the role of the sangha fulfils this role within Buddhism. The interaction between the ordained and lay sangha can inform the discussion surrounding religious expression (see Chapter 7). It can also provide an opportunity to discuss the importance, or lack thereof, of community in developing a person's identity and worldview. The development of the sangha over the years can form an important part of a religion developing to meet the needs of different groups and times.

The overwhelming question for both of these Three Jewels is with regard to how they provide refuge for Buddhists. Beginning with the idea of a refuge and its characteristics, a student can identify what purpose a refuge serves and how the dharma and sangha may meet those same needs. An important aspect of approaching the teaching of religion is to begin with concepts in the students' own experiences, and as such, looking at the teachings/rules and communities that provide this in a secular sense will provide a bridge to a Buddhist way of life. The *Big Ideas for Religious Education* (Wintersgill, 2017) highlight how the dharma fits with 'Words and Change' and sangha with 'Influence, Community, Culture and Power' (15). Teachers could ask the questions:

- How has the sangha developed over time?
- How has the sangha shaped traditions, laws, political systems, festivals, values, rituals and the arts?
- What is the power dynamic in the sangha that has led to positive (and negative) outcomes?
- What forms of literary genres are used in the dharma?
- How has visual and other forms of art have been used to express the dharma?
- What are the different views that will inform interpretation of the dharma?

These can be used to explore the importance of the dharma and the sangha throughout history, and today, and in Britain and beyond.

7

Expressions of belief

Within Buddhism expressions of belief are usually found in the way that a person lives. The chapter on The Middle Way (see Chapter 4) highlights that a person's outlook on life informed by the teachings of the Buddha find expression in every aspect of a person's life. To separate expressions of belief from a person's life would be anathema to the overall message of Buddhism. Indeed, Thich Nhat Hanh (2008) describes acts such as washing the dishes and eating a tangerine as mindful activities. It is therefore possible to speak of every act that a Buddhist performs as a potential expression of belief, though it may not be outwardly observable. This links, very much, with the discussion in the Series Editor's Foreword that outlines 'religion' as a modern and contested term. The neat structures that Western colonialists had constructed based on a Christian lens are not transferred to other religious traditions neatly no matter how hard people tried. Within the classroom this is one of the problems that a teacher will face when exploring Buddhism. When the General Certificate of Secondary Education (GCSE) specifications are explored in England, we note that sections such as 'Living the Buddhist Life' or 'Practices' deal with topics such as meditation, puja (both of which will be explored in the chapter) and ethics (see Chapter 8), alongside further expressions such as 'festivals' and life-cycle rituals. If one were to read the specifications, a person might be left with the impressions that festivals and rituals would have the same importance in Buddhism as within other traditions such as Christianity, Judaism or Hinduism as practised in the UK. While in areas around the world, festivals and life-cycle rituals have greater importance.

This is a result of the Department for Education issuing guidance for the reformation of the GCSEs that followed a common structure and tried to fit everything into a structure that had been inherited from a world religions paradigm. It is incumbent on teachers, who may need to teach within this structure, to highlight the reality of Buddhist living compared to that which is found in the specification and their attendant textbooks. For those teachers who are able to construct an approach to Buddhism not constrained by outside curricula, it will be useful to consider how to approach expressions of belief. How can the lived reality be reflected, and does a local expression or a more global understanding take precedence? Elsewhere (Holt, 2022) I have suggested that one of the five 'bridges' to ensure effective learning within the classroom is through the prioritization of local over global, but both have their place.

Throughout this chapter the main meditative practices will be explored from various Buddhist traditions, alongside other expressions such as puja or devotion. The various celebrations of festivals will be touched upon, as they have traditionally formed part of the teaching of Buddhism within the classroom. It will be at the teacher's own discretion how, or if, to use them in their teaching. At this stage of the development of a worldviews approach within England it is important to reflect on their inclusion or non-exclusion. Hopefully in the future this discussion will have been thought through and their appropriate place will have been found.

Meditation

Within the exploration of the Middle Way and the Threefold Path (see Chapter 4) the importance of meditation was discussed. It is the task of this chapter to build upon this and outline the meditative practices that are common within Buddhism. Buddhists will meditate in different ways including:

- quietening their mind;
- sitting in certain positions;
- controlling their breathing;
- fixing their mind on particular ideas; and
- using visual aids.

The focus of meditation is the control of the body and mind and the consideration of the self and requires one to ignore one's surroundings and focus on the self. Meditation can then be seen to go from oneself to the helping of others. Focussing on the mind and body is only the first stage of meditation; ultimately it goes beyond the self. It is through meditation that one gains the understanding to be truly without ego in one's thoughts and actions. The aim is to progress through the jhanas (dhyanas). The four form jhanas are:

1. A Buddhist enters a state of joy by being freed from the desire for sensual pleasures. The senses drift into the background and are unimportant. The first jhana, initially, may be a momentary experience of joy, but it can be trained to continue for longer periods of time, and people are eventually able to enter this jhana every time they meditate.
2. The second jhana brings an inner state of tranquillity. The mind is free of conscious thought; the mind is able to concentrate without conscious action.
3. In the third jhana a person gains a feeling of equanimity, where joy is replaced with bliss. A person is removed from the external world but is blissfully aware of their breathing and their body.

4. In the fourth jhana desire and aversion are overcome, and a state of perfect equanimity exist. A person does not feel things that are pleasant or unpleasant. A person stays in this state until they choose to come out of it for themselves. In this stage a person begins to explore the nature of existence and possibly begins to experience the formless jhanas – that are not tied to the body, namely, infinite space, infinite consciousness, infinite nothingness, neither perception nor non-perception.

Interpretations differ as to whether awakening is attained after the four jhanas, or after the formless jhanas (see Harvey, 2013), or even after a ninth stage of *nirodha samapatti*. Nirodha samapatti has been described as 'an extremely intense and deep state cultivated through meditation in which the mental and physical activities are temporarily suspended … Some Buddhist scholars have compared a meditator in Nirodha Samapatti to someone who is in a state of hibernation or suspended animation with no detectable vital signs' as 'there is cessation of perception (sanna) and feeling (vedana)' (Ubeysekara, 2020).

Samatha

Samatha meditation aims to bring about peace within the mind and is sometimes called tranquillity meditation. In essence what takes place is that the busy thoughts of a person's life are gradually calmed enabling the person to be at peace within themselves.

This builds on the Middle Way and especially the quality of 'Right Mindfulness'; in samatha this can be seen to refer to four different types of mindfulness:

- The body
- Feelings
- Mind
- Mental states

In the first practice of samatha the person focuses on each one of these for a short time to become aware of it, how it feels and allow it to calm and be at peace. Usually in samatha there is a focus for the mind, which can include:

- A person's own breath which is a very common focus. For example, focussing on one's own breathing enables a person to rid themselves of outside distractions and stresses. This is most commonly described as mindfulness meditation which will be explored further on.
- A candle flame
- A Buddharupa
- A picture

Through this concentration the person is able to settle down and achieve restfulness and peace where the mind is clear. This type of clarity is, however, only the first stage.

Other, higher, forms of consciousness (known as jhanas) can be sought through samatha meditation:

- Detachment/clarity
- Stillness
- A more defined joy
- Calm and peaceful consciousness

This form of mediation does not lead to enlightenment (and can be seen to distract from it as the person becomes happy with their peaceful state). They can lead to aspects of the early form (rupa) of *jhanas* (*dhyanas*).

To be efficacious in the path to enlightenment samatha has to lead to/be used in conjunction with vipassana. In some ways the difference between vipassana and samatha is that in samatha there is a focus on one action or thing, whereas in vipassana the various stages are focussed on to help a person gain insight into the nature of all things. Cousins (1984) suggests the difference between focus and intent:

> Samatha is explained as the medicine for craving, bringing freedom from sickness by liberation of heart, while vipassana is the medicine for the sickness of ignorance, bringing freedom from sickness in liberation of understanding. One developing samatha (fourth noble truth), comprehends matter (first truth), abandons craving (second truth) and realizes liberation of heart (third truth). One developing vipassana (fourth truth), comprehends the immaterial (first truth), abandons ignorance (second truth) and realizes liberation of understanding (third truth). (62)

Samatha, in some ways, can be seen to be the first stage of vipassana that is outlined further on.

Vipassana

Vipassana is also known as insight meditation, though sometimes it is also called mindfulness, as it aims to help the person develop insight into the true nature of things (enabling the person to then achieve enlightenment and nibbana). The ability to focus on one topic for a long time needs to be developed (hence why samatha is usually used as a preparation for vipassana). There are certain key features of vipassana:

- Vipassana is taught to a person by a master.
- Usually vipassana is carried out in the lotus position.
- The Buddhist tries to consider questions about themselves but will also focus on questions around the Four Noble Truths.
- They are trying to develop mentally so that they can look at themselves as if they were an outsider.

- They may not use objects as the purpose of vipassana is to see beyond the physical to the true nature of everything.

Another purpose of vipassana is to internalize the dhamma; it is not just theoretical concepts but a (the only) reality that becomes a part of the person. Seeing things as they really are enables a person to deal with other people in a positive manner no matter how they have been treated by them. In the *Satipatthana Sutta* the Buddha is reported to have taught insight or vipassana meditation as 'the direct path for the purification of beings, for the overcoming of sorrow and lamentation, for the disappearance of pain and distress, for the attainment of the right method, and for the realization of unbinding'. In this sutta the Buddha outlined three stages for the practice of insight meditation:

- 'The monk remains focused on the body in and of itself – ardent, alert, and mindful – subduing greed and distress with reference to the world.'
- 'One remains focused on the phenomenon of origination with regard to the body, on the phenomenon of passing away with regard to the body, or on the phenomenon of origination and passing away with regard to the body.'
- 'Or his mindfulness that "There is a body" is maintained (simply) to the extent of knowledge and recollection. And he remains independent, unsustained by [not clinging to] anything in the world.'

The twentieth-century Burmese monk, Mahasi Sayadaw (2015), developed *Practical Vipassana Techniques*, based on the aforementioned sutta. He outlined four basic exercises with a preparatory stage.

Preparatory stage: This is the setting of the scene, or the establishing of the conditions for the attainment of insight. There is a purification of the way that a person lives, and whether that person is lay or ordained it involves a living of the precepts required of a bhikkhu or bhikkhuni. It also involves trusting the teacher who is to help in the development of the meditative practice. Once this is established, a reflection on the 'Four Protections' that the Buddha offers during meditation: the Buddha, metta (loving kindness for all living things), the body (a rejection of the attachment necessitated by the body) and death (reflecting on impermanence and the cycle of samsara). With this preparation established a person sits on the floor with their legs crossed.

The first basic exercise: This involves a focus on the rising and falling as the person concentrates on their breathing. This enables those at the start of the process to be attentive, and ensure the mind is focussed and concentrated. A person should be 'totally aware of the movements of rising and falling as they occur in the course of normal breathing' (Sayadaw, 2015, 764).

The second basic exercise: While a person is aware of the rising and falling of breathing it is natural for mental activities to take place. When this happens, the person should make a mental note of the process occurring, such as reflection, imagination or even going if the person imagines going somewhere. These mental activities should be allowed to disappear, and the focus should return to the rising and falling of breathing.

The third basic exercise: The process of meditation takes time, and so a person's body may begin to express discomfort. Again, a person should note the feelings that arise in terms of bodily fatigue, ache and so on. These should be noted and reflected on, and then allowed to dissipate, before returning to a focus on the rising or falling. If the person needs to move or itch, because the discomfort becomes too much, they should note the deliberate movements, and then return to the rising and falling. Sayadaw warns that over time intensely painful sensations may arise; these may motivate a person to stop or to take a break, but if a person continues 'with determination [they] will most likely overcome these painful sensations and may never again experience them in the course of contemplation' (2015, 766). There may be involuntary movements or sways. Again, a person should make mental note of them and allow them to dissipate. If a person needs to stand, or drink, everything should be done purposefully with mental notes being made of everything. Everything should be mindful, deliberate and performed with complete awareness and focus. This focus can be practiced and should be present in every activity that a person performs throughout the day including the eating of a tangerine as described at the beginning of this chapter. There should be no distraction, but everything is attended to with complete focus and attention. With such focus, when a person returns to sitting and rising and falling, the person should be much more aware of contemplation. Thich Nhat Hanh (2012b) has suggested:

> It's very simple but very effective. When we bring our attention to our in-breath and our out-breath, we stop thinking of the past, we stop thinking of the future, and we begin to come home to ourselves. (12–13)

The fourth basic exercise: The purpose of the exercises up to this point has been to develop focus in attention and insight. It has been training a person to be insightful and focussed. 'The student who thus dedicates himself to the training day and night will be able in not too long a time to develop concentration to the initial stage of the fourth degree of insight (knowledge of arising and passing away) and onward to higher states of insight meditation (vipassana-bhavana)' (Sayadaw, 2015, 770).

The purpose of such mindfulness is to gain insight into the true nature of all things. Being aware of the way that body, mind and feelings function, will give an insight into their impermanence. For Theravada Buddhists this would focus on gaining that insight into the Four Noble Truths, and for Mahayana Buddhists it would be focussed on the emptiness of all things.

As with all Mahayana teaching, the gaining of insight or wisdom is not sufficient, and the purpose of meditation leads to further compassionate action. Thich Nhat Hanh (2012b) has outlined that:

Mindfulness is the basis of a Buddhist ethic. What does being mindful mean? It means, first of all, that we stop and observe deeply what is happening in the present moment. If we do this, we can see the suffering that is inside us and around us. We can practice looking deeply with concentration in order to see the causes of this suffering. We need to understand suffering in order to know what kind of action we can take to relieve it. (4)

Theravada Buddhists, and others, may also see that the purpose of all meditation is to help others, in a similar way to what the Buddha taught others. This, compassion may also be an outworking of the practice of the *brahma viharas* (sublime attitudes):

- Metta (loving kindness) bhavana (meditation).
- Karuna (compassion) bhavana.
- Mudita (joy) bhavana.
- Upekkha (equanimity) bhavana.

In metta-bhavana the concept and virtue of metta or loving kindness is focussed on and as such will develop within a person. Metta bhavana is usually seen to have five stages:

1. The person meditating will focus on metta for themselves and remembering how they have been loved.
2. This extends quite naturally into love towards those people who are close to the person meditator. This will usually be friend and family. Oftentimes a phrase such as 'May you be happy' will be repeated to express and emanate metta.
3. The third stage extends to a person they do not know, or have neutral feelings for. Again, a phrase expressing a hope for love for the person will be repeated.
4. This stage focuses on metta for 'enemies', meaning someone they have negative feelings towards. The focus is on developing and expressing metta for even those persons a person has unkind feelings towards.
5. The expression of metta is extended to all beings – a universal expression and hope for metta.

In some ways it sounds straightforward, but at each stage it involves a consciousness of the concept of metta and how the person is 'feeling'. It is not a checklist, but a transformation of a person's feelings and attitudes towards all things. Rather than a separate activity, Thich Nhat Hanh (2008) suggests that it is part of the practice of mindfulness. In his description of compassion for one's enemies, the focus on the person, heir background and motivations are cycled through many meditations and thoughts:

> Continue until you feel compassion rise in your heart like a well filling with fresh water and your anger and resentment disappear. Practice this exercise many times on the same person. (102)

As indicated by Hanh's feeling of compassion arising, metta bhavana is very close to karuna bhavana in developing and expressing feelings of compassion. The various stages or foci will be developed toward the person meditating, loved ones, neutral people, enemies and all beings. The focus will be on compassion and the desire to remove suffering from all beings' situations. Care should be taken to avoid pity which elevates the person feeling the pity, but instead it should be compassion which brings a person to the same empathetic level as those on whom they are focussing.

Mudita bhavana focuses on the joy for, and of, others. In repeating the stages of loved ones, neutral persons, enemies and all beings, Jennifer O' Sullivan (2018) suggests that the following phrase be repeated:

> I'm happy that you're happy.
> May your happiness last.
> May your happiness grow.
> May your happiness and good fortune radiate.

The phrases may differ, but the intention and the sentiment will be the same across the different forms of mudita bhavana. In each of these meditations, these virtues are carried through and focussed on in a mindful way in a person's life.

Upekkha bhavana works in a similar way to the first three brahma-viharas. In that, each is sought to be distributed throughout the universe. Upekkha or equanimity brings the other three brahma-viharas into balance and prevents them from becoming too focussed on the perceived reality of those things that form the focus of the meditation. It is a feeling of detachment, and a recognition that everything will rise and fall, and that everything is impermanent. Although detachment could be seen to be negative, in actuality, seeing things as they really are is a way of expressing love, compassion and joy. Gethin (1998) articulates it as:

> a state of calm balance with regard to the sufferings and pleasures of beings; it is likened to the attitude of a mother to a child that is busy with its own affairs, indicating that equanimity should not be misunderstood as mere indifference. (187)

The meditation will go through the similar stages as those already mentioned.

Chan/Zen/dhyana

Dhyana is a word that literally means meditation, suggesting the method used to bring clarity and focus to the mind. Chan is the Chinese translation of dhyana, and Zen is the Japanese translation.

Zen a school of Mahayana Buddhism developed in China and Japan. Zen (or Ch'an) means meditation and is based around the importance of mediation rather than scriptures. The goal of Zen Buddhism is satori (or individual enlightenment), which is the aim of all schools of Buddhism. Everything within Zen is oriented and directed towards satori.

In 520CE Bodhidharma travelled from India to China and founded the line of Zen masters there. He is credited with developing martial arts as a way of maintaining health and strength. Following his death there were five patriarchs (a Zen Master) in succession:

- Bodhidharma (from about 440 to about 528)
- Huike (487–593)
- Sengcan (?–606)
- Daoxin (580–651)
- Hongren (601–674)
- Huineng (638–713)

Zen Buddhism has split into two schools: Rinzai and Soto. Within the UK the Serene Reflection Meditation tradition is based within Soto Zen. Although dhyana is a word that refers to meditation it has specific relation to the meditation used within the Zen school of Buddhism. The purpose of meditation within Zen Buddhism is to focus within oneself to realize one's own buddha-nature. This type of meditation practiced in Zen is often called *Zazen*.

> Chan points directly to the human mind, to enable people to see their true nature and become buddhas. (Nan, 1997, 92)

Other things such as scriptures can help; but they are only important as they help to realize the goal of enlightenment and aid meditation. This approach is highlighted by D. T. Suzuki:

> To study Zen means to have Zen-experience, for without the experience there is no Zen one can study. But mere experience means to be able to communicate it to others; the experience ceases to be vital unless it is adequately expressible. A dumb experience is not human. To experience is to be self-conscious. Zen experience is complete only when it is backed by Zen consciousness and finds expression in one way or another. (1946, 110)

Zen is an experience of experience rather than of study. Zen is believed to have been taught by the Buddha Shakyamuni. He began the transmission of Zen to one of his disciples Kasyapa in the Flower Sermon. In this sermon the Buddha held up a white flower and just looked at it in his hand. Kasyapa is the only one who smiled in recognition. This led Kasyapa to be his successor; the Buddha is reported to have said:

> I possess the true Dharma eye, the marvellous mind of Nirvana, the true form of the formless, the subtle dharma gate that does not rest on words or letters but is a special transmission outside of the scriptures. This I entrust to Mahakasyapa. (Dumoulin, 1994, 9)

Knowledge of Buddhism is transmitted in gestures and actions (silence) rather than scriptures. Zen is a religion based on silent meditation that seeks enlightenment for people in the same way that Kasyapa experienced it in the Flower Sermon. This transmission is believed to have happened in parallel (but separate) to the scriptural transmission and thus developed into a distinct tradition. Soto emphasizes sitting silently in meditation while Rinzai emphasizes koan, which involves meditating on questions (which usually a teacher has given), for example, what is the sound of one hand clapping?

While the purpose of mediation is enlightenment, it is slightly differently understood. Through the help of a master it is possible to achieve enlightenment quickly through the attainment of perfect wisdom, or the ability to see things as they really are.

Hui neng (the sixth patriarch) had seen through the 'dust' to the true nature of things. Zen meditation may focus on riddles (*koan*) (particularly in China). Or it can focus on the gradual progression to truth through intense daily meditation. This could take the form of sitting and staring at a blank wall, the purpose being to train the mind to be clear of any 'dust' or interference. This concentrates on the individuals awareness of their own enlightenment; they will sit in the lotus position, put their hands in the dhyana mudra and keep their eyes open.

In other forms of Zen this type of meditation is known as *Shikantaza* (just sitting). Bielefeldt has suggested that 'the *T'ien-t'ai hsiao chih-kuan* ... probably represents the first practical manual of meditation available to-the Chinese' (1986, 133). The description that it contains of 'just sitting' seems straightforward. It outlines how to prepare oneself, and then:

> Having thus composed himself, the meditator is to relinquish all judgments and simply observe his thoughts as they arise; once observed, thoughts will cease, and eventually the mind will become unified ... the surface waves of the mind will subside, and the pearl of liberating wisdom beneath will appear of its own accord. (Bielefeldt, 1986, 135)

Visualization

Visualization while used throughout Buddhism is a particularly important aspect of meditation in Vajrayana (see Chapter 5) and Pure Land Buddhism (see Chapter 2).

In Vajrayana and wider Tantric Buddhism the centrality of visualization is suggested by Donald Lopez (2015b):

> Much tantric practice involves visualization; some Tibetan exegetes would argue that the distinguishing feature of tantric practice was to turn the goal into the path or visualizing oneself as the buddha that one seeks to become – imagining oneself with the body of a buddha, adorned with the thirty-two major marks and eighty secondary marks and seated resplendent on the throne at the centre of the mandala palace. Thus, mandalas came to be described in great detail, each with a different buddha at its centre. (471)

In Tantric Buddhism, mandalas and thangkas (thankas) serve more than merely a focus of meditation but as a means to visualization. In some traditions this will be to visualize the Buddha or bodhisattva, in others it is to identify oneself as the Buddha or the deity who is the focus of the mandala. Through this a Buddhist is able to connect with deities and bodhisattva who Matthieu Ricard describes as 'archetypes of knowledge, of compassion, of altruism, etc., which are objects of meditation and bring out these qualities in us through visualization techniques' (Faure, 2009, 60). Though Faure (2009) rejects this interpretation as the view of a Western elite highlighting the experiences that Buddhists describe of the reality of these experiences, and beings. Indeed, he suggests that the 'Dalai Lama himself has declared that he makes all his important decisions based on oracles delivered by his own personal soothsayer during trances whereby the latter is possessed by one of these fearsome deities of Tibetan Buddhism' (60). Avoiding this somewhat dismissive language, it is important to highlight that the visualizations serve an important purpose and are described as authentic experiences.

In addition to the development of qualities of the Buddha or the bodhisattva, in Vajrayana Buddhism, as a person is able to visualize themselves in the place of the Buddha, it is possible that they attain awakening as a part of this visualization process. In Vajrayana this type of 'intense' meditation where one identifies with the Buddha is only available to those who have been initiated and taught the various practices. The use of the mandalas as a focus for visualization are an important aspect of meditation and devotion..

In Pure Land Buddhism the *Amitayurdhyana Sutra* (Sutra on the Contemplation of Buddha Amitayus), Shakyamuni Buddha teaches Vaidehi the importance of, and how to visualize, the Pure Land (see Chapter 6). He outlines thirteen contemplations or visualizations of things in the Pure Land that should be undertaken:

1. The setting sun
2. An expanse of water
3. The ground filled with jewels
4. Trees full of flowers, leaves and jewels
5. Ponds
6. Various objects
7. The lotus throne of the Buddha
8. The image of Amitabha/Amida
9. Amitabha/Amida
10. Avalokitesvara
11. Mahasthamaprapta
12. Those wishing to be reborn in the Pure Land
13. Amitabha/Amida and the two bodhisattvas

For each of these he outlines the process. The example of the setting sun suggests:

> You and all other beings besides ought to make it your only aim, with concentrated thought, to get a perception of the western quarter. You will ask how that perception

is to be formed. I will explain it now. All beings, if not blind from birth, are uniformly possessed of sight, and they all see the setting sun. You should sit down properly, looking in the western direction, and prepare your thought for a close meditation on the sun; cause your mind to be firmly fixed on it so as to have an unwavering perception by the exclusive application of your mind, and gaze upon it in particular when it is about to set and looks like a suspended drum. After you have thus seen the sun, let that image remain clear and fixed, whether your eyes be shut or open; such is the perception of the sun, which is the First Meditation (*Amitayurdhyana Sutra*).

This visualization will enable the person meditating to develop qualities and the familiarity with Amida and his Pure Land to be reborn there. Thus, visualization is an important aspect of Pure Land Buddhist meditation.

Puja/devotion

Puja is a sanskrit word which means 'worship', which may not be the most accurate description for the acts of devotion that a Buddhist will undertake. Other words that are often associated with puja include *garava* (respect/esteem) and *saddha* (Skt: *sraddha*), which is usually translated as faith. Worship is perhaps a useful shorthand to help others understand the nature and purpose of that which is being undertaken. While meditation can be categorized as an act of devotion, there are many elements to what is commonly called 'puja' that is separate to, though interconnected with, the meditative practices that have been explored earlier on.

Saddhatissa (1978) argues that the translation of saddha as faith is incorrect, and his alternate translation suggests one aspect of Buddhist devotion that forms the basis of what is commonly termed puja:

> Firstly, it is a confidence born out of understanding of the Four Noble Truths. Secondly, *it is a feeling of reverence or esteem a follower accords to a personality* or a set of doctrines. (137, emphasis added)

Observing examples of Buddhist puja the focus on the reverence shown to a personality has, perhaps, the most resonance. This can be seen to form a part of what is termed Buddhanusmrti (Pali: Buddhanussati) or meditation on the virtues of the Buddha. Central to this in many traditions is the image of the Buddha or bodhisattva. Whether in the vihara or in the home there will most likely be a shrine with an image of the Buddha or a bodhisattva as its focus. There are many different images (*buddharupa* meaning 'form of the awakened one') of the Buddha Shakyamuni, all of which remind people of the various events of his life, and the virtues that he exhibited. As within puja, so within the classroom, these different buddharupas can be used to help understand the example that the Buddha set, and the inspiration that he is to Buddhists.

Each of the buddharupas may contain aspects of the marks of a great being (see Chapter 3), which a Buddhist can reflect upon. The commonalities between many rupas include:

- Long fingers and toes
- Long nose
- Long earlobes
- A head protuberance (urna)
- Broad shoulders

Examples of buddharupas include:

- Fearless or Protection Buddha

    In this rupa the Buddha is seated with his right hand raised facing outward. This reminds the observer of protection as the raised hand could be seen to be a shield; and that as a result of this a person may be less fearful. It is seen to be a protection against the Three Poisons of craving, ignorance and hatred/aversion.

- The Meditation Buddha

    In this rupa the Buddha is seated with his legs crossed in a double or single lotus position. Both the Buddha's hands lie in his lap with the palms up. On occasion an alms bowl can be placed on his lap. Sometimes the Buddha's eyes are shown as nearly fully closed. This is a calming Buddha, that enables a person to seek calm in their devotion and in their lives through meditation. This rupa is often known as *amithabha* (boundless light) Buddha.

- Earth-Touching Buddha

    This is one of the most common buddharupas and is often described as the 'callling the earth to witness' Buddha. The legs are crossed, with the left hand resting in the lap. The right hand, with the palm towards the Buddha, points towards the ground. It is associated with the enlightenment of the Buddha, who, upon overcoming Mara and his daughters, touched the earth and called upon her to witness that he was now fully awakened.

- Nirvana/Reclining Buddha

    This image of the Buddha on a table lying on his right hand side is said to depict the final moments of the Buddha's life and his entrance into parinirvana. A reflection on this event can help a Buddhist realize the inevitability of death and the impermanence of all things. It can also serve as an inspiration to attain parinirvana.

Figure 7.1 The teaching Buddha (seated Buddha Shakyamuni, 965 or 1025. Gilt bronze, 8 1/2 x 7 1/4 x 4 3/4 in. [21.6 x 18.4 x 12.1 cm]). Brooklyn Museum, gift of the Asian Art Council in memory of Mahmood T. Diba and Mary Smith Dorward Fund, 1999.

Source: Creative Commons-BY (Photo: Brooklyn Museum, 1999.42_SL1.jpg).

- The Medicine Buddha

This Buddha is shown with a bowl of herbs in his left hand resting upon his lap. The right hand is shown pointing downwards with the palm facing away from the Buddha. Linking with the idea of the Four Noble Truths as a medical formula, it is possible to suggest that he is bringing the cure/medicine to the world. The position of the right hand is a *mudra* representing the giving of a blessing to humanity.

- The Ascetic Buddha

  This may be one of the most jarring images of the Buddha as he is emaciated. It reflects the time that he lived as an asectic (see Chapter 3). It reminds people of the futility of harsh asceticism and the need to live a Middle Way. Sildatke has articulated the positive importance of the image: 'It is not a symbol of death and resurrection but of self-empowerment and overcoming of suffering by the human spirit. It is a manifest to Buddha's unbelievable will and dedication and therefore an iconic image for Buddhist worshippers and followers on his path alike' (Voon, 2016).

- The Teaching Buddha (see Figure 7.1)

  This image of the Buddha is usually depicted in art when the Buddha is teaching and shows particuallry the moment when he is teaching his First Sermon (see Chapter 3). In being seated in front of the Buddha, as his original followers were, a Buddhist can take inspiration from his teachings. Both hands are showing the same mudra, but at different angles. The right hand is raised with the hand pointing outwards, while the left hand is foldted in the lap or across the chest.

Buddhaghosa suggests that the results of this practice 'in addition to complete confidence, mindfulness, understanding, and merit' is that the devotee 'comes to feel as if he (sic) were lviing in the Master's presence'. The activity is therefore 'designed specifically to evoke not only the memory of a buddha, but also his living presence' (McMahan, 2002, 149). The devotion, or puja, that is undertaken will sometimes have elements of the practices and objects mentioned further on.

The use of a buddharupa, as indicated earlier on, is not limited to representations of the Buddha Shakyamuni. Nor are they limited to the rupa of being a symbolic representation of the Buddha. Many Buddhists will recognize the nature of the rupa being a springboard to greater devotion and focus:

> This is not worshipping an idol as the statue is just there as a remidner of the Buddha and his teaching. It is not like praying to God: 'We don't know where he is. He cannot hear you or answer your prayers.' The offerings are made to show respect to the man and his teachings, 'to say thank you to the Buddha for bringing his teachings'. (Cush, 1990, 46)

Fowler (1999) recognizing the seeming incongruity of devotion to the Buddha within Theravada Buddhism, as it is not taught that he is a cosmic presence, suggests that the main focus of the puja is the dhamma. There, are, however many Buddhists who through the cosmic presence of the Buddha imbue devotion to the rupa and the rupa itself with greater power and meaning. The story is told of King Pasenadi of Kosala in the *Kosalabimbavannana*. King Pasenadi would often go to the Buddha for guidance and created what is believed to have been the first image of the Buddha. If the Buddha was away the King would be able to pay his respects to him, and to make offerings. The Buddha approached the image, at which point the rupa began to rise to show respect to the Buddha. The Buddha stopped the image and said that after his death, the image would represent him and be a vehicle for his teachings. This highlights the purpose of the rupas of both being a source and an inspiration of his dharma, and also a reminder of his life.

For many Buddhists the rupa is more than a physical object. There is a ceremony to imbue the statue with the attributes of the Buddha:

> This is done by a meticulous process, which adheres to a comprehensive set of rules, varying among different traditions, and incorporating manuals, sacred sounds, and elaborate rituals – for example, an eye-opening ceremony which is believed to transform a mere likeness into a holy presence. The potency of images that carry the qualities of the Buddha is also reflected in the fact that many are considered to have supernatural powers, perhaps enabling wishes to come true for those who venerate them. (Wang, 2021, 56–7)

As indicated there are images that are given biographies that entwine those who venerate it with the life of the Buddha. One example of such is *The Chronicle of the Emerald Buddha* (Notton, 1932), which tells the story of the legend and travels of the Emerald Buddha beginning with its fashioning by Indra and Vishnu in the first century, until it found its way to Thailand's Wat Phra Kaeo (Temple of the Emerald Buddha) (Roeder, 1999). It has great significance for the people of Thailand today with it marking the changing of the seasons.

Other bodhisattvas will also be used as objects in devotion. In a similar manner to the rupas of Buddha Shakyamuni, the hope of the devotee is that these rupas will remind them of the bodhisattva's teachings and attributes. Through the focus on the image a person can sit in the presence of the devotee, and the qualities and teachings can be channelled. Examples of bodhisattva include:

- Avalokitesvara who exhibits especially the quality of karuna (compassion).
- Guanyin (Kannon) a female incarnation of Avalokitesvara also related to compassion.
- Prajnaparamita seen to be a female personification of wisdom.
- Maitreya seen as the future Buddha of this world (see Chapter 6).

The steps to the bodhisattva path are elucidated earlier on (see Chapter 5) and may form a part of the devotion offered to the rupas of each of the bodhisattva.

In describing puja in the home or in a vihara it will follow some general principles, but the exact nature of such will vary from person to person. Usually:

> When Buddhists enter a temple or shrine room in which an image of a buddha is installed, they may go before the image, kneel down and bow three times so that their forehead touches the floor. This is a very formal action. The three bows represent the Buddha, dhamma and sangha. (Erricker, 2001, 102)

Generally speaking the three main parts of Buddhist puja are bowing in front of the Buddha, making offerings and chanting. The Buddhist will make offerings of rice or food and light incense daily. In doing so a Buddhist might chant mantras and repeat the Three Refuges. Oftentimes aids to worship maybe used; a Buddhist can use any or none of these in their meditation. The use of a buddharupa has already been discussed, but objects often found in devotional activities help Buddhist along the path and to channel their focus. Examples may include:

- *Incense* suggests that the dharma is spread to all areas of the world.
- *Candles* are a symbol of the dhamma that extinguishes the darkness of ignorance.
- *Flowers* are used to reflect the fragility and impermanence of all things. In one Buddhist vihara visited by the author in Manchester, UK, the flowers were replaced by Lego structures, again suggesting the impermanence of everything.
- *Prayer flags* are flags with prayers or sutras written on them. There are generally seen to be of two types: horizontal flags or *Lung ta*, which are attached to a string. The second type of flag is usually on a vertical pole and are called *Darchog*. These are often decorated with a horse in the middle with three flaming jewels (representing the Buddha, the dharma and the sangha), with mantras written around the outside. In each corner are pictured four powerful animals significant in Tibetan Buddhism: the dragon, the garuda, the tiger and the snow lion (Clark, 2022). On the Lung ta the flags are usually arranged in groups of five colours:
  - Blue representing space
  - White representing the air and wind
  - Red representing fire
  - Green representing water
  - Yellow representing earth (see Clark, 2002).

  Prayer flags do not, as commonly believed, carry prayers to deities, rather they spread the blessings of the dharma throughout the universe. One of the most common mantras printed on prayer flags is *om mani padme hum*, the mantra of Avalokiteshvara, which send compassion throughout the six realms.
- *Prayer wheels* combine a mantra *om mani padme hum* with a movement (mudra). The mantra is written around the outside of the wheel and the mudra's movement is attained by spinning the wheel clockwise with wrist movement. Inside the prayer wheel is a scroll with the mantra repeated fufty0 times. It is believed by some that

spinning the wheel by one revolution will evoke fifty blessings sent out to the six realms. Both the prayer wheel and the flags evoke a sense of responsibility beyond the individual; the practice of Buddhism is about the blessing of all of existence.

- *Malas* are a string of beads used in devotion and meditation usually to count the mantras that are being recited.
- *Stupa* is a small version of the stupas that serve to mark places where relics of the Buddha are believed to be buried. They serve as a reminder of the Buddha and the impermanence of everything.
- *Mandala*s are patterns created to represent spiritual reality and form a focus for meditation in many Buddhist traditions. Their use in visualization techniques have been explored earlier. The creation of the mandala, in some traditions, is as important as the focus on the mandala itself; examples include sand mandalas that take many days to create, and then they are destroyed in a symbolic representation of impermanence. In Vajrayana Buddhism there will often be a Buddha or a deity at the middle of the mandala.
- *Thangka/thanka* is a cloth wall-hanging of a Buddha or Bodhisattva and aroused in a similar way as a rupa to focus the mind and develop specific qualities. They can also be used in visualization.
- *Singing bowls* are used to produce a single note to focus the mind.

The Buddhist may also use their body in worship. For example, putting your hands together in front of your face or chest is a sign of respect and is often performed in front of the rupa. Alternatively the worshipper may touch their chest, lips and foreheads to show that they are worshipping with the body, speech and mind. To show further respect a Buddhist might bow, kneel or lie flat before the buddharupa; this is common within Tibetan Buddhism.

Puja in the vihara differs from that in the home because a Buddhist will usually have the aid of a bhikkhu, bhikkhuni or equivalent in the ordained sangha to assist them in their worship – they will often perform ceremonies and read sutras. Offerings are also made to the bhikkhus and bhikkhunis. In the home it will be much more informal, with a smaller shrine and more personal worship. No one else needs to be involved and there is no set time, or structure.

Festivals

In mentioning festivals within Buddhism it is important to note that not all festivals are celebrated by all Buddhists. Many will be distinct to countries, as Buddhism has adopted local practices and customs. These have been repurposed in many cases to reflect Buddhist teaching. There will also be some Buddhists who consider some of the

Expressions of Belief

celebrations to go against Buddhist principles and they will be seen to go to excess. Celebrations and festivals may include:

- *Parinirvana/Nirvana Day* is celebrated my many Mahayana Buddhists in February.
- *Asalha Puja Day/Dharma Day* usually takes place in July and celebrates the first teaching of the Buddha.
- *Abhidhamma Day* is usually celebrated in April to remember when the Buddha went to Tusita heaven to teach his mother.
- *Avalokitesvara's Birthday* is celebrated in March by many Mahayana Buddhists to celebrate the Bodhisattva ideal.
- *Bodhi Day* remembers the enlightenment of the Buddha.

Thoughts for the classroom

Within this chapter time has necessarily been taken to explore the various expressions of Buddhist devotion. It is interesting that when meditation is taught within the classroom, it is generally taught quite briefly and summarized with aspects of mindfulness, while recognizing that there are different types. This chapter has shown that there is much more to meditation and dependent on the age and understanding of the students that it is important to make this clear. This book has only been able to scratch the surface of the various types of meditation but the complexity has been recognized. Particularly interesting is the exploration of Vajrayana Buddhism. It is simple to teach mandalas and thangkas as focus for meditations, and that is the purpose that they serve for many Buddhists. However, being able to explore them as part of the visualization techniques of tantra would be a focus for comparison of the various methods used to seek awakening. This, again, draws upon the diversity or messiness of Buddhism as not being able to generalize with any degree of accuracy.

The second way that meditation is 'used' within the classroom is to have children undertake some meditation exercises. This is a controversial aspect of teaching religion and worldviews that I have discussed elsewhere (Holt, 2022) in exploring the suitability of experiential approaches to learning. This is something that a teacher needs to consider carefully before undertaking such approaches. The concerns that people may express are twofold. Firstly, the mundanification of what are 'spiritual' or 'sacred' practices. How does the teacher safeguard against making the sacred mundane, as it does not have the same intents and purposes as within Buddhism. In using 'meditation' as an activity (see further on) it could be that it is being cheapened. There are questions that need to be asked as teachers consider activities that might replicate religious experience in a vacuous way. As such a teacher needs to be very conscious of the reasons why they are doing something and the aim of the activity. Do the benefits outweigh the potential concerns? Does this activity desanctify some of the religious actions of Buddhism and make them mundane?

The second concern is that students are being asked to 'perform' a Buddhist ritual act by engaging in meditation. The purpose of such an activity is to have pupils feel what it is like. As indicated by the previous concern, without the same purpose and belief supporting it, it is impossible to get the same feeling. Within the classroom there seem to be an inconsistent approach to the re-enactment of, or participation in, ritual acts. For example, the re-enactment of a wedding may be considered fine, whereas the repeating of ritual actions of prayer would not. Where is the line drawn, and how do teachers know what is appropriate or not?

Buddhist meditation is an interesting case, in the sense that while it has not been secularized, the concept of mindfulness, and mindful breathing, has. It is not unusual for mindfulness classes to be held in community centres, workplaces, hospitals and schools. Is mindfulness a Buddhist approach, or has it been appropriated and transformed into something else? Liz Bucar (2022) raises this issue with regards to meditation, though her focus is Hindu meditation; the same discussion can happen around Buddhist meditation or mindfulness:

> To me, it seemed clear the techniques were grounded in, as Paul Tillich would say, an ultimate concern ... By engaging in the techniques, and feeling their benefits, we were implicitly externalising the religious ideas behind them as well ... I wanted him to acknowledge that we were in an ethical grey area when we offered these techniques to students without mentioning these religious connections. (221)

There is a possibility that there is a difference between meditation and mindfulness. There is a range of literature that suggests that mindfulness may be a secularization of a Buddhist concept and as such care should be taken over its use in the classroom. For some this is a conscious attempt. Indeed, Candy Gunther-Brown (2019) suggests that one of secular mindfulness's 'founders' Jon Kabat-Zinn

> devised an apparently secular program to 'take the heart of something as meaningful, as sacred if you will, as Buddha-dharma and bring it into the world in a way that doesn't dilute, profane or distort it, but at the same time is not locked into a culturally and tradition-bound framework that would make it absolutely impenetrable to the vast majority of people. (168)

This sounds like a well-meant task, but Gunther-Brown suggests that Kabat-Zinn ' "bent over backward" to camouflage his understanding of mindfulness as the "essence of the Buddha's teachings" ' (2019, 168).

From a Buddhist perspective, it is possible to suggest that secular mindfulness is not Buddhist, as its ultimate aim is far removed from the mindfulness of Buddhism. Ronald Purser (2019), building on the work of Miles Neale (2011), has described it as 'McMindfulness' meaning that it is 'oversold and commodified' and stripped from its ethical basis from Buddhism (Purser, 2019, 17). It is about reducing stress rather than addressing the causes of suffering, and as such it reinforces the status quo. Donald Lopez (2012) echoes this when he suggests that mindfulness should be not about stress reduction, for the Buddha 'sought to create stress, to destroy complacency, in order to lead us to a state of eternal stress reduction, that state of extinction called nirvana'. Thus, teachers may feel it appropriate to use forms of mindfulness recognizing that it is not Buddhist but has been appropriated in a secular way for the modern world.

One example that might be used is the example of a teacher asking students to eat an apple. Their task, in a similar way to the way Thich Nhat Hanh suggested eating a tangerine, was to eat an apple, and only concentrate and think about how they ate the apple and what they learned. This was not a meditation, but served as a way to have students be in the moment and consider how this could be done with intent and what was learned by being in the moment. Is this, therefore, a more appropriate activity than engaging in a meditation. The appropriateness of mindfulness in the classroom is too big a discussion for the scope of this book, but it is something that we, as teachers, need to consider.

One activity that I have carried out in the classroom with students from eight to eighty years of age is a guided imagination. This was not related to Buddhism but could be. The idea was to go on a journey to a happy/special place. This is an example not of a meditation but an imagination that enabled students to understand how to be in the moment and be still. One colleague who carried this out received a complaint from a parent because the teacher had called it a meditation, and the parent did not want their child participating in other religion's activities. Therefore, it is apparent that the framing of the activities carried out in experiential learning is important; they should not be replicating religious activities.

In Chapter 2 we explored the use of religious objects in the classroom. The devotional and meditative activities of Buddhists are a further opportunity to use these objects in the classroom, whether they are the buddharupas, mala beads, thangkas or mandalas. Objects are a valuable resource when teaching in the classroom, but teachers need to be clear how and why they are using them. They, too, are subject to mundanification. In exploring the imagery of the rupas the subtlety of symbolism can be explored. One of the temptations may be to complete an activity such as colouring in a mandala template. This type of activity should be treated with caution, as it could be a way to fill time, rather than having students engage with some beliefs and practices that may deepen their knowledge of Buddhism. Though some may disagree, and suggest that 'mindful' colouring can be a way to understand how it might be to live in the moment, and not be subject to distractions. As with every activity that is planned for the classroom, the teacher needs to be confident that they have thought through why students are being asked to complete it.

Although obvious expressions of Buddhism have been explored, this is not to suggest that these are the limits and there is nothing else. Indeed, Phra Nicholas Thanissaro (2011) has suggested that in focussing on meditation there are often important elements of lived Buddhism that are missed:

> Aspects of home practice such as respect (as distinct from tolerance), filial piety, chanting and bowing, mentioned frequently in the home context, were not mentioned by any of the children in connection with class-room presentation. (69)

Indeed, there are innumerable elements of Buddhist rituals that have not been explored in this chapter. If there are local Buddhist communities, having the voices of Buddhists articulating the everyday nature of the Buddha's teachings and the virtues of Buddhism is crucial. They provide an authenticity that is central to a worldviews approach to teaching religion. Todd Lewis (2017) suggests that there are 'twelve major holy days' or monthly Uposatha days that are observed, monastic rituals, merit transfer rituals, pilgrimages, and also it should be noted that there is a constant formulations of new Buddhist rituals' such as '*boke fuji* amulets introduced into Japan to combat senility' or a new procession in Nepal (142). There are always opportunities to expand the rituals explored in the classroom.

Part 2

Contemporary issues

8

The ethical dimension

When considering the ethical dimension of Buddhism there is a temptation to treat it in a similar way that may be found in other religions. Fujiwara (2019) identifies this tendency as the 'Islamicisation of Buddhism' within the religion and worldviews classroom (248). The terminology that Fujiwara uses is problematic, but the tendency he is describing is one with which teachers will need to be aware of. This is the tendency to weigh decisions based on the rules that have been laid down; in Fuhiwara's example, he suggests that a Muslim weighs their choices against the guidance for what is halal or haram. While somewhat simplistic this may be extended to the application of ethics and morality in other religious traditions. This tendency may be overly simplistic in all religions, but at this point, within Buddhism, it is important to note that ethical living is not a transactional activity. Buddhists do not practise the Eightfold Path or the Five Precepts because it will lead to a reward, whether karmic or otherwise. Although it should be noted at this point that in Chapter 2 that for some, or many, Buddhists they are happy with rebirth into higher realms, and as such there may be a focus on karma in an individual's life. The teaching of Buddhism, however, is that the development of character or of virtues is that which is most important in terms of an ethical outlook. The purpose is the process of becoming so that awakening can be realized. The Buddha is reported to have taught:

> The non-doing of any evil, the performance of what's skilful, the cleansing of one's own mind: this is the teaching of the Awakened. (*Dhammapada*, 183)

Within Buddhism there can be different motivations behind ethical actions, but all ethical actions can be seen to be outworkings of the development of wisdom and compassion. As a Buddhist moves along the path, the living of ethical principles are less focussed on the individual, and more on how compassion can be expressed towards others. One Buddhist has expressed her view as to the ethical expression of Buddhism:

> I behave kindly and help others around me and work to spread joy around me in any way shape or form.

The ethical living of Buddhists is informed by the example of the Buddha, the teaching of the Buddha and the sangha, meaning that the sources of authority are the Three Jewels. In reality, however, these are guidelines and it is the individual in whom the final responsibility rests; as Thich Nhat Hanh has expressed of the Five Precepts, they are 'intended not to be an absolute but a path to walk on' (2014, 36). Throughout this chapter we will explore various ethical guidelines such as the Five Precepts, the virtues of metta (loving kindness) and karuna (compassion), and how these may be underpinned by the *paramitas* (perfections) and find expression in the lives of Buddhists today. It bears repeating that these are not checklists to be ticked off; they can, indeed become hindrances in that 'there is a danger that one can become dogmatically attached to them' (Whitaker and Smith, 2018, 54). They are but guiding principles that help along the path to awakening.

Metta

Metta is the teaching that a Buddhist must strive for universal loving kindness (see Chapter 7). Bodhisattvas are a great example of the attitude that needs to be developed within everybody. Examples include Avalokitesvara (infinite compassion) and Tara (female infinite compassion). Having achieved buddhahood they take it upon themselves to show others the way. There is a legend told of a Zen bodhisattva who enters villages and blesses each of them with his hands – there is no discrimination. In tandem with metta-bhavana (see Chapter 7), metta as a virtue is developed in stages:

- Within oneself (not in an egotistical sense but recognizing our ability to love and be loved).
- Friends and loved ones.
- Neutral people (perhaps a stranger).
- Enemies.
- The whole of nature.

Metta suggests that Buddhists should view the whole world as a parent views her baby. As well as the stages that a person must pass through, metta could also be seen to be developed in gradations, from goodwill to friendship and then love to others. However, the goal of metta is for it to become an integral part of a person – they have been trained over the years to show metta. Thus, it becomes a spontaneous action rather than an action motivated by the desire for merit. Although meditation and study of scriptures and bodhisattvas can contribute towards the training of the mind in how to view others, the main way that metta can be developed is by the practising of it. As we move forward in this chapter it will be evident how metta underpins other aspects of Buddhist ethics.

Karuna

In a similar way to metta, karuna is a virtue that all people should seek to have in their lives. As has been noted throughout this book, a distinguishing feature of Buddhism is compassion. This compassion extended through the various stages outlined in metta. In Mahayana Buddhism, karuna is the driving force behind the putting off parinirvana, so that a bodhisattva can choose to be reborn to show compassion to all beings and help them seek awakening.

Karuna is linked very much to metta but focuses on the helping of those who suffer and are experiencing the dukkha. This can be achieved through the offering of dana (generosity – one of the Theravada and Mahayana paramitas). A Buddhist should do all they can to alleviate the suffering of others.

The ultimate act of karuna is the leading towards enlightenment, and hence the example of the Buddha and bodhisattvas should be sought. Within Mahayana Buddhism the bodhisattvas can be 'prayed' to for the purpose of transferring merit and thus alleviate suffering. The focus of this help is the whole of the natural world and building on metta, the XIV Dalai Lama has said:

> The main theme of Buddhism is altruism based on compassion and love ... Those engaged in the practice of compassion feel much happier internally – more calm, more peaceful – and other people reciprocate that feeling ... [I]t is necessary to have great compassion, caring about the suffering of others and wanting to do something about it. In order to have such a strong force of compassion, first you must have a strong sense of love which, upon observing suffering sentient beings, wishes that they have happiness. (2012, 43–4)

Buddhists should therefore be aware of the world around them and if opportunities arise to help others they should act on it, either by teaching the principles of dharma or by providing means to alleviate someone's immediate suffering.

The importance of metta and karuna as the basis of Buddhist ethics cannot be overstated. Expressed together they will hopefully form the character of a person, and the way that a person lives will quite naturally reflect these two virtues. As we move through the rest of this chapter it will be important to note how they influence the application and living of further Buddhist principles. Although not to be explored in detail, the paramitas of both Theravada and Mahayana (see Table 8.1) can be seen to be expressions of wisdom/insight, metta and karuna.

The Five Precepts

The Five Precepts (Skt: *pancasila*; Pali: *pancasila*) are seen to be the most oft used expression of ethics for a lay Buddhist (there are additional precepts for the ordained, or in the case of Mahayana, the vows of a bodhisattva). They are listed as:

1. Refrain from taking life.
2. Refrain from taking what is not given.

Table 8.1 The Paramitas of Mahayana and Theravada Buddhism

Mahayana paramitas (see Chapter 5)	Theravada paramitas
Dana (generosity)	*Dana* (generosity)
Sila (morality)	*Sila* (morality), proper conduct
Ksanti (patience)	*Nekkhamma* (renunciation)
Virya (effort or vigour)	*Panna* (wisdom)
Dhyana (concentration)	*Viriya* (effort or vigour)
Prajna (wisdom or insight)	*Khanti* (patience)
Upaya (skilful means)*	*Sacca* (honesty)
Pranidhana (determination)*	*Adhitthana* (determination)
Bala (power)*	*Metta* (loving kindness)
Jnana (knowledge)*	*Upekkha* (equanimity)

*These four were added in the *Ten Stages Sutra*

3. Refrain from sexual misconduct.
4. Refrain from wrong speech.
5. Refrain from intoxicants that cloud the mind.

Each of these precepts will be explored in turn, but in tandem with the restrictions that the precepts place on Buddhists, there are also positive aspects to the living of them (see Table 8.2). In turn, Thich Nhat Hanh (2014) has expressed the Five Precepts as aspects of living mindfully (see Table 8.2), and together with the other expressions they help a Buddhist understand how each can be developed in their life.

The First Precept

In the *Brahmajala Sutta* it is recorded:

> Abandoning the taking of life, the contemplative Gotama abstains from the taking of life. He dwells with his rod laid down, his knife laid down, scrupulous, merciful, compassionate for the welfare of all living beings.

Sometimes the precept not to kill any living or sentient being is expanded to include not to harm any living thing. In this sense, the restriction is much broader and potentially much harder to live. It is important to note that there is an intentionality behind the action. It has been noted that a person who adopts a vegetarian lifestyle will inevitably kill bacteria and perhaps insects incidentally in the act of living. This is

Table 8.2 Three Approaches to the Five Precepts

Five Precepts	Five Positive Precepts	Five mindful precepts (Thich Nhat Hanh, 2014)
Refrain from taking life.	Act with loving kindness in protecting and sustaining life.	Reverence for life.
Refrain from taking what is not given.	Generosity.	True happiness – meaning that one is generous in thought, word and action.
Refrain from sexual misconduct.	Respect and support healthy relationships.	True love.
Refrain from wrong speech.	Say what is true and helpful; speaking with compassion.	Deep listening and loving speech.
Refrain from intoxicants that cloud the mind.	Practice mindfulness to be able to discern the truth behind all things.	Nourishment and healing.

where the exploration of beliefs such as karma help a person understand the efforts that they must make to not kill or harm any living being. The converse of this precept gives further insight into understanding how life should be protected and sustained through intentional action and the development of compassion and loving kindness. The absence of killing an enemy does not mean that a person is compassionate but is merely the first step on the path of not wishing ill-will towards them. Metta-bhavana and karuna-bhavana are thus important mindful activities to develop the character of not wishing harm on any living thing.

The precept perhaps begins with the injunction not to kill humans. Indeed, in the Vinaya one of the things that a bhikkhu can do to be expelled from the order of monks is to take a life intentionally. In defining the act of killing, the *Vinaya* suggest:

There are five factors for the full offense here.

1. Object: a living animal.
2. Perception: one perceives it to be a living animal.
3. Intention: one knowingly, consciously, deliberately and purposefully wants to cause its death.
4. Effort: whatever one does with the purpose of causing it to die.
5. Result: it dies as a result of one's action (*Vinaya. Buddhist Monastic Code*, 7).

Within Buddhist ethics and the modern world there can be seen to be various intersections with the First Precept and the killing of a human being.

War

These may include killing in a war, euthanasia and abortion. In a discussion with regards to right livelihood earlier (see Chapter 4) it was suggested that motive may serve as an ameliorating factor in killing. For example, if a soldier kills a person to protect others than it might be possible for it to be justified. Indeed, this justification through motivation might be extended to euthanasia when it is motivated out of compassion and it is used to prevent further suffering. These 'exceptions' are not universally accepted and are an area for debate. Indeed, it should be noted that the five factors for the full offense mentioned earlier do not mention any mitigating circumstances, and if one were to consider the actions of war, euthanasia and abortion, then all five criteria can generally be seen to be met (though the perception of a foetus as a living being may be debated). Damien Keown outlines that motivation can still lead to an unwholesome action:

> While motive is of great importance in Buddhist ethics it does not by itself guarantee moral rightness. If it did, it would be impossible to do wrong from a good motive. We see here that the Buddha felt this was only too possible. (Keown, 1995a, 63)

What does this mean, therefore, for these ethical issues? There are varying interpretations within Buddhism, in some ways depending on which interpretation or which text is given most prominence. A story from the Jataka tales and a past life of the Buddha Shakyamuni highlights the possibility of justification for killing:

> While on board a ship, Shakyamuni [Buddha] discovers that there is a robber intent on killing all five hundred of his fellow passengers. Shakyamuni ultimately decides to kill the robber, not only for the sake of his fellow passengers but also to save the robber himself from the karmic consequences of his horrendous act. In doing so, the negative karma from killing the robber should have accrued to Shakyamuni but it did not. (Victoria, 2006, 225–6)

The suggestion may be that in preserving the lives of many others, then it is possible that a Buddhist is living the positive aspects of the First Precept in preserving life. Buswell and Lopez (2014) suggest that skilful means is extended to include some aspects of what might be perceived to be wrong action:

> Certain texts suggest, however, that an advanced bodhisattva or buddha not only may, but must, break conventional precepts (including monastic vows) if doing so will be beneficial. (871–2)

Though only with reference to 'advanced' beings there might be an area of interpretation that would allow the employment of skilful means when motivated by compassion. Indeed, while advocating non-violence, the Dalai Lama is reported to have said 'in April 2009 ... that 'wrathful forceful action' motivated by compassion, may be 'violence on a physical level' but is 'essentially nonviolence' (Jenkins, 2011).

Conversely, in *Yodhajiva Sutta* a soldier comes to the Buddha and asks him, as he has heard, whether when a soldier dies in battle he is reborn in the realm of the devas. The Buddha avers answering, but when pressed tells the soldier that:

> When a professional warrior strives & exerts himself in battle, his mind is already seized, debased, & misdirected by the thought: 'May these beings be struck down or slaughtered or annihilated or destroyed. May they not exist ... Now, there are two destinations for a person with wrong view, I tell you: either hell or the animal womb.

It would appear that there are different views within Buddhism. The use of violence by soldiers will find its proponents, and its justifications, in the writing of the Buddha. What is clear is that violence towards others motivated by anything other than compassion is wrong. The use of compassion to save others is perhaps justified, but this is not automatic and there is a range of views within Buddhism.

This is not to suggest that the use of violence for reasons other than compassion is not undertaken by Buddhists. Whether these actions could be considered to be Buddhist, or merely unwholesome actions inspired by the Three Poisons, is an area for discussion. This seems to be a particular issue in Myanmar with the persecution of Muslims by the Buddhist majority. One suggestion is that a bhikkhu, Wirathu, has been described as 'The Face of Buddhist Terror' (Beech, 2013). He is accused of preaching anti-Muslim hatred and of inciting violence. He denies inciting violence, but his rhetoric has been used by Buddhists in their targeting of Muslims in Myanmar. Indeed, one Buddhist abbot has suggested:

> He sides a little towards hate ... This is not the way Buddha taught. What the Buddha taught is that hatred is not good, because Buddha sees everyone as an equal being. The Buddha doesn't see people through religion. (Hodal, 2013)

Whatever the truth, Muslims are being persecuted by Buddhists. As with all religions there are actions of its adherents that are out of step with their teachings. This is not an aspect of Buddhism to be focussed upon in the classroom, but neither is it one that should be shied away from if students raise the incongruity of world events.

We have diverted slightly from a discussion of the rights and wrongs of serving as a soldier. That there is an ambiguity of interpretation in discussing the service of a soldier, or violence, in a protective and compassionate means is evident within Buddhism. The question of issues such as abortion and euthanasia raise different issues in the sense that while it may be a compassionate motive, they are not used to prevent the suffering of others (for the most part) but to end the suffering of the 'self'.

Abortion

The issue of abortion may hinge on the issue of whether the foetus is a living being. If it is not, then not all of the five factors are present. The *Maha Tanhasankhaya Sutta* seems to suggest that consciousness or life begins in the womb:

> Monks, the descent of the embryo occurs with the union of three things ... when there is a union of the mother & father, the mother is in her season, and a gandhabba is present, then with this union of three things the descent of the embryo occurs. Then for nine or ten months the mother shelters the embryo in her womb with great anxiety, as a heavy burden.

Gandhabba usually refers to a consciousness ready for rebirth. It appears that the moment of conception brings together these three things in a womb: sperm, egg and gandhabba. Therefore, the embryo is a living being, and as such abortion is condemned in the Vinya and also in the Jataka where a story 'thus refers to abortion-mongers in a hell, along with matricides and adulterers' (Harvey, 2000, 315). It may be, however, that there is a question as to the age of the foetus, Trevor Ling (1969) suggests:

> In general it can be said that in Theravada Buddhist countries the moral stigma which attaches to abortion increases with the size of the foetus. This is an aspect of the general Buddhist notion that the seriousness of the act of taking life increases with the size, complexity and even sanctity of the being whose life is taken. (58)

Damien Keown (1995a), however, suggest that Ling's interpretation is erroneous, and the gradation of size only applies when killing animals, not humans. The skilful means elucidated earlier when a person is able to kill to prevent injury to another, seems to focus the harm towards a perpetrator of injury rather than someone who is not causing harm as in the case of a foetus. Interestingly, this may open up the possibility of allowing an abortion if a mother's life is at risk, as the harm is being 'caused' by the foetus and the suffering of the mother and her imminent death would be avoided. Phillip Lesco (1987) reporting a conversation with Ganden Tri Rinpoche suggests that there is an exception for the saving of a mother's life but not for her mental health:

> If the mother's life is truly endangered by continuation of the pregnancy so that both lives are at stake, it is permissible to abort the foetus. Much less clear is the situation of implied threat to the mother's mental health. Here it is extremely difficult to predict the outcome upon her health and, therefore, aborting the foetus would not be permissible. (217)

As with the taking of life by a soldier, there appears to be a slight diversity of view within Buddhism with regards to abortion. The overwhelming teaching is to protect life; but if it is to be done out of compassion then there will be Buddhists who would accept abortion in certain circumstances.

Euthanasia

Many of the teachings necessary for a discussion of euthanasia have already been discussed with relation to the motivation of compassion and the necessity of preventing further suffering. There are, however, teachings that would suggest that for many Buddhists the use of active euthanasia may be rejected, while elements of compassion may lead to an alternative view. The Dalai Lama (2012) suggests that the state of mind at the time of a person's death is of paramount importance as they prepare to be reborn:

> Since the mind at the time of dying is a proximate cause of the continuation into the next lifetime, it is important to use the mind near the time of death in practice. No matter what has happened in terms of good and bad within this particular lifetime, what happens right around the time of death is particularly powerful. Therefore, it is important to learn about the process of dying and prepare for it. (194)

In some ways this statement could be used to argue both sides of euthanasia. If a person is suffering, then they are unable to prepare themselves, and the circumstances of death would be unfavourable. Whereas, if one is seeking death then this may also be an unfavourable circumstance for death. Damien Keown (1995b) suggests that there is a distinction to be made between 'the person who rejects medical care with the express purpose of ending his life, and the person who resigns himself to the inevitability of death after treatment has failed and the medical resources have been exhausted' (954).

In exploring the acceptance of suitability of euthanasia, many Buddhists would prefer to focus on the compassion that can be expressed to the person while they are living. Groups such as the Buddhist Hospice Trust in the UK seek 'to provide on request, where possible, spiritual friendship and compassionate sharing for those who are seriously ill, dying or bereaved' (Buddhist Hospice Trust, n.d.). The focus is on ensuring that people are able to have a good death, without intervention. However, there is a seeming acceptance of passive euthanasia where treatment is withdrawn. Buddhaghosa suggests:

> If one who is sick ceases to take food with the intention of dying when medicine and nursing care are at hand, he commits a minor offence (dukkata). But in the case of a patient who has suffered a long time with a serious illness the nursing monks may become weary and turn away in despair thinking 'when will we ever cure him of this illness?' Here it is legitimate to decline food and medical care if the patient sees that the monks are worn out and his life cannot be prolonged even with intensive care. (Takakusu & Nagai, 1975, 2:467)

Again, there is ambiguity in Buddhist teaching and practice surrounding euthanasia. The overwhelming injunction is to preserve life, but could skilful means provide jsutification for acting on compassion to end the suffering of a person in this life? This would seem to be dependent on the situation and interpretation of the individual. As, in all circumstances, 'individuals must follow their consciences, which should be informed by reflection on scriptural teachings, custom and tradition, and the opinions of distinguished teachers' (Keown, 1995a, 952).

Vegetarianism

This is perhaps one of the things that people outside of Buddhism know about Buddhist ethics: Buddhists are vegetarian. The question is: are they? The injunction to not kill any living thing is interpreted to extend to all animal life. Saddhatissa (2016) suggests that the underlying philosophy behind this attitude is that of compassion. Buddhists do not consider that man is made in the image of a deity and therefore fundamentally different from other living beings; on the contrary, we consider that man is akin to animals although he represents a higher stage of evolution. Since life is dear to all beings we Buddhists regard even the least significant life to be sacred and therefore try to develop loving kindness to all without limit, preference or prejudice. (94)

The Buddha is seen to condemn the eating of animals (including fish). In the *Mahaparinirvana Sutra* the Buddha is reported to have said:

> I do not permit my sravaka disciples to eat meat ... One who eats meat kills the seed of great compassion. (Page, 2007, 52)

In a Mahayana view, the reports of the Buddha eating meat are explained as skilful means:

> In order to save beings, he shows [pretends] that he eats meat. Though he [seems to] eat meat, in actual fact he does not. O good man! Such a Bodhisattva does not even take pure food. How could he eat meat? (*Mahaparinirvana Sutra*, Page, 2007, 53)

There is, however, ambiguity across the traditions of Buddhism. Earlier it was noted that the punishment for a bhikkhu killing a human was expulsion. The punishment for the killing of a living being, other than a person, is 'expiation' or the making of amends, suggesting a distinction between human life and other forms of life. There is less karmic consequence for the killing of animals than there is for humans, suggesting that the prohibition is not complete. In *Sihasenapativatthu* the Buddha is reported to have accepted that even bhikkhus may be able to eat meat if offered:

> One should not knowingly consume meat made [killed] for the sake of a monk. Whoever should consume it: an offense of wrong doing. I allow fish and meat that is pure in three respects: One has not seen, heard, or suspected (that it was killed on purpose for a monk).

Therefore, if an animal has been killed already, but not specifically for the bhikkhu, then they can eat what is offered. Interestingly, despite the seeming prohibition of eating meat in Mahayana, the Dalai Lama is mostly vegetarian, meaning that 'His Holiness's kitchen in Dharamsala is vegetarian. However, during visits outside of Dharamsala, His Holiness is not necessarily vegetarian' (Routine Day, n.d.). One Buddhist has expressed the nuanced view of vegetarianism within Buddhism:

> We are aware that all life is connected and we are sustained by each other and the planet. So respect for life is part of that. We all have karma and whether I was a cow in my past life or a Pharaoh I've no idea, but I'm as grateful to any animal for letting me sustain my life as I would a grain of rice. Next time perhaps the animal that sustained me might be reborn as a human who knows. In Nichiren Buddhism all beings have buddha nature but to sustain life we all have a part to play. I think the attitude is the important

thing I certainly feel less cruel conditions for animals are important and that should be taken into account. But as I say that's where I am now. Another person who practices my particular form of Buddhism may completely disagree with eating animals and that's entirely up to them.

Building on the First Precept and the compassion that should be evident for all living things, it would appear that vegetarianism is an aspiration. Many Buddhists will adopt a vegetarian lifestyle, but it is not as prescribed as perhaps teachers in the classroom are used to teaching.

The Second Precept

In the *Brahmajala Sutta* it is recorded:

> Abandoning the taking of what is not given, the contemplative Gotama abstains from taking what is not given. He takes only what is given, accepts only what is given, lives not by stealth but by means of a self that has become pure.

Although focussed on stealing, there are many extensions to this precept of only taking that which is freely given. The prohibitions can extend to cheating, gambling and receiving things to which a person is not entitled. The consequences of gambling are outlined in the *Sigalovada Sutta*:

> There are, young householder, these six evil consequences in indulging in gambling:
>
> **(i)** the winner begets hate,
> **(ii)** the loser grieves for lost wealth,
> **(iii)** loss of wealth,
> **(iv)** his word is not relied upon in a court of law,
> **(v)** he is despised by his friends and associates,
> **(vi)** he is not sought after for matrimony; for people would say he is a gambler and is not fit to look after a wife.

The impact that such deceptions have on a person's character lead to them not being trusted, and being subject to greed and desire, and causing the degradation of others.

Within Zen the idea of stealing has been expanded to include other aspects of life such as 'The theft of time ... Yamamoto Gempo Roshi used to call this kind of stealing the greatest felony of all' (Aitken, 1984, 28). I think it can also be expanded to include a discussion of social justice and also environmentalism.

Social justice

Inherent in stealing, taking that which is not yours, is taking more than is your share. This may be a stretch to an extent, but when the positive aspect of this Precept is considered, the opposite of dana or generosity is selfishness. Aitken (1984) suggests that:

our slums and skid rows are clear symptoms of an economy that is manipulated here and abroad to provide a base of unemployment so that competition for jobs will keep wages at a minimum, and stockholders will realize maximum profits. The natural world is exploited for short-term benefit to a 'fortunate' minority, while other people, animals, plants, and the earth organism itself suffer. (30)

This links, very much, with the values and goals of Engaged Buddhism. Utilizing Thich Nhat Hanh's (2017a) Fourteen Principles, it is possible to highlight some that directly link with social justice and the alleviation of suffering:

> 4. Do not avoid contact with suffering or close your eyes before suffering. Do not lose awareness of the existence of suffering in the life of the world. Find ways to be with those who are suffering, including personal contact, visits, images, and sounds. By such means, awaken yourself and others to the reality of suffering in the world.
> 5. Do not accumulate wealth while millions are hungry. Do not take as the aim of your life Fame, profit, wealth, or sensual pleasure. Live simply and share time, energy, and material resources with those who are in need...
> 10. Do not use the Buddhist community for personal gain or profit, or transform your community into a political party. A religious community, however, should take a clear stand against oppression and injustice and should strive to change the situation without engaging in partisan conflicts...
> 13. Possess nothing that should belong to others. Respect the property of others, but prevent others from profiting from human suffering or the suffering of other species on Earth.

This call to ensure that all have sufficient for their needs, rather than the accumulation of wealth for the self, lies at the heart of the Buddha's message. Just as asceticism and hedonism were rejected, so extreme wealth and poverty should be avoided. A Buddhist can always give of themselves if they do not have money or resources to alleviate the suffering of others. This is motivated by compassion and loving kindness. Just as bodhisattvas are moved by compassion for the plight of all beings, this is an ideal that all Buddhists should be working towards.

Oftentimes in classrooms the focus is on the headline catching ethical issues such as abortion, but the far more pressing issues for the world are social justice and the environment (see further on). The exploration of the work of Engaged Buddhism, and Buddhism more widely in seeking for social justice, is central to the virtues that Buddhism teaches.

Environmentalism

When deciding where to include environmentalism in a discussion of Buddhist ethics, there are arguments to include it in the First Precept or the Second Precept. The damage that humanity is doing to the planet is 'killing' the environment in terms of the destruction of habitats, trees, animals and all manner of living things. This is often due to the greed of humans in stripping the planet of its natural resources. In so doing, global warming is a reality and there are threats to all living things. As such, and to repeat aspects of the Fourteen Principles of Engaged Buddhism, Buddhists are to 'live simply' and to prevent the 'suffering of other species'. This can only be done through a Buddhist environmentalism. Within Buddhism, responsibility for the earth has not been given by some deity, but is the result of the interconnectedness of all things, indeed, Thich Nhat Hanh (1998b) has suggested that 'harming nature is harming ourselves, and vice versa' (41).

There is a suggestion that because the environment is a 'modern' concern it does not form part of Buddhist ethics. The argument is that people in the modern world are erroneously trying to apply teachings such as the interdependent nature of all things, and the buddha-nature, in ways that were never intended to justify an environmental activism. Many would reject this as a narrow view of Buddhism, which is a worldview that can meet the challenges of the modern world. One activity and movement that has adopted activities to highlight the issues facing the environment is the Thai tree ordination movement. With the concern around deforestation in Thailand some monks symbolically ordain trees and because 'Buddhist monks are held with such high esteem in Thai culture, these rituals stop the destruction of trees' (Fuller, 2022, 102). This is just a small example, and it would appear that there is an attempt to more closely link Buddhist teaching and environmental ethics, that can have a significant impact on the natural world:

> The seed of environmental ethics is contained in Buddhist literature and nurturing this can lead to a philosophy of nature which is bound to have a profound effect on the protection of natural resources and of nature as a whole. (Sahni, 2007, 1)

It might be a surprise to students to learn of an ambiguity in Buddhist approaches to the environment. It would be interesting to explore the plurality of views within Buddhism, and how beliefs expressed in the past are being interpreted today, and how they can lead to an engaged Buddhism that cares for the environment.

The Third Precept

In the *Brahmajala Sutta* it is recorded:

> Abandoning uncelibacy, the contemplative Gotama lives a celibate life, aloof, refraining from the sexual act that is the villager's way.

For a lay precept the restriction does not extend just to celibacy but includes sexual misconduct. This is an ambiguous term, especially in the modern world. Sexual misconduct is a contextual, cultural and societal norm. It could be seen that any sexual conduct that causes harm (linked with the First Precept) would be rejected. It is, therefore, self-evident that any kind of sexual assault or coercion is to be rejected and avoided. This has become an important topic in Buddhist communities across the globe, in a world where the power dynamics involved in sexual relationships are an important part of consent and misconduct. Buddhist communities have not been immune to this, and it is important to note elements of this within the classroom as appropriate. Ann Gleig and Amy Langenberg (2021) suggest that for older students 'the ethical complexities surrounding consent and power inequity in cases of sexual violation are particularly alive for ... students, who often possess a rich if vernacular language for describing sexual violence' (2021, 146). This is a sensitive area, and teachers should approach topics with care and consider whether such elements are appropriate for the maturity and experiences of the class.

Also condemned by the Buddha in the *Parabhava Sutta* is adultery:

> Not satisfied with one's own wives, he is seen among the whores and the wives of others – this is the cause of his downfall.

In the fourth century the definition of sexual misconduct was explained by Vasubandhu in his *Abhidharmakosabhasyam*:

1. Intercourse with a forbidden woman, that is, the wife of another, one's mother, one's daughter or one's paternal or maternal relations;
2. Intercourse with one's own wife through a forbidden orifice;
3. Intercourse in an unsuitable place: an uncovered spot, a shrine or forest;
4. Intercourse at an unsuitable time: when the wife is pregnant, when she is nursing or when she has taken a vow. Some say: when she has taken a vow only with the consent of her husband (Pruden, 1992, 651–2).

The assumption here would appear to be that sexual activity is between a man and a woman, between a husband and a wife. There are examples in the Vinaya of restrictions against sexual contact with *pandakas* (translations vary but usually include men who engage in same-sex relationships, or inter-sex people) and sexual activity that did not involve the vagina. It could be suggested that these were reflective of the societal norms of the time. There are further condemnations of same-sex relationships:

> Likewise, endless varieties of punishments in a future life are described for the wrong deed of sexual intercourse between two men. The one who commits misconduct with boys sees boys being swept away in the Acid River who cry out to him, and owing to the suffering and pain born of his deep affection for them, plunges in after them. (*Saddharma-smrtyupasthana Sutra*)

This approach to same-sex relationships as an example of sexual misconduct has also been re-stated by the Dalai Lama:

> Something may be considered improper in terms of organs, time, and place – when sexual relations involve inappropriate parts of the body, or when they occur at an unsuitable

time or place. These are the terms Buddhists use to describe sexual misconduct. The inappropriate parts of the body are the mouth and the anus, and sexual intercourse involving those parts of the body, whether with a man or a woman, is considered sexual misconduct. Masturbation as well. (Dalai Lama, 1996, 46)

This again could be a reflection of the cultural context within which the Dalai Lama lived and taught. Nearly twenty years later the Dalai Lama seemed to have changed his views when he suggested that 'if two people, a couple, really feel that way, it's more practical, more satisfaction, and both sides fully agree, then okay!' (Molloy, 2014). Paul Fuller (2022) notes these attitudes throughout history and currently; indeed, he suggests that the Dalai Lama still sees same-sex relationships as misconduct. He recognizes that these attitudes are most likely a result of cultural norms rather than being based on the Buddha's teachings.

In this context it is possible to suggest that in today's society that Buddhists should adopt a more accepting attitude towards same-sex relationships. Master Hsin Yun has reflected this attitude:

> People often ask me what I think about homosexuality. They wonder, is it right, is it wrong? The answer is, it is neither right nor wrong. It is just something that people do. If people are not harming each other, their private lives are their own business; we should be tolerant of them and not reject them. (Sujato, 2012b)

Adopting this approach to Buddhism draws on different aspects of Buddhist teachings; that of compassion and loving kindness, and also the idea that that which is harmful should be avoided. In terms of compassion and loving kindness, many Buddhists would suggest that adopting homophobic attitudes would cause suffering to those with same-sex attraction and in relationships. Although many may see the celibate lifestyle of a bhikkhu or bhikkhuni to be preferable, if that is not adopted then there is no more harm inherent in a same-sex than a heterosexual relationship. The thing that makes something 'wrong' is the harm or suffering that it causes. When Thich Nhat Hanh (2014) explores the positive aspect of this precept it is with regard to 'True Love'. It is interesting that his explanation does not refer to specific sexual activity but the intention behind it:

> Knowing that sexual desire is not love, and that sexual activity motivated by craving always harms myself as well as others, I am determined not to engage in sexual relations without true love and a deep, long-term commitment made known to my family and friends ... am committed to learning appropriate ways to take care of my sexual energy and to cultivating loving kindness, compassion, joy, and inclusiveness – which are the four basic elements of true love – for my greater happiness and the greater happiness of others. (61–2)

Compassion and loving kindness should lie at the heart of sexual relationships, rather than greed, desire and attachment. As with the other aspects of the Five Precepts, the intention of the Buddhist in their actions is paramount. However, this is an area that is developing within Buddhism and it should be noted when we teach that there are different attitudes within Buddhism.

The Fourth Precept

In the *Brahmajala Sutta* it is recorded:

> Abandoning false speech, the contemplative Gotama abstains from false speech. He speaks the truth, holds to the truth, is firm, reliable, no deceiver of the world.

In subsequent elements of the sutta, divisive speech, abusive speech and idle chatter are similarly condemned. There are consequences for the person who participates in speech that is harmful. For an individual Buddhist it would seem self-evident that a person should refrain from any conversation or words that would cause harm to others, whether it is true or otherwise. Again, the intention behind the words is important. Are they designed to build up or to tear down?

There is, however, ambiguity in what constitutes harmful speech if it is determined by the intention behind it. Hurtful speech could be used to warn people of the wrongness of their actions, or it might be used in a way to protect others who are vulnerable. In some ways words and their interpretation are open to the whim of the speaker and the hearer. The motivation of compassion and loving kindness can lead to expressions that some may find offensive. Paul Fuller (2022) in his discussion of ethnocentric engaged Buddhism suggests some reasons that might motivate 'violence' which could also be seen to include rhetoric that is violent. These reasons or motivating situations for condemnation include:

- the idea that the dharma might be disappearing
- the idea that Buddhist identity is under threat
- the concern that Buddhism needs protecting (see 149).

The compassion for Buddhists might lead to action. Indeed, Wirathu suggests that this is his motivation behind the divisive rhetoric that he uses against Muslims:

> I am defending my loved one ... like you would defend your loved one. I am only warning people about Muslims. Consider it like if you had a dog, that would bark at strangers coming to your house – it is to warn you. I am like that dog. I bark. (Oppenheim, 2017)

Fuller (2022) recognizes the danger and possible offense that using examples from Myanmar may cause. Suggesting that some people will argue that 'Engaged Buddhism is compassionate in nature, and the subjects described ... describe an enraged or angry form of Buddhism' (142). This is the breadth that a worldviews approach to teaching religion brings. The 'mainstream' and perhaps 'authentic' expression of Buddhism focuses on the avoidance of language that is harmful and divisive, but there are individuals for whom offensive rhetoric is an expression of what they feel to be right. It would be very interesting in the classroom for students to explore the teachings of the Buddha and how they are reflected in the speech of Buddhists. This kind of activity helps students understand the cultural influence on the living of a religion.

As with all the precepts there is a positive aspect to their living rather than just avoiding the negative:

> I am committed to cultivating loving speech and compassionate listening in order to relieve suffering and to promote reconciliation and peace in myself and among other people, ethnic and religious groups, and nations. Knowing that words can create happiness or suffering, I am committed to speaking truthfully, using words that inspire confidence, joy, and hope. (Hanh, 2014, 79)

A Buddhists speech must be motivated by insight and loving kindness. This finds its expression in the kind and truthful words that people speak with one another.

The Fifth Precept

In the *Sigolavada Sutta* the dangers of intoxicants are recorded:

> There are, young householder, these six evil consequences in indulging in intoxicants which cause infatuation and heedlessness:
>
> **(i)** loss of wealth,
> **(ii)** increase of quarrels,
> **(iii)** susceptibility to disease,
> **(iv)** earning an evil reputation,
> **(v)** shameless exposure of body,
> **(vi)** weakening of intellect.

The use of alcohol particularly is forbidden by this Precept. It is seen to have a deleterious impact on those who break it. One story from Mongolia warns of the dangers of breaking the Fifth Precept. A Buddhist lama (spiritual master) was travelling among the nomadic tribes. The people would give him food and lodging in exchange for his blessings. One evening he was offered lodging by a young woman who lived alone. She made it conditional that he would have to do one of three things: sacrifice a goat, sleep with his hostess or drink alcohol. He decided on the last of these options, thinking that drinking alcohol was the least harmful of the three. One drink led to another, however, and before long he was drunk. In this state, the sound of the goat started to annoy him so much that he went out and killed it, and when he woke up the next morning he found he had been to bed with the hostess! Whatever the truth of this story it is evident that it can have negative impacts. Though for some Buddhists the prohibition is about becoming intoxicated rather than partaking of small amounts.

Tobacco does not seem to be covered by the Fifth Precept, maybe because it was not known by the Buddha, or maybe it is because of the focus on the clouding of the mind rather than its negative impact on a person's health. Thich Nhat Hanh (2014) suggests that the avoidance on things that distract and consume the mind are what this Precept is about:

> I am determined not to gamble, or to use alcohol, drugs, or any other products which contain toxins, such as certain websites, electronic games, TV programs, films, magazines, books, and conversations. I will practice coming back to the present moment to be in touch with the refreshing, healing, and nourishing elements in me and around me, not letting regrets and sorrow drag me back into the past nor letting anxieties, fear, or craving pull me out of the present moment. (103)

The positive aspect of this Precept can focus on the clarity of mind provided by mindfulness and meditation, and therefore that which seeks to cloud the mind should be avoided.

The role of women

In the *Soma Sutta* the bhikkhuni, Soma, is tempted by Mara when he questions her ability as a woman.

> Then Mara the Wicked, wanting to make the nun Soma feel fear, terror, and goosebumps, wanting to make her fall away from immersion, went up to her and addressed her in verse:

> That state's very challenging;
> it's for the sages to attain.
> It's not possible for a woman,
> with her two-fingered wisdom.

> Then Soma, knowing that this was Mara the Wicked, replied to him in verse:

> What difference does womanhood make
> when the mind is serene,
> and knowledge is present
> as you rightly discern the Dhamma.
> Surely someone who might think:
> 'I am woman', or 'I am man',
> or 'I am' anything at all,
> is fit for Mara to address.

This highlights the truth within Buddhism that there is no fixed self, and that if a person becomes attached to concepts such as gender they are missing the point that they are merely perception. Therefore it could be suggested that many Buddhists would see a complete equality of women. This does not, however, tell the whole story.

Buddhism, as with any religion, is susceptible to cultural norms, which throughout history have been fairly patriarchal. It may not have meant the subjugation of women at different points but possibly a marginalization or an erasing of the female voice from events and discourse.

The inclusion of women within the ordained sangha since the time of the Buddha is often pointed to as an indicator of the full equality of women since the beginning; indeed, it has been described as 'a radical experiment for its time' (Murcott, 1991, 4). While this is true, and the inclusion of a female sangha would have been radical for the time, the process through which it came about reinforces elements of the societal view of women that was present at the time. Following the death of her husband, and the Buddha's father, Mahapajapati Gotami requested ordination into the sangha three times. Each time she asked the Buddha refused. After the Buddhist had left to go to Vesali, Mahapajapati Gotami cut her hair, donned yellow robes and walked the one hundred and fifty miles to see the Buddha. After such a long walk she arrived to see the Buddha with swollen feet and dirty. Crying she stood outside waiting to see the Buddha when she was approached by Ananda, who queried her dishevelled state. Ananda intervened on her behalf and requested that she be ordained; the Buddha again refused three times.

> So Ananda put the request in a different way. Respectfully he questioned the Buddha, 'Lord, are women capable of realising the various stages of sainthood as nuns?'
> 'They are, Ananda,' said the Buddha.
> 'If that is so, Lord, then it would be good if women could be ordained as nuns,' said Ananda, encouraged by the Buddha's reply.
> 'If, Ananda, Maha Pajapati Gotami would accept the Eight Conditions it would be regarded that she has been ordained already as a nun.'
> When Ananda mentioned the conditions to Maha Pajapati Gotami, she gladly agreed to abide by those conditions and automatically became a nun. Before long she attained arahantship. The other Sakyan ladies who were ordained with her also attained Arahantship. (Buddhanet, 2008)

It would appear that the Buddha was reticent to ordain women. The reason for this in unclear; some suggest that it is because the life of a bhikkhuni would be extremely difficult, or that he was merely testing Gotami to see if she was truly determined. However, on the ordination of women, the Buddha is reported to have taught that his dharma would no longer last in the world for a thousand years; rather it would only last for five hundred years. Despite this, many women are praised in the teachings of the Buddha; these include:

- Khema for her wisdom
- Dhmmadinna for her teaching of the dharma
- Bhaddakaccana for her great insight

There are many others, including Yasodhara, the wife of the Buddha, who was ordained at the same time as her mother-in-law.

There are also indications that elements of a woman's role outside of the ordained sangha are somewhat relational. The *Mallika Sutta* tells of a conversation between the Buddha and King Pasenadi, who is disappointed at the birth of his daughter:

> Well, some women are better than men,
> O ruler of the people.
> Wise and virtuous,
> a devoted wife who honours her mother in law.
> And when she has a son,
> he becomes a hero, O lord of the land.
> The son of such a blessed lady
> may even rule the realm.

On the one hand, women are of infinite worth, while on the other hand they are of this worth because of her abilities as a wife and a mother. Again, this is perhaps countercultural for his time, but today it seems somewhat archaic to many Buddhists. It does, however, provide a justification for expanding the rights and role of women within a society that is now more accepting.

It is important in the classroom to utilize examples of women who have been important for the development of Buddhism, while also being honest and recognizing some of the challenges that have been faced throughout history. In reclaiming a feminist lens it is important for Buddhists and teachers to challenge elements of patriarchy and reinforce the teachings of the Buddha that can support the full inclusion of women. This will, perhaps, mean challenging some of the cultural norms still evident within society. It will be important to explore whether aspects of the narrative that perpetuates are cultural accretions, or truths that cannot be overcome. Naomi Appleton (2011) highlights that within Theravada, while a woman is able to attain arahantship, they are unable to be a bodhisattva (in the Theravada understanding), as is shown through the Jataka tales, that once the decision is made, rebirth as woman is impossible. Similarly, in some forms of Mahayana, 'a woman must become a man before becoming a Buddha. Stories of magical sex change that comment upon the illusory nature of gender exist in some of the most influential Mahayana texts' (34). While on the other hand there are lines of female *lamas/tulkus:*

- In the fifteenth century CE, the bodhisattva/buddha Vajravarahi was seen to have been reborn as Princess Chokyi-dronme who was known as Samding Dorje Phagmo. She was the first of a line of tulkus that continue today.

- In the late nineteenth century Shugseb Jetsun Rinpoche was acknowledged as a tulku.

As was noted earlier on, however, there still continues to be obstacles to the widespread ordination of women (see Chapter 6), which could be seen to be based on the cultural norms of such places. A similar example in the UK occurred when Christmas Humphreys requested a Zen teacher but when Jiyu Kennett was nominated (a British female Zen roshi), Humphreys refused her, asking instead for a male, Japanese teacher.

While the teachings of Buddhism can be used to articulate a radical feminism, it would appear that some do not think that this is the conclusion that Buddhism leads to. This could be because of interpretation of teachings, or it could be because of the cultural context within which Buddhism flourishes. There have been movements in recent years, but Byrne (2012) issues a warning to those who immediately equate Buddhism with gender equality:

> Essentially my argument is that Feminist Buddhologists run the risk of overemphasizing the egalitarian teachings of the Buddha at the expense of adequately addressing the misogyny and discrimination against women that can be found both textually and practically in Buddhist traditions. (181)

In exploring a feminist approach to Buddhism, both strands need to be engaged with in the classroom.

Thoughts for the classroom

In this chapter we have only touched on elements of some ethical issues. There are many issues in the modern world that have not been explored; issues such as abortion, euthanasia, environmentalism and vegetarianism. This does not mean that others are not important, but that the ones that are included are indicative of the way that Buddhists strive to make ethical decisions. Their approaches to ethics are drawn from the underpinning beliefs that are described in the rest of the book. What is notable, however, is the issue of interpretation. In most of the issues explored there is scope for personal decision making, and this must be based on a person's interpretation of how best to show wisdom and compassion. Within vegetarianism and same-sex relationships we have seen that there are views on both sides, and they raise issues for conceptions of authority and interpretation. It is important in exploring many ethical issues to recognize the differing worldviews and cultural contexts among Buddhists around the globe. Some 'traditional' Buddhists who like the status quo use interpretive lenses from that cultural perspective, whereas younger, and perhaps more Westernized, Buddhists view Buddhism through their own lenses. Maybe within Buddhism there is room for both approaches, but the importance of recognizing the deeply held views of others is paramount in gaining understanding.

9

Authority and diversity in the Buddhist world

At the end of the Introduction to this book we listed a number of Buddhist traditions that are to be found within the UK. In some ways these only scratch the surface as there are many 'non-sectarian' groups as well as groups who meet around Buddhist principles in people's homes. Throughout the remainder of the book up until this point both Mahayana and Theravada traditions and sources have been mentioned and drawn upon. It is important to note this twofold presentation (or threefold if we include Vajrayana as we did earlier [see Introduction]) but it is not the whole story. In this chapter we will explore a variety of different traditions that can be found in the UK and around the world. As this task is undertaken it is important to note the concept of authority in each and whether that authority can be extended beyond that particular tradition. It is interesting that there are many teachings and beliefs that go across the various Buddhisms, and the approach of this book in articulating some of the central concepts of the dhamma has been to utilize a range of writers who are drawn from different traditions with the understanding that they can help articulate what certain things may mean for many Buddhists. Examples include Thanissaro Bhikkhu who would be identified with the Theravada tradition, whereas the Dalai Lama is from Tibetan Buddhism, and Thich Nhat Hanh would fall within Zen. It will not be possible to identify every tradition or individual worldview that expresses Buddhism in this chapter, but hopefully in identifying some of the larger groups a better understanding of the diversity within Buddhism can be developed.

Before exploring three traditions to be found within the UK and beyond it is important to note two things:

1. The history, presence and development of Buddhism within the UK will be explored in much greater detail in Chapter 10.

2. In light of the Series Editor's Foreword alongside the Introduction to this book (see earlier on) to outline the various traditions is to miss the rich diversity of individual worldviews that will be a panoply of different approaches to, and across, Buddhism. There will be individuals who utilize selected aspects of more recognized organized worldviews. The presentation further on is not to negate this worldviews approach, but

the delineations do exist and it will be useful to establish them to enable a context to the worldviews of individuals.

The three chosen ones are not to suggest that this is the limit of expressions found within the UK. There are many more to be found. The three chosen ones of Soka Gakkai International, New Kadampa Tradition and Triratna develop existing understandings raised by more 'traditional' expressions of Theravada and Mahayana Buddhism. Each, in their own way, has shown a development of Buddhism for the modern world. They also claim large membership in the UK and as such are fairly vocal in the Buddhist groups around the country.

Nichiren Buddhism

Within the UK there are various groups from the Nichiren tradition including Soka Gakkai International UK, Nichiren Shu UK, Rissho Kosei-kai UK and Nichiren Shoshu Hokkeko. There are various differences between each of these groups, but all trace lineage to Nichiren, a thirteenth-sentury Buddhist teacher who is believed by many to have been a bodhisattva. The largest of the Nichiren traditions is Soka Gakkai International; as such this section will explore the teachings and beliefs that seem to be consistent across the traditions and then will explore specifically Soka Gakkai International.

Nichiren, as already mentioned, was a Buddhist teacher in thirteenth-century Japan. From about the age of twelve (approximately 1233) Nichiren studied at Mount Hiei in Kyoto, and other temples in Japan, as part of Tendai Buddhism, as well as studying aspects of Pure Land Buddhism. In his study of Pure Land Buddhism he understood through the teachings of Shinran that 'a single recitation of *namu amida butsu* ('Homage to Amitabha Buddha') ensured rebirth in the pure land of Amitabha' (Lopez, 2015b, 637). Within Tendai Buddhism he also found a tradition that established the *Lotus Sutra* as the pre-eminent teaching, and that all other sutras were examples of the Buddha's skilful means in establishing 'provisional teachings tailored for specific audiences' (Lopez, 2015b, 638).

On 28 April 1253 Nichiren returned to his home temple at Seicho-ji. Here he was to reflect on his twenty years of study and meditation. On the summit of Mount Kiyosumi, Nichiren made his first public declaration of *Namu Myoho Renge Kyo* ('Devotion to the Mystic Law of the Lotus Sutra' or 'Glory to the Dharma of the Lotus Sutra') establishing one of the central tenets of Nichiren Buddhism.

Just as Shinran had suggested the chanting of Amitabha's name could ensure rebirth in the Pure Land, Nichiren established the Lotus Sutra and the chanting of *Namu Myoho Renge Kyo* as the way to attain freedom from rebirth. Everything was now to be focussed on the teachings of the *Lotus Sutra*; his declaration of the *Lotus Sutra* was the reason that Shakyamuni Buddha had come to earth; Nichiren outlined this in *Kanjinhonzonshø*:

I can say that the Buddha appeared in this world not for the people on Mount Grdhrakuta during the last eight years of his teaching. The Buddha appeared in this world for the people who live in the Age of the Right Teachings of the Buddha, the Age of the Counterfeit of the Right Teachings of the Buddha, and the Age of Degeneration. Furthermore, I can say that the Buddha appeared in this world not for the people who lived in the two thousand years from the beginning of the Age of the Right Teachings of the Buddha to the end of the Age of the Counterfeit of the Right Teachings of the Buddha but for people like me, who live at the beginning of the Age of Degeneration. (Senchu, 2003, 108)

For Nichiren, the 'Hinayana' and the preliminary Mahayana practised since the time of the Buddha had been emblematic of the counterfeit teachings of the Buddha. It was only the *Lotus Sutra* that would bring people to liberation.

Stone (2003) has suggested that the pronouncing of *Namu Myoho Renge Kyo*, the refocussing of Tendai, the rejection of Pure Land and the divisions that ultimately led to the establishment of Nichiren Buddhism 'were probably more complex and unfolded over a longer time' than is suggested by the pronunciation outlined earlier on (246). Nichiren was driven from or unable to stay at Seicho-ji because of the divisions being caused. His rhetoric can be seen to be polemic as he rejected the Pure Land and condemned some of the practices of Tendai Buddhism despite their focus on the *Lotus Sutra*. He moved to Kamakura and lived at Matsubagayatsu. Here he attracted followers and patrons, and his teachings began to spread.

Nichiren allied the 'degeneration' of Buddhism with some of the calamities that affected Japan. He found himself angering the ruling elites of Japan, as they refused to acquiesce to his teachings and a return to pure Buddhism. As a result of his teaching he was exiled to Izu where he continued his study and writing. It was here that he established his 'five principles' (*gogi*) that establishes the pre-eminence of the *Lotus Sutra*.

> It sets five standards from which to evaluate the depth or shallowness and the superiority or inferiority of all the Buddhist doctrines originated from the Buddha, these five standards being the teaching (of the sutra), the propensity (the spiritual endowments of the learner), the time (the demands of the age), the country (where the doctrine is practised), and the order (before and after the propagation of the doctrine or the preceding doctrine under which the doctrines were practised). Nichiren concluded from those five standards, that the Hokke (Lotus) Sutra was the superior one. (Nakamura, 1964, 396)

Space does not allow for a full biography of Nichiren; however, his denunciation of Buddhist practice within Japan, exiles, opposition and the gathering of followers continued at a brisk pace throughout his life. As the focus on the *Lotus Sutra* grew, Nichiren became identified with a figure from the text, Bodhisattva Superior Conduct, who was the leader of the bodhisattvas who appeared from beneath the earth when the Buddha gave the Lotus Sutra on Eagle's Peak.

Soka Gakkai International UK

Nichiren continued in various guises and schools within Japan, but we first fast forward to 1928 and the conversion of two educators, Tsunesaburo Makiguchi and Josei Toda, to Nichiren Buddhism. In November 1930 they published the first volume Soka Kyoikugaku Taikei (*The System of Value-Creating Pedagogy*). They saw Nichiren as a way to reform education and, also, provide social justice within society. Accused of sedition for refusing to place a Shinto amulet in homes and temples, Makiguchi, Toda and other leaders of Soka Gakkai were imprisoned. Makiguchi died in prison, but when Toda was released he began a series of activities including speeches and fundraising to prepare for the re-establishment of Soka Gakkai; this took place in 1951. Soka Gakkai engaged in proselytization and it quickly grew. Soka Gakkai is dedicated to 'developing the positive human potentialities for individual happiness and for global peace and prosperity' (SGI, 1996, 2).

> Daisaku Ikeda (b. 1928) ... became president in 1960, founded Soka Gakkai International in 1975 and expanded SGI into a worldwide movement as a lay branch of Nichiren Shoshu Buddhism. (Bluck, 2006, 89)

In the early 1960s it was introduced into the UK when businessmen who had worked in Japan returned with Japanese wives who were members of Soka Gakkai (Wilson, 2000: 355). Wilson (2000) sees the growth of Soka Gakkai in Britain as being a reaction against the traditional beliefs and practices that were no longer seen to be able to meet the needs of the modern world. Buddhism, and Soka Gakkai, met this need. In 2022, Soka Gakkai UK reported that there over 620 local groups across the UK and a membership of over 14,000. Some see it as the largest Buddhist group.

Earlier it was indicated that Soka Gakkai is a lay branch of Nichiren, and Stephen Batchelor (1994) suggested that it is 'the largest lay religious organization in the world' (150). This is as a result of a conflict with wider Nichiren Shoshu. For the most part, there had been cordial, or at least polite relationships between Nichiren shoshu and Soka Gakkai until in 1991 when Soka Gakkai were excommunicated by the Nichiren Shoshu. The disagreements came to a head surrounding the issues of leadership, the role of priests and the laity, and 'the organizational problem of a small provincial priestly order suddenly growing into a mammoth national and international community of believers.' Nichiren Shoshu has the ordained leaders and as such 'claims that it is the sole custodian of religious authority and dogma, while the Soka Gakkai leadership argues that the sacred writings of Nichiren, not the priesthood, represent the ultimate source of authority, and that any individual with deep faith in Nichiren's teachings can gain enlightenment without the assistance of a priest' (Metraux, 1992, 326). The origins seem to be a question of authority. Should a lay organization be subject to the ordained members of the community?

One notable practice is the chanting or repetition of *Nam-myoho- renge-kyo* (Glory to the Dharma of the Lotus Sutra). This phrase, as well as being repeated, is written on a gohonzon (see Figure 9.1), and repetition takes place in front of it:

Figure 9.1 Gohonzon.
Source: Crazysigns, CC BY-SA 3.0 https://creativecommons.org/licenses/by-sa/3.0.

It is most readily understood as a symbol of ultimate reality, a mandala or map of the spiritual forces of the universe, which was devised by Nichiren himself. The most prominent feature of a gohonzon is an inscription in calligraphy of the phrase 'Nam-myoho- renge-kyo,' which is surrounded by signs for bodhisattvas and lesser deities drawn from Japanese traditions. The gohonzon is not an icon or a sacred image in the conventional sense of the terms but an abstract representation of Buddha as a universal essence or principle. (Seager, 2006, 33)

One Buddhist has described her acts of devotion:

I sit in front of my Buddhist altar and I recite two chapters of the Lotus Sutra as well as chanting the phrase Nam MyoHo Renge kyo (the sutras title) until I feel refreshed and invigorated.

It is also indicative of the ability to practice Buddhism and realize one's own buddha-nature without a priest. When a person chants the Daimoku (Nam-myoho- renge-kyo) they purify the area around the gohonzon, which then becomes the Kaidan (which is believed to be the high sanctuary of Buddhism). The high sanctuary or Kaidan in Nichiren Shoshu believe this has been erected at the foot of Mount Fuji. As such, the priests control access to it.

Other aspects of Soka Gakkai which set it apart from other traditions of Buddhism surround the establishment of three themes as its focus in its charter:

- Peace
- Culture
- Education (see Lebron, 2012).

These three aspects have been central to their work around the world. Soka Gakkai International has promoted petitions and activities that have raised the promotion of peace, established schools in different countries and sponsor arts programmes and performances. This can be seen to be a part of their desire to share their teachings but also represent key aspects of Buddhist belief.

Soka Gakkai has sometimes been described a going beyond Theravada and Mahayana, and as such could be a different way of perceiving Buddhism and taking refuge in the sangha. Authority is not through the ordained members of the community but through the seeking within to discover the buddha-nature.

The New Kadampa Tradition

In 1991 the New Kadampa Tradition was founded by Tibetan monk Kelsang Gyatso in a split from wider Tibetan Buddhism. Kelsang Gyatso felt that elements of Tibetan Buddhism were becoming too syncretistic under the guidance of the Dalai Lama; he felt that the teachings of Tsongkhapa, the fifteenth-sentury founder of Gelugpa, was a pure form of Buddhism. It was felt that his message, and therefore the message of Buddhism, did not need diluting or shifting to accommodate Western practices and sensibilities. Rather than draw on aspects of other traditions of Buddhism, Gyatso felt that the message and practices should remain undiluted. The New Kadampa Tradition website highlights the applicability of this message to the modern day:

> Modern Kadampa Buddhism is a special, practical presentation of Buddha's teachings that is particularly suited to the modern day. It was introduced into contemporary society by the world-renowned meditation master and scholar Venerable Geshe Kelsang Gyatso Rinpoche.
> Modern Kadampa Buddhism preserves the meaning and intention of Buddha's original teachings while presenting them in a clear and systematic way that anyone of any nationality, age or gender can easily understand and put into practice. (NKT-IBU, 2022b)

It has been further observed that:

> The organisation is not simply maintaining that it represents Buddhism adapted for westerners; it is also striving to underline its separation from the Tibetan Gelug sect and emphasize the point that the West – via the NKT – is now the guardian and custodian of the pure tradition of Tsongkhapa in the modern world. From a NKT viewpoint, Geshe Kelsang has played a unique role in the transmission of Tsongkhapa's pure teachings, and the organisation and study structures he has created in the West are now believed to protect and preserve a tradition that is all but lost in its indigenous Eastern context. (Kay, 2004, 88–9)

The focus on the purity of the message and the inheritance of the teachings of Tsongkhapa has seemed to find 'success' in the UK and throughout the world, 'According to the NKT itself, by 2022 there were 1,300 NKT centres worldwide, though this number includes small groups along with established centres' (Blomfield, 2022).

There were other that exacerbated and solidified the split with the wider Gelugpa tradition. In 1996 the Dalai Lama suggested that Dorje Shugden, a Tibetan deity who was traditionally seen as a protector should not be worshipped. Dorje Shugden occupies a contentious place within Tibetan Buddhism, with some seeing him as a demon rather than a deity. Kelsang Gyatso expands the explanation of who Dorje Shugden is. Georges Dreyfus (2011) suggests that:

> Kelsang Gyatso's Western New Kadampa Tradition seems to be unique among Shukden followers in going as far as to claim that this deity is fully enlightened and hence must be considered a proper object of refuge and worshiped as such. (74)

In response to the Dalai Lama's decree, supporters of Gyatso and members of the New Kadampa Tradition protested when the Dalai Lama spoke at events in the West. As a result of these protests, and the refusal to acquiesce to the prohibition, Kelsang Gyatso was removed from his association with the Sera monastic community who also retracted his geshe degree. This, in essence, formally split the New Kadampa Tradition from wider Tibetan Buddhism.

This could have been problematic as authority within Tibetan Buddhism and the lineage of ordination is important. However, in spite of the split with wider Tibetan Buddhism, New Kadampa Buddhists, under the direction of Kelsang Gyatso, would argue that the lineage of authority has continued. Modern Kadampa suggests:

> After Je Tsongkhapa, the New Kadampa lineage flourished for hundreds of years, reaching the present day through immensely pure lineage Gurus such as Je Phabongkhapa and Vajradhara Trijang Rinpoche.
>
> In recent years, this precious lineage has been preserved and promoted throughout the world by the contemporary Buddhist Master, Venerable Geshe Kelsang Gyatso Rinpoche, the present day lineage holder. (NKT-IBU, 2022b)

Based on the teachings of Kelsang Gyatso there are three educational programmes offered by New Kadampa:

- *The General Programme:* This 'is an ideal starting point for those interested to find out more about the practical application of Buddhism and meditation to modern life. It consists of a wide range of events from regular weekly classes and entry level courses to Tantric empowerments and long retreats. All the teachings are based on books by Venerable Geshe Kelsang Gyatso Rinpoche' (NKT-IBU, n.d.-)

- *The Foundation Programme:* This focuses on enabling 'practitioners to deepen their knowledge and experience of Buddhism' (NKT-IBU, n.d.). This is done through the study of five topics based on the writings of the Buddha Shakyamuni and the associated commentaries of Kelsang Gyatso:
  - The stages of the path to enlightenment
  - Training the mind
  - The heart sutra
  - Guide to the bodhisattva's way of life
  - Types of mind, based on the commentary 'How to Understand the Mind'

- *The Teacher Training Programme:* This is designed to expand a person's understanding of Buddhism and prepare to be teachers. It is done through the study of twelve topics based on the writings of the Buddha Shakyamuni and the associated commentaries of Kelsang Gyatso:
  - The stages of the path to enlightenment
  - Training the mind

- The heart sutra
- Guide to the bodhisattva's way of life
- Types of mind
- Guide to the Middle Way
- Vajrayana Mahamudra
- The bodhisattva's moral discipline
- Offering to the spiritual guide
- Vajrayogini tantra
- Grounds and paths of secret mantra
- The practice of Heruka body mandala

The meditation and study centres are focussed on teaching and meditation. There is also a strong emphasis on the role of the teacher. The three education courses offer a pathway to ordination that seems less restrictive than other forms of Buddhism. Kelsang Gyatso summarized the Vinaya in ten principles:

> Throughout my life I will abandon, killing, stealing, sexual conduct, lying and taking intoxicants. I will practice contentment, reduce my desire for worldly pleasures, abandon engaging in meaningless activities, maintain the commitments of refuge, practise the three trainings of pure moral discipline, concentration and wisdom. (Waterhouse, 1997, 211–12)

New Kadampa is an interesting case study in terms of authority, in the sense that the only books that are studied are those written by Kelsang Gyatso, suggesting that he may be the only authorized interpreter of the teachings of the Buddha. The role of the teaching is significant too. Both of these elements of authority have led to criticism from within and without the order. There is a suggestion by those who have left that it is an authoritarian regime that seeks to restrict what is taught and the actions of members:

> NKT seems to newcomers like an open, welcoming organization, it becomes increasingly restrictive and controlling once practitioners are drawn inside. 'The NKT has two different faces: one is for the media and the public, and the other is for the people inside the NKT. (Hertog, 2018)

The 'authoritarian' nature of leadership has also led to accusations of abuse by teachers. Kelsang Gyatso, prior to his death in 2022, had stepped back, and the community is now led by an elected General Spiritual Director who is appointed for a period of eight years.

The New Kadampa Tradition is an interpretation of Tibetan Buddhism for the West, as suggested by its ordination vows. It does seek to maintain and observe the teachings of the Buddha; this is accomplished through the interpretation of such by Kelsang Gyatso.

Triratna (formerly Friends of the Western Buddhist Order)

Triratna (formerly Friends of the Western Buddhist Order [FWBO]) is one of the largest Buddhist groups in the UK (Kay, 2004), though numbers, except on a local level, are difficult to confirm. Sam Littlefair (2018) suggests that by 2017 the 'ordained sangha operated in 26 countries and reported a membership of 2200, with 30% of members in India'; however, this only records those who are ordained, not those who are affiliated in any of the other ways. The tradition describes itself as:

> A worldwide movement of people who try to engage with the Buddha's teachings in the conditions of the modern world. Neither monastic nor lay, we are simply Buddhists, at varying stages of commitment and understanding, adopting to the best of our ability in our lives the ethical standards of the Dharma. (The Buddhist Centre, n.d.d)

The FWBO changed its name in 2010 to Triratna to reflect a greater focus on the Three Jewels to which all Buddhists go for refuge: The Buddha, the dharma and the sangha. A further reason for the name change surrounded the expansion of the tradition beyond the West and an increasing number of members in India. The nomenclature of 'Western' seemed incongruous in light of this, though there were many of its members who 'were sorry to lose the word 'Western' from the name; being known as 'Western Buddhists' was meaningful to them' (Vajragupta, 2010, 175).

The name change does not change the history and the desire to develop a Buddhism for the modern world that focuses on the Three Jewels. It is often seen to be an anomaly among Buddhist groups within the UK. Robert Bluck (2006) has compared Triratna with other expressions of Buddhism which have

> sprung from a single Asian Buddhist tradition – whether Theravada, Tibetan or Japanese – with varying degrees of adaptation to a new context in Britain. The Friends of the Western Buddhist Order (FWBO) does not fit into this pattern but consciously draws on and adapts a range of Buddhist teachings and practices from several schools. (152)

It seeks to be ecumenical, in the sense that it draws on elements from many different traditions within Buddhism. It differs from the 'non-sectarian' groups within the UK because it has an hierarchical structure whereas 'most nonsectarian groups tend to be loose-knit egalitarian affairs' (Coleman, 2001, 116).

The FWBO was founded by Sangharakshita (Dennis Lingwood, 1925–2018). Its organization and beliefs are inherently tied up with the life and teachings of Sangharakshita; he, himself, suggested that 'the Dharma studied, practised, and propagated by Order members is the Dharma as elucidated by me' (Sangharakshita, 1990, 21); this is done in such a way that the dharma is 'translated by me from the terms of Eastern culture into the terms of Western culture' (Sangharakshita, 1990, 24). It will, therefore, be useful to trace the biography of Sangharakshita, the development of Triratna and then the central beliefs of the tradition.

Sangharakshita

Sangharakshita was born Dennis Lingwood in 1925 in London. A heart condition meant that much of his childhood was spent confined to his bed. He took the opportunity to read, something which continued after his convalescence. His readings included books from the East, the first of which was

> Madame Blavatsky's *Isis Unveiled*. Upon reading the *Diamond Sutra*, a perfection-of-wisdom sutra, and the *Platform Sutra*, a Chan text, he determined to be a Buddhist, and took refuge from a Burmese monk in London. (Lopez, 2002, 187)

Indeed, reading those two sutras at the age of sixteen helped Lingwood realize 'I was, in fact, a Buddhist and always had been' (Sangharakshita, 1992, 8).

After being conscripted at the age of eighteen, Lingwood served as a radio engineer in India, Ceylon (Sri Lanka) and Singapore. While in Sri Lanka, Lingwood developed a relationship with local Hindu swamis, and it seems he was determined to become a monk. On being transferred to Singapore he resumed his contact with Buddhists, having been disappointed by the the attitude of some in Sri Lanka and India. While in Sri Lanka, and after hostilities had ended, it is said that 'after the war he stayed on in India [and f]or two years he lived as a wandering mendicant' (The Buddhist Centre, n.d-a). Chryssides and Wilkins (2008) suggest that while hostilities had ceased, Lingwood's leaving of the army was essentially a desertion (48). While in India until 1964 Lingwood travelled around and studied under a number of teachers that helped his understanding of the dharma. These teachers and associated included:

- The future Buddharakshita who was his travel companion.
- Mata Anandamayi.
- Ramana Maharishi.
- Swamis of Ramakrishna Mission.
- U Chandramani ordained him a novice Theravada monk in May 1949 (receiving the name of Sangharakshita).
- When he was fully ordained in 1950 he had U Kawinda as his preceptor (upadhyaya), and Jagdish Kashyap as his teacher (acharya).
- Jagdish Kashyap was his teacher at Varanasi University.
- Lama Govinda who sparked an interest in Tibetan Buddhism.
- Dhardo Rinpoche, the Gelug Lama under whom he learned more about Tibetan Buddhism, having become somewhat disillusioned with Theravada.

- Dhardo Rinpoche who ordained him in the Mahayana tradition.
- Yogi Chen, a Ch'an teacher.
- Bhimrao Ramji Ambedkar was someone with whom Sangharakshita worked. After Ambedkar's death Sangharakshita continued to work with Dalits in Indian society.

Each of these figures provided a wide experience of Buddhism for Sangharakshita, which would serve as a prelude to the development of the ecumenical FWBO. Having returned to the UK in 1964 Sangharakshita was asked to help out at Hampsted Heath Vihara in London, from which he was expelled while on a trip to India a couple of years later. On returning to the UK in 1967 he felt constrained by the Buddhism taught and practiced by the Buddhist Society and the Hampsted Heath Vihara and set up the FWBO.

Beliefs and practices

As is suggested by the name 'Triratna' the focus is on the Three Jewels: the Buddha, the dharma and the sangha. During his time in India and its environs Sangharakshita become somewhat disillusioned with the lack of focus that were seemingly placed on these aspects of Buddhist teaching by many Buddhists. Stephen Batchelor (1994) has noted while going for Refuge that there is nothing new in Buddhist terms; for Lingwood, later Sangharakshita, 'among many Buddhists had degenerated into the pious repetition of formulae' – that this central aspect had become a mere 'preliminary step to be superseded by the more "serious" commitments of taking the monastic... vows' (334). The Three Refuges, in the eyes of Sangharakshita, are 'the key to the mystery of existence' (Batchelor, 1994, 335).

There are different levels to going for Refuge. This centrality of going for Refuge is shown during the ordination ceremony. The ceremony is in two parts: the private and the public. In the private ceremony the ordinand meets with their private preceptor. The preceptor is to confirm that their going for Refuge is heartfelt and honest. Once the two have repeated the going for Refuge together, the ordinand is given a Buddhist name that may reflect some of their 'qualities and spiritual potential', followed by a mediation of a 'special meditations practice' (Vajragupta, 2010, 107), which is usually a 'specific visualization practice or sadhana as their main practice, visualizing a particular Buddha or bodhisattva and reciting the appropriate mantra' (Bluck, 2006, 157). These visualizations are particularly important and also personal.

The second, public, aspect of the ordination is normally attended by family members, friends and people from the Triratna community. Again, the ordinand will chant the Three Jewels; this time they will do it in community with the other people being ordained. The ordination concludes with a white *kesa* being placed around their neck. This kesa is a white length of cloth/scarf that is worn around the neck, on each end is embroidered the Three Jewels as a reminder of the Refuge they have taken and the importance of it in their teaching.

At this ordination a person will accept and take upon themselves the Ten Precepts and the Ten Positive Precepts (see Table 9.1).

Particularly of interest to the teacher and to the student in the classroom may be the comparison of the Five/Ten Precepts (Pansils) explored earlier in Mahayana and Theravada traditions (see Chapter 8) and their relation to the Precepts of Triratna Buddhism. It is evident that the first five are similar/identical in nature. The final five are linked to the Mahayana precepts but do not reflect those taught in Theravada. The reason for such, especially is the adaptation of Buddhist teachings for the modern world or, in Triratna terms, the removal of cultural accretions from the teachings and practices of Buddhism. For example, the precept of not touching gold or silver (money) from the precepts of Theravada is seen to be an aspect that is impossible within today's society. This may be seen as a contextual teaching that has no relevance in today's society.

The living of the Ten Positive Precepts is also an area rich for exploration in the classroom. What do each of these mean in terms of a positive living of a Buddhist ethic?

Table 9.1 The Ten Precepts and Ten Positive Precepts of Triratna Buddhism

The Ten Precepts	The Ten Positive Precepts
I undertake the item of training which consists in abstention from killing living beings.	With deeds of loving kindness I purify my body.
I undertake the item of training which consists in abstention from taking the not-given.	With open-handed generosity I purify my body.
I undertake the item of training which consists in abstention from sexual misconduct.	With stillness, simplicity, and contentment I purify my body.
I undertake the item of training which consists in abstention from false speech.	With truthful communication I purify my speech.
I undertake to abstain from taking intoxicants.	With words kindly and gracious I purify my speech.
I undertake the item of training which consists in abstention from frivolous speech.	With helpful communication I purify my speech.
I undertake the item of training which consists in abstention from slanderous speech.	With harmonious communication I purify my speech.
I undertake the item of training which consists in abstention from covetousness.	Abandoning covetousness for tranquillity I purify my mind.
I undertake the item of training which consists in abstention from hatred.	Changing hatred into compassion I purify my mind.
I undertake the item of training which consists in abstention from false views.	Transforming ignorance into wisdom I purify my mind.

Source: Lokabandhu, 2013.

What is interesting in the declaration of each of the precepts (whether the 'original' or the positive) is that they are framed as aspirations. There is a recognition that people will fall short but that Buddhism is about living life in a way that will train a person's ethical sensitivity.

A further practice that lies at the heart of Triratna Buddhism is meditation. Based on the writings of Sangharakshita (2012) in *The Purpose and Practice of Buddhist Meditation: A Sourcebook of Teachings* there are five stages or *dhyanas* that are described. In an interesting exploration of the purpose of the stages, Maitreyabandhu (2015) explains that the nature of humanity is that of a drunkard being shown the way home by a guide. The drunkard gets cross with seemingly contradictory advice such as go left, or go right. They cannot see what the guide can; they do not realize the danger they are in. Maitreyabandhu highlights that the guide in this allegory is the Buddha, and that through his teachings a person can realize the nature of existence and are able to navigate the treacherous path.

> The path home has five stages or aspects. We begin by developing a fit mind – we need to sober up and cultivate the first two stages of 'integration' and 'positive emotion'. Then it dawns on us that our 'drunken self' is getting us into trouble, and that we need to let go of that self. This brings about the third and fourth stages: 'spiritual death' resulting in 'spiritual rebirth'. We see things clearly and know, really know, what life is for. Woven through this journey is the fifth stage/aspect, that of 'spiritual receptivity' – being open to our direct experience, to the guide, and to the nature of things. (2)

While we will now discuss them as separate stages, it is important to note that Sangharakshita (n.d.) offers a caveat: 'These stages are not rigidly demarcated; like the colours of the rainbow, one fades into another by imperceptible degrees' (2). The five stages themselves are seen to be:

- *Integration:* This is a stage that is characterized by mindful breathing; it is where everything starts coming together (or integrates) for the Buddhist and the mind begins to be shut off from the world. In the 'ordinary' world everything seems to be so fragmented, and everything is separate, but with a nod to dependent origination, the purpose or result of this stage comes together in the consciousness. This is a meditation that focuses on a single object that may also be breath, or an object. This is used as an object to develop awareness. This dhyana or stage is the foundation for all that follow.
- *Positive emotion or inspiration:* This is a stage that arises out of the integration to the idea of something outside of the self. Something at a much deeper level that is much more pure than a realization of the nature of the interconnectedness of all, something that inspires a person to action.

> This dhyana links with metta bhavana, the meditation of loving kindness. Just as inspiration leads to a positive outlook, so does this stage lead to positive emotion and the desire to act for the benefit of others.

- *Spiritual death:* In this stage there is the death of the self, the realization that the objectification of things, including the self, is dissipated. Fundamental to this stage is the Recollection of the Six Elements: earth, water, fire, air, space and sonsciousness. This is a practice based on the teaching of the Buddha in the *Dhatu-vibhanga Sutta*. Using the passage from this sutta about the earth, one can see the process of realization, and the letting go of perception and the earth:

    And what is the earth property? The earth property can be either internal or external. What is the internal earth property? Anything internal, within oneself, that's hard, solid, and sustained (by craving): head hairs, body hairs, nails, teeth, skin, flesh, tendons, bones, bone marrow, kidneys, heart, liver, membranes, spleen, lungs, large intestines, small intestines, contents of the stomach, feces, or anything else internal, within oneself, that's hard, solid, and sustained: This is called the internal earth property. Now both the internal earth property and the external earth property are simply earth property. And that should be seen as it has come to be with right discernment: *'This is not mine, this is not what I am, this is not my self.' When one sees it thus as it has come to be with right discernment, one becomes disenchanted with the earth property and makes the earth property fade from the mind.* (*Dhatu-vibhanga Sutta*; emphasis added)

    This stage enables a person to move on to the next dhyana of meditation.

- *Spiritual rebirth:* In the previous stage the true nature of reality is realized, and the 'mundane' self dies; in its place the 'transcendent' self arises. It is at this point that visualization exercises will begin in the meditative practices of a Buddhist.

    'The visualized figure before you; the figure of a Buddha, the figure of a Bodhisattva, sublime and glorious though it may be, is, in fact, you – is the new you – you as you will be if only you allow yourself to die' (Sangharakshita, 1978, 7).

    The visualization practice of each individual is unique and is reflective of the bodhisattva ideal being the major focus of a Triratna Buddhist's search for awakening.

- *Receptivity and spontaneous compassionate activity:* This is often called the 'just sitting' stage or 'formless' meditation. In Triratna the practice is described thus:

    Just Sitting is a space of non-action in which anything can emerge. Often the fruit of the previous practice only emerges when you stop 'doing' it. (The Buddhist Centre, n.d.-c)

Subhuti (2009) suggests that 'just sitting' should follow each previous stage. If a person conducts mindfulness of breathing it should be concluded/followed with a period of just sitting. The same for metta bhavana and so on. It is different to mindful breathing meditation in the sense that a person is not focussing on an object (see earlier on), the attention is not floating aimlessly but is aware of everything around them.

The first two stages of this path are usually associated with *samatha* meditation; while the final three are linked with *vipassana*. In the past, particularly in the time of

Sangharakshita, it would appear that the more in-depth practices of vipassana were only taught after a long process of preparation:

> Only after the full preparatory work of attaining the jhanas is accomplished are practitioners encouraged to move on to the vipassana or to take up the various options drawn from Mahayana and Vajrayana traditions. (Bell, 1994, 210)

It would appear that this informal prohibition is beginning to change and vipassana is being introduced earlier, maybe 'because the ordination process now takes longer, but also because the technique is beginning to be seen as safe and beneficial even for fairly new meditators (Bluck, 2006, 157).

In the classroom it is interesting to note the influences on the meditative stages of Triratna. In being a self-declared ecumenical organization, one that draws together the various traditions, an observer would expect to see the syncretization of other traditions, as well as Western influences. Harry Oldmeadow has described it as 'perhaps the most successful attempt to create an ecumenical international Buddhist organization' (Oldmeadow, 2004, 280).

Conversely, One Buddhist commented that the Triratna tradition is a 'hybridisation that has utilised aspects of different traditions and corrupted them with Western influences'. It is important to note the different ways that Triratna describes itself and also how it has been received by others within Buddhism. Whereas, syncretization was seen to be positive in the outlining of Buddhism in the Introduction, the way that this is negated with engagement with the West may seem to be a double standard. Indeed, the developmental years of the, then, FWBO were seen to be 'a self-enclosed system and their writings have the predictability of those who believe they have all the answers' (Bunting, 1997). In the words of James Coleman (2010):

> In its early days, FWBO members had a reputation among other British Buddhist groups as being rather brash and standoffish, but this book is evidence that they, like Western Buddhism in general, have mellowed with age.

The need to connect with the wider Buddhist world seems to have increased over the years. Examples include the joining of the European Buddhist Union and the Network of Buddhist Organizations

Within the sangha the traditional organization of monks and laity evident in other forms of Buddhism is broken down. The sangha itself has no set rules apart from the precepts – some members of the order work full time for the order others hold down jobs in the 'outside' world. Whatever the role that they fulfil they will strive to adopt Buddhist principles in their everyday life. The sangha is a non-monastic order, is self-sufficient and doesn't adopt a vow of poverty – this enables the work of order to be carried out in a simpler and more effective way. The community is designed to be self-sufficient and not reliant on outside donors, who may donate with an expectation of influence. Instead there are 'Right Livelihood' projects based in the local Triratna Centres that will help with the funding and running of the centre and the support of the wider community.

The sangha has been extended to all of those who have gone for refuge and is generally seen to be much more inclusive than in other forms of Buddhism. There are generally seen to be four types of people associated with Triratna:

- Beginner (someone who is new to Triratna)
- Friend (a regular practitioner)
- Mitra (a person who has publicly declared their desire to be a Buddhist within the Triratna context)
- Order member (someone who has gone for Refuge and been ordained into the Triratna Buddhist Order and has been recognized as such by the Preceptors' College) (The Buddhist Centre Development Team, 2019).

The order actively participates in outreach work and seek to present the teachings of Buddhism in as positive light as possible. While still emphasizing the Buddha's teachings they also emphasize the positive side of the teaching, for example, not harming any living thing also focuses on deeds of loving kindness. A look at any of the individual centre's activities will enable an indication of the activities that take place therein. These may include:

- Meditation classes of different types and levels.
- Classes on Buddhism and its various teachings, again aimed at different levels.
- Community building through such activates as meetings and mindful cleaning.
- Puja services.
- Eight Step Recovery Meetings based on the teachings of the Buddha.
- In addition to these there may be mindfulness sessions, school visits and shops of Buddhist materials.

Controversy

Triratna is an established Buddhist community in the UK and throughout the world, and it could be suggested that they have 'successfully' adapted the dharma for the Western world. It is still, however, a tradition that does not sit neatly within the UK or within the wider Buddhist tradition. Although he was ordained a Theravada monk and studied under a number of teachers (see earlier on), questions remain in wider Buddhism about his spiritual lineage. However, in the Triratna community, it has been described as a 'friendly hierarchy' (Rawlinson, 1997, 503) and the idea of an ordained sangha has been transcended through a communal approach. There are, however, still order members known as *dharmacharis* and *dharmacharinis* (dharma-farers), and *mitras* (friends). It does not take away the fact that ordinations are outside of the traditional methods surrounding the number of monks and so on; but the ordination and lineage seems to have been reimagined for the modern world.

It is also interesting that when Suella Braverman was appointed as UK attorney general in 2020, the appointment was met with critical newspaper articles that questioned the past of the Triratna community. *The Observer*, for example, ran a headline: 'Attorney general Suella Braverman belongs to controversial Buddhist sect. Founder of the Triratna order was accused of sex abuse; victim has spoken out about cabinet minister's new role' (Doward, 2020). This highlights aspects of the history of Triratna that they have had to overcome throughout the years. Reports emerged in the 1970s and 1980s that Sangharakshita and others engaged in sexual misconduct, coercion, dogmatism and misogyny. In Bunting's (1997) newspaper report there were member testimonies of forced homosexual activities perpetrated by Sangharakshita as a form of spiritual abuse, abusing his position of power. The Triratna Buddhist Community (2018) took these actions seriously, and in 2018 published a report outlining what had been done within the community to address the abuses and outline what would be done moving forwards. The community today is transparent about the issues in their history and on their website outline to the public the steps taken and how they continue to address concerns today, which begins with a statement of 'Apology and Regret' (The Buddhist Centre, n.d.-b). There is still work to be done to include Triratna within the UK to move past their history to enable practitioners, teachers and students to move past this controversy. Indeed, during the research for this book one teacher in an English school questioned why, with its history, Triratna was found in examination specifications.

Thoughts for the classroom

Within the established Mahayana and Theravada traditions the question of authority lie upon the teachings of the Buddha and the sangha. It is interesting, in exploring three expressions that are popular in Britain today, to see that each one has adapted the question of authority for the modern world. For Soka Gakkai and Triratna this has involved the breaking down of the traditional separation between the ordained and the lay sangha. For the New Kadampa Tradition this has been about the establishment of an orthodoxy, where the interpretation of the Buddha's teachings appear to be in the hands of one person. While, in all forms of Buddhism there continues to be an autonomy that, to an extent, is both amplified and restricted within these traditions.

These three traditions also show the need for teachers to go beyond 'traditional' representations. At various points in this book we have explored the importance of recognizing Theravada and Mahayana understandings, but it is evident that even this level of diversity is insufficient. Aspects of Zen or Pure Land Buddhism have only been

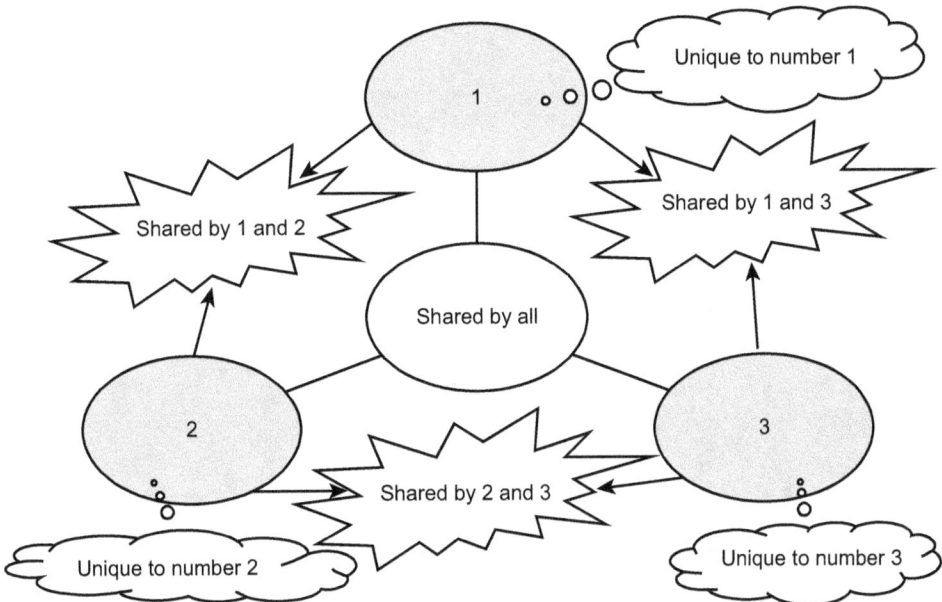

Figure 9.2 Similar and different.

briefly touched upon. Each of these expressions challenge assumptions about what Buddhism is, what it teaches and how it is practised. How a teacher includes all of this diversity will depend on the understanding of students, but the opportunity to recognize this messiness is key. One activity that often works is an activity where students are invited to compare aspects of three traditions, practices or beliefs (see Figure 9.2). In the context of this chapter the title of this similar and different activity could variously be 'authority', 'sangha' or 'beliefs' and then explore them from the three perspectives.

10

Buddhism and contemporary Britain

Throughout the previous chapters there have been many examples expressed of how Buddhism is lived in Britain today. This is an important aspect in striving to teach Buddhism in the classroom. Chapter 9 explored some of the traditions that can be found within the United Kingdom. It is interesting that as each of these have developed it is against the background of Western modernism and post-modernism. In this way it could be argued that, as noted by Travers Christmas Humphreys, that a 'Western form of Buddhism must in time emerge' (Humphreys, 1958, 126); indeed he felt that there was already an approach to Buddhist belief and practice that he described as 'eclectic' or maybe in more simplistic terms pick 'n' mix (Humphreys, 1956, 6; 1968, 80). This is something that has remained within the conversation around Buddhism in the UK; indeed, in 1994, Stephen Batchelor saw this as having not occurred and that instead there was a 'spectrum of adaptation' that included those who wanted to maintain a 'pure' form to others who wanted to strip Buddhism of cultural accretions (Batchelor, 1994, 337, 379). This 'Westernisation' of Buddhism in the UK may also be supported with the 2011 Census data in England and Wales. In this Census 178,453 people identified as Buddhist. There is no data available to unpick the traditions followed, but an interesting note is the associated birthplace and ethnicity data (see Figure 10.1).

This would suggest that the majority of Buddhists in the UK are from a 'Western' background. There is a greater unpacking of the data needed, but this may necessitate an understanding and exploration of Buddhism within the UK. Work in this area has been ongoing throughout the years but is an area rich for exploration and updating. Some important works include:

- Ian P. Oliver (1979) *Buddhism in Britain*
- Deirdre Green (1989) *Buddhism in Britain: Skilful Means or Selling Out?*
- Denise Cush (1990) *Buddhists in Britain Today*
- Robert Bluck (2006) *British Buddhism. Teachings, Practice and Development*

Table 10.1 Census Data. Buddhism in England and Wales

Buddhism in England and Wales

Country of birth	Ethnicity
UK 66,522	White 59,040
Far East 59,931	Chinese 34,354
South Asia 9,847	Asian 13,919
	Mixed 4,647
	Black 1,507
	Other 34,036

Source: Office for National Statistics (2003 and 2004).

This chapter will chart the history of Buddhist in Britain but also the diversity of the lived experience of Buddhists in the UK today. Chapter 9 strove to provide a background for the different groups in the UK and the nuances of belief and practice; this chapter will be much more about how Buddhism is, and has been, experienced over the past century or more.

Buddhism arrives in the UK

The history of Buddhism in Britain began in the nineteenth century, building on interest in Buddhism through the colonial experiences of people who had been in government service. The various events in the development of Buddhist presence in the UK are outlined as follows:

- The nineteenth century established in the colonial mind what Buddhism was. In line with the discussion in the Introduction, British society seemed to conflate or create an image of the Buddha and Buddhism that fitted with Victorian values and ideas of religion.

- In 1881 the Pali Text Society was organised by T. W. Rhys Davids. Rhys Davids stated that the goal of this society, which still exists today, was to 'render accessible to students the rich stores of the earliest Buddhist literature now lying unedited and practically unused in the various manuscripts scattered throughout ... Europe' (Oliver, 1979, 22). This reflected the encounters of the Empire, in that the Buddhism with which people were most familiar was the Theravada of colonies such as Burma (now Myanmar), Thailand and Sri Lanka.

- In 1907 the Buddhist Society of Great Britain and Ireland was formed in London. T. W. Rhys Davids was its first president. This was a confluence of academics and students interested in the study of Buddhism and others who were attracted by Buddhism. This tension perhaps led to it being later combined with the Buddhist Lodge and established again as the Buddhist Society in 1924 with Christmas Humphreys as president.

- In 1925 Anagarika Dharmapala, a Sri Lankan Buddhist, brought the Maha Bodhi Society to the UK. The Maha Bodhi Society was founded by Dharmapala and the British journalist Edwin Arnold. Along with the Buddhist Society, the Maha Bodhi Society would serve as one of the central focuses for the development of Buddhism in the UK.

- In 1927 D. T. Suzuki published *Essays in Zen Buddhism*, which introduced Zen thought into Britain. He visited the Buddhist Society in 1936 and those who met with him felt that 'an hour with a Zen master was worth weeks of literary study' (Humphreys, 1968, 41).

- The growth of Buddhism was slow, and some of its presence in the UK was due to the immigration of people from Burma, Sri Lanka and China. Some British Buddhists went to different areas of Asia to study under teachers and some received ordination. These newly ordained monks in the 1940s and 1950s include Nanavira Thera and Nanamoli Bhikkhu. It is important to note the importance of these 'British' monks; indeed, Humphreys (1955) celebrated William Purfurst (ordained in 1954 in Thailand as Kapilavaddho) as 'our own bhikkhu' heralding 'a new chapter in the history of Buddhism in England'(174–5).

- The Buddhist Society published their own 'Twelve Principles of Buddhism' in 1945 as 'a clear-cut Western presentation' of Buddhism (Humphreys, 1968, 47). Humphreys tried to get these adopted throughout the world at the Second World Buddhist Conference in Tokyo in 1952.

- In 1954 the Dhammakaya tradition was brought to the UK by Kapilavaddho Bhikkhu, and subsequently the English Sangha Trust in 1955 was founded.

- In 1954 the London Buddhist Vihara opened.

- In 1962 Peggy Kennett, later Jiyu-Kennett, became a novice Zen nun, becoming fully ordained in Japan in 1963. As indicated earlier (see Chapters 8 and 9), she was to return to Britain as a Zen Master, but Humphreys averred asking instead for a Japanese man.

- In 1966 a British woman, Freda Bedi, was the first Western woman to be ordained in Tibetan Buddhism.

- In 1967 the first Tibetan Buddhist Centre (Kagyu Samye Ling) was organised by Choje Akong Tulku Rinpoche and Chogyam Trungpa Rinpoche.

- In the late 1960s Shenpen Hookham became a Tibetan nun, and became a lama, and as part of her vocation began to teach the dharma to people in the West. Her autobiography *Keeping the Dalai Lama Waiting & Other Stories: An English Woman's*

Journey to Becoming a Buddhist Lama is an insight into her life journey through Buddhism.

- Since the 1960s many new and imported Buddhist groups and centres have been organised, all seeking to establish a Buddhism that meets the needs of the Western world. Some do this through an emphasis on the traditional elements of Buddhism, others reinterpret beliefs and practices such as the breaking down of barriers within the sangha. There are also groups such as 'secular' Buddhism that in a similar way to modern Buddhism tries to peel away the layers of mysticism and develop a worldviews that is rational and perhaps focussed on the psychological aspects of Buddhist worldviews.

- In 1993 the Network of Buddhist Organisations was established to draw together the disparate groups of Buddhism.

A narration of the history of Buddhism does not tell the whole story of Buddhism. There are many elements of Buddhism that have permeated the culture of Britain. These might include mindfulness classes or the importance of meditation. It will be interesting to see what the next stage of development of Buddhism within the UK will be. It is a religion that has not been as studied as others, and as such there is perhaps a superficial understanding of what it is and what it teaches in the wider populace. This has begun to be overcome through the high-profile teachings and examples of people like the Dalai Lama and Orlando Bloom. With an increase in understanding comes a greater scrutiny. As such, the exploration of issues such as the environment, the place of women and social justice (see Chapter 8) will receive greater attention. This may be constructive and positive, or it may be negative. Only time will tell.

Syncretism

As outlined earlier one of the perceived strengths of Buddhism has been its ability to adapt to the culture and practices of the countries in which it is found. This was particularly evident in an exploration of Tibetan and Japanese Buddhism. To an extent this has happened in the UK, particularly as elements of Triratna and other particularly Western traditions have been explored. It is possible to see, as in other countries, a symbiotic relationship between Buddhism and British culture. Although mindfulness is now firmly established in the secular sphere, it is undeniable that the Buddhist underpinning of such has permeated its practice. The end purpose of awakening may have disappeared, but the mindfulness and calmness of mind has been adopted through the many different workplace practices.

It is also possible to see the adoption of Buddhist practices and beliefs into people's everyday lives, without the formal adoption of Buddhism in terms of going for refuge. Sometimes it is possible to hear throwaway comments about being a Buddhist Christian, meaning that people have adopted certain Buddhist practices that complement their Christian beliefs. For many, though, this is not a throwaway comment, or the adoption of a couple of practices, but a deeply held belief. Rose Drew (2011) has presented a nuanced description of people who she describes as 'dual-belongers', meaning:

> In the most unequivocal cases of Buddhist Christian dual belonging, people practise within both traditions, belong to a Buddhist and a Christian community, identify themselves as fully Buddhist and fully Christian and have made a formal commitment to both traditions (usually through baptism and the taking of the three refuges). (4)

Indeed, the Catholic priest and theologian Paul Knitter (2013) has suggested he is a Buddhist Christian, or maybe a Christian Buddhist. This is, perhaps, one area of potential exploration in the classroom. Students and teachers are often used to drawing lines of demarcation between religions, but it would appear that those lines are less rigid than has traditionally been assumed. There are important questions that this kind of dual belonging raises, in that it challenges the 'truth claims' of religion in seeking to reconcile seemingly contradictory beliefs. Drew (2011) highlights this when she asks:

> How is this possible when, for example, God is so central to Christianity yet absent from Buddhism; when Christians have faith in Jesus Christ while Buddhists take refuge in the Buddha; when Christians hope for heaven and Buddhists hope for nirvana; and when Buddhists and Christians engage in different practices? (1)

Which is reinforced by Knitter (2013) when he asks 'Am I still a Christian?' (xiii). In some ways this links back to the exploration of the representation of Buddhism in *The Simpsons*, where Lisa is able to observe Christmas with her family. This is an area that is rich for exploration and one that will provide many different questions and answers.

Countercultural

In the Introduction to this book we explored the work of John Strong (2015) in exploring the diversity of Buddhist traditions through the examination of the various places of worship in Lumbini. It is possible to complete a similar exercise for England. Emma Tomalin and Caroline Starkey (2016) published a report for Historic England entitled *A Survey of Buddhist Buildings in England*, which is a rich resource to begin this exploration. Tomalin and Starkey recognize the limitations of their study as they suggest that a large number of Buddhist meetings happen in people's homes, and as such their research was only able to identify 190 Buddhist buildings. In terms of traditions the breakdown is:

> Out of the 190 buildings 59 are from the Theravada tradition; 69 are from Tibetan traditions, with 39 of those from the New Kadampa Tradition (NKT); 29 are from different East Asian traditions; and 33 are what we are calling non-sectarian, with 25 of these from Triratna (previously called Friends of the Western Buddhist Order). (5)

These buildings serve a number of purposes including, but not limited to:

- Buddhist practice
- Celebrating Buddhist festivals
- Community activities for Buddhists
- Monastic Buddhist living quarters
- Lay community living quarters
- Buddhist retreats
- Buddhist schools
- Buddhist businesses
- A place where Buddhist practice sessions are offered to all

This reflects the view of one Buddhist who suggests:

> We are free to practise without any restrictions. There are centres here of most of the different traditions, and some wonderful teachers live here and are available while other great teachers visit often.

In exploring the different designs and functions of these Buddhist buildings students will be able to see the eclectic nature of Buddhism. This is an important aspect of teaching Buddhism beyond the places of a Buddhist majority around the world. Students need to be aware of the reality of Buddhism in Britain today, and while monasteries and temples around the world are stunning, and the portrayal of oversized Buddha statues are awe inspiring, this is not the lived experience of Buddhists in Britain today. For some Buddhists, the community aspect of Buddhism is central, while for others it is a very individual practice. This diversity should be recognized alongside the 'essential' aspects of Buddhist belief and practice. Not all Buddhists go to retreats, and many Buddhist viharas are used to provide services for the local community.

Some elements of Buddhist life can be seen to be countercultural in the twenty-first century, and it may be this that appeals to people. The egalitarian message of Buddhism that rejects a focus on the material can be seen to be a way out of the 'rat race' that people may not find fulfilment through. This counterculturism is not, however, something that is always positive. One Buddhist has commented:

> The culture is extremely materialistic and does not value spiritual practice, so one has to be determined to pursue a course of action and to hold values that go against the prevailing culture.

This shows some of the challenges of living as a Buddhist in the modern world. Life may be simpler in that religious freedom is more ingrained, and the greater proliferation of mindfulness and vegetarianism (if that is a part of Buddhism), but there are still challenges that mean attachment, desire and aversion are everyday influences that need to be lived alongside.

Thoughts for the classroom

Throughout this chapter we have explored the place of Buddhists in Britain. Sometimes the focus is on developing Buddhist identity so that the beliefs, teachings and practices are not watered down. On the other hand, Buddhists are aware of an increasing awareness of their place within, and from, wider society. As Buddhism has developed there has been the need for Buddhists to find greater representation of the needs of their communities and the individuals therein. Some of this has been able to happen through the development of representative voices within society, and these are also voices that can be used in the classroom.

Buddhists in the public eye have raised the awareness of the wider society of Buddhism and Buddhist principles. Examples include:

- Eric Lubbock (1928–2016) was a Member of Parliament and also of the House of Lords
- Tom Baker, an actor in *Dr Who*; he occasionally described himself as Buddhist or living according to Buddhist principles
- Jonny Wilkinson, an ex-England rugby player
- Adewale Akinnuoye-Agbaje, an actor possibly most famous for playing Mr. Eko in *Lost*.
- David Bowie, a musician, studied Buddhism and lived elements of a Buddhist life.
- Benedict Cumberbatch, an actor 'describes himself as a Buddhist – "at least philosophically"' (Wells, 2016).
- Naomi Watts, a British actress
- Orlando Bloom, a British actor

The most important examples that we use in the classroom are those from our local area. The diversity of the Buddhist experience in the UK is significant and should find expression in our classrooms. Unfortunately this has not always been the case.

Buddhism is a religion that transforms the individual as they understand the nature of existence. Sometimes in our writing and teaching we forget that everything in Buddhism has its root in this teaching. Nothing in the Buddhist worldview makes sense without an understanding of sunyata, the Four Noble Truths and the purpose of existence in the arahant and bodhisattva ideals. It is my hope that as we explore Buddhism as a lived religion, it will become more than a list of observable phenomena but that it will reflect the reality of Buddhist life. It is only then that the richness and diversity of Buddhism can be understood by those we teach.

Notes

INTRODUCTION

1   As part of the teaching of religions and worldviews within the classroom I think it is important that we use vocabulary that is not Christianized. As such in Hinduism we use 'mandir' rather than 'temple'. In Buddhism there are many different words such as: vihara, chaitya, stupa, wat and pagoda. I will try, as far as is possible, to use Buddhist terms, but here, as in other places, the original authors use anglicized words, and in many forms of 'Western' Buddhism these terms have been adopted.

3 THE BUDDHA

1   This understanding of Buddha Gautama as a bodhisattva would be accepted by most Buddhists; there is, however, a distinctive Mahayana understanding of the term which will be explored in Chapter 3.

Reference list

All urls have been accessed on 28 April 2023.

Aitken, R. (1984). *The Mind of Clover: Essays in Zen Buddhist Ethics*. San Francisco: North Point Press.

Ammerman, N. T. (2021). *Studying Lived Religion: Contexts and Practices*. New York: New York University Press.

Apple, J. (2014). *The Irreversible Bodhisattva (Avaivartika) in the Lotus Sutra and Avaivartikacakrasutra*. Semantic Scholar. https://www.semanticscholar.org/paper/The-Irreversible-Bodhisattva-(avaivartika)-in-the-Apple/4cc24223ba6ec8e32b19b9dca36ae7cadc7c0267

Appleton, N. (2010). *Jataka Stories in Theravada Buddhism: Narrating the Bodhisatta Path*. Abingdon: Routledge.

Appleton, N. (2011). In the Footsteps of the Buddha? Women and the Bodhisatta Path in Theravada Buddhism. *Journal of Feminist Studies in Religion*, 27(1), 33–51.

Aristotle, & Ross, D. (2009). *The Nicomachean Ethics* (Oxford World's Classics). Oxford: Oxford University Press.

Armstrong, K. (2000). *Buddha*. London: Phoenix.

Batchelor, S. (1994). *The Awakening of the West: The Encounter of Buddhism and Western Culture*. London: Aquarian Press.

Batchelor, S. (2015). Translator's Introduction. In Shantideva, *A Guide to the Bodhisattva's Way of Life* (pp. vii–viii). Dharamsala: Library of Tibetan Works and Archive.

Beal, S. (2003). *Romantic Legends of Sakya Buddha: A Translation of the Chinese Version of the Abhiniskramana Sutra (1875)*. Whitefish: Kessinger Publishing Co.

Beech, H. (2013, July 1). The Face of Buddhist Terror. *Time*. https://content.time.com/time/subscriber/article/0,33009,2146000,00.html

Bell, S. (1991). *Buddhism in Britain - Development and Adaptation*. Doctoral thesis, Durham University.

Bernert, C. (2018). *Words of a Gentle Sage: Collected Teachings of Khenchen Appey Rinpoche* (Vol. 1). Kathmandu: Vajra Books.

Bhikkhu, T. (2014, Spring). There Is No Self. Nope, Never Said That, Either. – The Buddha. *Tricycle. The Buddhist Review*. https://tricycle.org/magazine/there-no-self/

Bhikkhu, T. (2018). *Noble Strategy. Essays on the Buddhist Path* (rev. ed.). Metta Forest Monastery: Valley Centre.

Bhikkhu, T. (2022, August 8). 7 Things the Buddha Never Said. *Lion's Roar*. https://www.lionsroar.com/what-the-buddha-never-said/

Bielefeldt, C. (1986). Ch 'ang-lu Tsung-tse and Zen Meditation. In P. Gregory (Ed.), *Tradiitons of Meditation in Chinese Buddhism* (pp. 129–62). Honolulu: University of Hawai'i Press.

Blomfield, V. (2022, October 14). Kelsang Gyatso Obituary. *The Guardian*. https://www.theguardian.com/world/2022/oct/14/kelsang-gyatso-obituary

Bloom, C. (2023). *The Bloom Review: Does Government 'Do God?' An Independent Review into How Government Engages with Faith*. https://assets.publishing.service.gov.uk/government/uploads/system/uploads/attachment_data/file/1152684/The_Bloom_Review.pdf

Bluck, R. (2006). *British Buddhism. Teachings, Practice and Development*. Abingdon: Routledge.

Bodhi, B. (1994). *The Noble Eightfold Path. The Way to the End of Suffering* (rev. ed.). Kandy: Buddhist Publication Society.

Bodhi, B. (1995). *Transcendental Dependent Arising: A Translation and Exposition of the Upanisa Sutta*. Access to Insight. https://www.accesstoinsight.org/lib/authors/bodhi/wheel277.html

Bodhi, B. (2003). *Abhidhammatha Sangaha. A Comprehensive Manual of Abhidhamma. Pali Text, Translation and Explanatory Guide*. Onalaska: Pariyatti.

Bodhi, B. (2010). Arahants, Bodhisattvas, and Buddhas. *Access to Insight*. https://www.accesstoinsight.org/lib/authors/bodhi/arahantsbodhisattvas.html

Bodhipaksa. (2007, Summer). What You're Made Of. *Tricycle. The Buddhist Review*. https://tricycle.org/magazine/six-element-practice/

Bowie, R. A., Panjwani, F., & Clemmey, K. (2020). *Texts and Teachers. Opening the Door to Hermeneutical RE*. Canterbury: National Institute of Christian Education.

Brahm, A. (2015). *Who Ordered This Truckload of Dung?* Somerville: Wisdom Publications.

Brazier, D. (2014). *Buddhism Is a Religion. You Can Believe It*. Malvern: Woodsmoke Press.

British Library. (n.d.). *Coloured Illustrations of Buddhist Heavens and Hells*. British Library Collections. https://www.bl.uk/collection-items/buddhist-cosmology

Brunnhozl, K. (2012). *The Heart Attack Sutra. A New Commentary on the Heart Sutra*. Ithaca: Snow Lion Publications.

Bucar, L. (2022). *Stealing My Religion. Not Just Any Cultural Appropriation*. Cambridge: Harvard University Press.

Buddhaghosa, B., & Nanamoli, B. (2010). *The Path of Purification. Visuddhimagga*. Colombo: Buddhist Publication Society.

Buddhanet (2008) *Maha Pajapati Gotami, Founder of the Order of Nuns*. https://www.buddhanet.net/e-learning/history/pajapati.htm

Buddhharakkhita, A. (1985). *The Dhammapada: The Buddha's Path of Wisdom*. Kandy: Buddhist Publication Society.

The Buddhist Centre. (n.d.-a). *A brief biography of Sangharakshita: 1925–2018*. The Buddhist Centre. https://thebuddhistcentre.com/bhante

The Buddhist Centre. (n.d.-b). *Addressing Ethical Issues in Triratna*. The Buddhist Centre. https://thebuddhistcentre.com/stories/ethical-issues/

The Buddhist Centre. (n.d.-c). *Just Sitting*. The Buddhist Centre. https://thebuddhistcentre.com/text/just-sitting

The Buddhist Centre. (n.d.-d). *What is Triratna?*. The Buddhist Centre. https://thebuddhistcentre.com/page/about-us

The Buddhist Centre Development Team. (2019). *How Triratna Works. Being a Brief Guide to Its Mission, Size, Activities, Structure, Roles, Responsibilities, and Funding*. Buddhist Centre. https://thebuddhistcentre.com/system/files/groups/files/how_triratna_works.pdf

The Buddhist Hospice Trust. (n.d.). *FAQ*. The Buddhist Hospice Trust. https://buddhisthospice.org.uk/faqs/

Bunting, M. (1997, 27 October). The dark side of enlightenment. *The Guardian, G2 supplement*, 1–4.

Buswell, R., & Lopez, D. (2014). *The Princeton Dictionary of Buddhism*. Princeton: Princeton University Press.

Byrne, J. (2013). Why I Am Not a Buddhist Feminist: A Critical Examination of 'Buddhist Feminism'. *Feminist Theology, 21*(2), 180–94.

Cantwell, C., & Kawanami, H. (2016). Buddhism. In L. Woodhead, C. Partridge & H. Kawanami (Eds.), *Religions in the Modern World* (3rd ed., pp. 73–112). Abingdon: Routledge.

Cantwell Smith, W. (1991). *Meaning and End of Religion*. Minneapolis: Fortress Press. (Original work published 1962).

Chogyel, T. (2015). *The Life of the Buddha*. New York: Penguin.

Chryssides, G. D., & Wilkins, M. Z. (2008). *A Reader in New Religious Movements: Readings in the Study of New Religious Movements*. London: Continuum International Publishing Group.

Clark, T. (2022). *The Prayer Flag Tradition*. prayerflags.com. https://www.prayerflags.com/pages/the-prayer-flag-tradition

Cleary, T. (1993). *The Flower Ornament Scripture: A Translation of the Avatamsaka Sutra*. Boston: Shambhala.

Coleman, J. W. (2001). *The New Buddhism: The Western Transformation of an Ancient Tradition*. Oxford: Oxford University Press.

Coleman, J. (2010, November 4). Hard and Valuable Lessons. *Lion's Roar*. https://www.lionsroar.oom/hard-and-valuable-lessons/

Commission on Religious Education. (2018). *Religion and Worldviews: The Way Forward. A National Plan for RE*. London: Commission on RE.

Conze, E. (1978). *The Prajna-paramita Literature*. Tokyo: Reiyukai.

Conze, E. (2001). *Buddhist Wisdom. The Diamond Sutra and the Heart Sutra. Vintage Spiritual Classics*. New York: Random House.

Cooling, T. (2002). Commitment and Indoctrination: A Dilemma for Religious Education? In L. Broadbent & A. Brown (Eds.), *Issues in Religious Education* (pp. 44–55). New York: Routledge.

Cooling, T., Bowie, B., & Panjwani, F. (2020). *Worldviews in Religious Education*. London: Theos.

Cousins, L. S. (1984). Samatha-yāna and Vipassanā-yāna. In G. Dhammapala, R. F. Gombrich & K. R. Norman (Eds.), *Buddhist Studies in Honour of Hammalava Saddhātissa* (pp. 56–68). Nugegoda: Hammalava Saddhatissa Felicitation Volume Committee.

Crenshaw, Kimberlé (1989). Demarginalizing the Intersection of Race and Sex: A Black Feminist Critique of Antidiscrimination Doctrine, Feminist Theory and Antiracist Politics. *University of Chicago Legal Forum*, 1989 (1), 139–68.

Cush, D. (1990). *Buddhists in Britain Today*. London: Hodder & Stoughton.

Dalai Lama. (1995). *Commentary on the Thirty Seven Practices of a Bodhisattva*. Dharamsala: Library of Tibetan Works and Archives.

Dalai Lama. (1996). *Beyond Dogma. Dialogues and Discourses*. Berkeley: North Atlantic Books.

Dalai Lama. (2009). *For the Benefit of All Beings: A Commentary on the Way of the Bodhisattva*. London: Shambhala.

Dalai Lama. (2012). *Kindness, Clarity and Insight*. Boston: Snow Lion.

Dalai Lama, & Chodron, T. (2014). *Buddhism. One Teacher; Many Traditions*. Somerville: Wisdom Publications.

Davids, C. A. (1878). *Buddhist Birth-Stories (Jataka Tales): The Commentarial Introduction Entitled Nidanakatha, the Story of the Lineage*. Translated from V. Fausböll's edition of the Pali text by T. W. Rhys Davids. London: Routledge.

Dawa-Samdup, L. K., & Baldock, J. (2013). *The Tibetan Book of the Dead*. London: Arcturus Publishing Ltd.

Dayal, H. (1970). *The Bodhisattva Doctrine in Buddhist Sanskrit Literature*. Delhi: Motilal Banarsidass.

Dhammadharo, A. L. (1994). *What is the Triple Gem?* Berkeley: DharmaNet International.

Dhammasami, K. (2019). Wheel of Life: Philosophy and Ethics. In J. Igunma & S. May (Eds.), *Buddhism. Origins, Traditions and Contemporary Life* (pp. 75–164). London: British Library.

Dharmachakra Translation Committee. (2013). *The Play in Full. Lalitavistara*. Boudhanath: 84000.

Dossett, W. (2020, June 2). *Is Pure Land Buddhism Buddhism?* TRS Chester Religious Studies Webinars. https://vimeo.com/channels/1613728/425790053

Doward, J. (2020, February 15). Attorney General Suella Braverman Belongs to Controversial Buddhist Sect. *The Observer*. https://www.theguardian.com/politics/2020/feb/15/new-attorney-general-suella-braverman-in-controversial-buddhist-sect

Drew, R. (2011). *Buddhist and Christian?: An Exploration of Dual Belonging*. Abingdon: Routledge.

Drewes, D. (2015). Oral Texts in Indian Mahayana. *Indo-Iranian Journal*, *58*(2), 117–41.

Dreyfus, G. (2011). The Predicament of Evil: The Case of Dorje Shukden. In M. D. Eckel & B. L. Herling (Eds.), *Deliver Us From Evil: Boston University Studies in Philosophy and Religion* (pp. 57–74). London: Continuum.

Dumoulin, H. (1994). *Zen Buddhism: A History (India & China)*. Translated by James W. Heisig & Paul F. Knitter. New York: MacMillan.

Easton, C., Wright, A., Goodman, A., Hibberd, T., & Wright, A. (2019). *A Practical Guide to Critical Religious Education: Resources for the Secondary Classroom*. London: Routledge.

Eddy, G. (2012). *Becoming Buddhist Experiences of Socialization and Self-Transformation in Two Australian Buddhist Centres*. London: Continuum.

Edwards, R. (1984). Pu-tai-Maitreya and a Reintroduction to Hangchou's Fei-lai-Feng. *Ars Orientalis*, *14*, 5–50.

Erricker, C. (2001). *Teach Yourself: Buddhism* (New ed.). London: Hodder & Stoughton.

Faure, B. (2009). *Unmasking Buddhism*. Chichester: Wiley-Blackwell.

Ferguson, G. (2022, July 27). What 'No Self' Really Means. *Lion's Roar*. https://www.lionsroar.com/what-no-self-really-means/

Foulk, T. G. (1995). Daily Life in the Assembly. In D. S. Lopez (Ed.), *Buddhism in Practice* (pp. 455–72). Princeton: Princeton University Press.

Fowler, M. (1999). *Buddhism. Beliefs and Practices*. Brighton: Sussex Academic Press.

Fujiwara, S. (2019). Buddhism in RE Textbooks in England: Before Shap and After the Call for Community Cohesion. *Religion & Education*, *46*(2), 234–51.

Fuller, P. (2005). *The Notion of Ditthi in Theravada Buddhism*. London: Routledge.

Fuller, P. (2022). *An Introduction to Engaged Buddhism*. London: Bloomsbury.

Gethin, R. (1998). *The Foundations of Buddhism*. Oxford: Oxford University Press.

Gethin, R. (2004). Wrong View (miccha-ditthi) and Right View (samma-ditthi) in the Theravada Abhidhamma. *Contemporary Buddhism*, 5(1), 15–28.

Gethin, R. (2022). Abhidhamma: Theravada Thought in Relation to Sarvastivada Thought. In S. B. Thompson (Ed.), *Routledge Handbook of Theravada Buddhism* (pp. 227–42). Abingdon: Routledge.

Gleig, A., & Langenberg, A. P. (2021). Collaboration as Care: Teaching Sexual Abuse in American Buddhism. *Journal of Feminist Studies in Religion*, 37(1), 145–7.

Gombrich, R. (1988). *Theravada Buddhism: A Social History from Ancient Benares to Modern Colombo*. London: Routledge and Kegan Paul.

Gombrich, R. (2010). The Buddha's Thought. *Revue Internationale de Philosophie*, 253(3), 315–39.

Gombrich, R. (2011). *How Buddhism Began. The Conditioned Genesis of the Early Teachings* (2nd ed.). London: Routledge.

Goodson, M. (2022, July 2). *The Vimalakirti Sutra Stories Retold*. Zen Gateway. https://www.thezengateway.com/teachings/the-vimalakirti-sutra

Green, D. (1989). Buddhism in Britain: Skilful Means or Selling Out?. In P. Badham (Ed.), *Religion, State and Society in Modern Britain* (pp. 277–91). Lampeter: Edwin Mellen Press.

Gunther-Brown, C. (2019). *Debating Yoga and Mindfulness in Public Schools: Reforming Secular Education Or Reestablishing Religion?* Chapel Hill: University of North Carolina Press.

Gyato, G. K. (1995). *The Bodhisattva Vow. A Practical Guide to Helping Others* (2nd ed.). Ulverston: Tharpa.

Haneda, N. (2012, May). Sangha. *The Dharma Breeze*, XVIII(1), 1–3.

Hanh, T. N. (1992). *Old Path. White Clouds: The Life Story of the Buddha*. London: Rider.

Hanh, T. N. (1998a). *The Heart of the Buddha's Teaching*. London: Rider Books.

Hanh, T. N. (1998b). *Interbeing: Fourteen Guidelines for Engaged Buddhism*. Berkeley: Parallax Press.

Hanh, T. N. (2008). *The Miracle of Mindfulness: The Classic Guide to Meditation by the World's Most Revered Master*. London: Ebury Publishing.

Hanh, T. N. (2009). *You Are Here: Discovering the Magic of the Present Moment*. Boston: Shambhala.

Hanh, T. N. (2012a). *Awakening of the Heart: Essential Buddhist Sutras and Commentaries*. Berkeley: Parallax.

Hanh, T. N. (2012b). *Good Citizens: Creating Enlightened Society*. Berkeley: Parallax Press.

Hanh, T. N. (2012c). *The Insight That Brings Us to the Other Shore*. Plum Village. https://plumvillage.org/wp-content/uploads/2014/09/2014-Thich-Nhat-Hanh-New-Heart-Sutra-letter-cc.pdf

Hanh, T. N. (2014). *Mindfulness Survival Kit: Five Essential Practices*. Berkeley: Parallax Press.

Hanh, T. N. (2017a, April 12). The Fourteen Precepts of Engaged Buddhism. *Lion's Roar*. https://www.lionsroar.com/the-fourteen-precepts-of-engaged-buddhism/

Hanh, T. N. (2017b). *The Heart of Understanding: A New Translation of the Heart Sutra with Commentaries*. Berkeley: Parallax.

Hanh, T. N. (2017c). *The Other Shore: A New Translation of the Heart Sutra with Commentaries*. Berkeley: Palm Leaves Press.

Harrison, P. (1998). The Pratyutpanna Samadhi Sutra. Translated from the Chinese (Taisho, Vol. 13, No. 418) by Lokaksema. In B. D. Kyokai (Ed.), *BDK English Tripitaka 25–11, 25–111* (pp. 1–116). Berkeley: Numata Center for Buddhist Translation and Research.

Harvey, P. (2000). *An Introduction to Buddhist Ethics: Foundations, Values, and Issues*. Cambridge: Cambridge University Press.

Harvey, P. (2013). *An Introduction to Buddhism: Teachings, History and Practices*. Cambridge: Cambridge University Press.

Harvey, P. (2021a). What Is Seen as Reborn, According to Buddhism? In E. Harris (Ed.), *Buddhism in Five Minutes* (pp. 96–8). Sheffield: Equinox.

Harvey, P. (2021b). What Splits Were There in Buddhism in the Early Centuries? In E. Harris (Ed.), *Buddhism in Five Minutes* (pp. 188–92). Sheffield: Equinox.

Hayes, R. P. (2018). The Buddha. In J. Powers (Ed.), *The Buddhist World* (pp. 487–95). Abingdon: Routledge.

Hertog, J. (2018, Winter). The One Pure Dharma: The New Kadampa Tradition Is Controversial—and Growing. Why? *Tricycle. The Buddhist Review*. https://tricycle.org/magazine/the-one-pure-dharma/

Hinnells, J. (2010). *The Penguin Handbook of the World's Living Religions*. London: Penguin.

Hodal, K. (2013, April 18). Buddhist Monk Uses Racism and Rumours to Spread Hatred in Burma. *The Guardian*. https://www.theguardian.com/world/2013/apr/18/buddhist-monk-spreads-hatred-burma

Holt, J. D. (2019). *Beyond the Big Six Religions: Expanding the Boundaries in the Teaching of Religions and Worldviews*. Chester: University of Chester Press.

Holt, J. D. (2022). *Religious Education in the Secondary School: An Introduction to Teaching, Learning and the World Religions*. Abingdon: Routledge.

hooks, bell (1994). *Teaching to Transgress. Education as the Practice of Freedom*. London: Routledge.

Hultzsch, E. (1925). *Corpus Inscriptionum Indicarum: Vol. I. Inscriptions of Asoka*. Oxford: Clarendon Press.

Humphreys, C. (1955). Our Thirtieth Anniversary Celebrations, *Middle Way*, 29(4), 171–6, 183.

Humphreys, C. (1956). Buddhism in the West. *Middle Way*, 31(1), 6–10.

Humphreys, C. (1958). Zen comes West. *Middle Way*, 32(4), 126–30.

Humphreys, C. (1968). *Sixty Years of Buddhism in Britain*. London: Buddhist Society.

Hüsken, U., & Kieffer-Pülz, P. (2011). Buddhist Ordination as Initiation Ritual and Legal Procedure. In U. H. Neubert (Ed.), *Negotiating Rites, Oxford Ritual Studies Series* (pp. 255–76). New York: Oxford Academic.

Inagaki, H., & Stewart, H. (2003). *The Three Pure Land Sutras* (rev. ed.). Berkeley: Numata Center For Buddhist Translation & Research.

Jackson, R. (1997). *Religious Education: An Interpretive Approach*. London: Hodder.

Jackson, R., Ipgrave, J., Hayward, M., Hopkins, P., Fancourt, N., Robbins, M., Francis, L, & McKenna, U. (2010). *Materials Used to Teach about World Religions in Schools in England*. Warwick: University of Warwick.

Jain, K. (2021, November 2). *Modi's Diwali Extravaganza Shows Why We Need to Tell the Many Stories of Rama*. Religion News Service. https://religionnews.com/2021/11/02/modis-diwali-extravaganza-shows-why-we-need-to-tell-the-many-stories-of-rama/

Jayawichrama, N. (Trans.) (2006). *Nidanakatha of the Jatakathakatha*. Sagaing: Sitagu Inernational Buddhist Academy.

Jenkins, S. (2011, May 11). It's Not so Strange for a Buddhist to Endorse Killing. *The Guardian*. https://www.theguardian.com/commentisfree/belief/2011/may/11/buddhism-bin-laden-death-dalai-lama#:~:text=Killing%20protects%20others%20from%20the,understand%20what%20%22nonviolence%22%20means

Jones, C. V. (2021). What Are the Main Contemporary Divisions in Buddhism? In E. Harris (Ed.), *Buddhism in 5 Minutes* (pp. 193–8). Sheffield: Equinox.

Jones, J. (1949). *The Mahavastu* (Vol. 1). London: Luzac & Co.

Josephson, J. A. (2012). *The Invention of Religion in Japan*. Chicago: University of Chicago Press.

Junghare, I. Y. (1988). Dr. Ambedkar: The Hero of the Mahars, Ex-Untouchables of India. *Asian Folklore Studies*, *47*(1), 93–121.

Kay, D. N. (2004). *Tibetan and Zen Buddhism in Britain: Transplantation, Development and Adaptation*. Abingdon: Routledge.

Keenan, J. (2000). *The Scripture on the Explication of Underlying Meaning*. Translated from the Chinese of Hsiian-tsang (Taisho, Vol. 16, No. 676). Los Angelese: Numata Center for Buddhist Translation and Research.

Keown, D. (1995a). *Buddhism and Bioethics*. London: Macmillan.

Keown, D. (1995b). Viewpoint. End of life: The Buddhist view. *The Lancet,* 366, 952–5.

Keown, D. (2003). *A Dictionary of Buddhism*. Oxford: Oxford University Press.

Keown, D. (2013). *Buddhism. A Very Short Introduction* (2nd ed.). Oxford: Oxford University Press.

Keown, D., & Prebish, C. (2010). *Encyclopedia of Buddhism*. Abingdon: Routledge.

Knitter, P. (2013). *Without Buddha I Could Not Be a Christian*. London: Oneworld.

Lealman, B., & Robinson, E. (1983). *The Mystery of Creation, Teacher's Handbook*. London: CEM.

Lebron, R. E. (2012). *Searching for Spiritual Unity ... Can There Be Common Ground?: A Basic Internet Guide to Forty World Religions & Spiritual Practices*. Bloomington: Crossbooks Publishing.

Lecso, P. A. (1987). A Buddhist View of Abortion. *Journal of Religion and Health*, *26*(3), 214–18.

Lewis, T. (2017). Conveying Buddhist Tradition through its Rituals. In T. Lewis & G. DeAngelis (Eds.), *Teaching Buddhism: New Insights on Understanding and Presenting the Traditions* (pp. 122–50). New York: Oxford University Press.

Lewis, T., & deAngelis, G. (2016). *Teaching Buddhism: New Insights on Understanding and Presenting the Traditions*. Oxford: Oxford University Press.

Ling, T. O. (1969). Buddhist Factors in Population Growth and Control: A Survey Based on Thailand and Ceylon. *Population Studies*, *23*, 53–61.

Lion's Roar Staff. (2003, September 1). Ask the Teachers: 'If there is no self, who is it that keeps getting reincarnated?'. *Lion's Roar*. https://www.lionsroar.com/ask-the-teachers-13/

Lion's Roar Staff. (2010, September 4). Ask the Teachers: Does 'No-Self' Contradict Rebirth? *Lion's Roar*. https://www.lionsroar.com/ask-the-teachers-31/

Lion's Roar Staff. (2018, May 12). The Buddhist Teachings on Rebirth. *Lion's Roar*. https://www.lionsroar.com/just-more-of-the-same/

Littlefair, S. (2018, October 30). Sangharakshita, Founder of Triratna Buddhism, Dead at 93. *Lion's Roar*. https://www.lionsroar.com/sangharakshita-founder-of-triratna-buddhism-dead-at-93/

Lopez, D. S., Jr. (1995a). *Buddhism in Practice*. Princeton: Princeton University Press.

Lopez, D. (1995b). *Curators of the Buddha: The Study of Buddhism Under Colonialism*. Chicago: University of Chicago Press.

Lopez, D. S. (2002). *A Modern Buddhist Bible: Essential Readings from East and West*. Boston: Beacon Press.

Lopez, D. S. (2012, Winter). The Scientific Buddha: Why Do We Ask That Buddhism Be Compatible with Science? *Tricycle. The Buddhist Review*. https://tricycle.org/magazine/scientific-buddha/

Lopez, D. S. (2015a, January 23). Ghosts, Gods, and the Denizens of Hell: Of Buddhism's Six Alternately Wretched and Blissful Realms, Only Ours Offers a Shot at Complete Liberation. *Tricycle. The Buddhist Review*. https://tricycle.org/article/ghosts-gods-and-denizens-hell/

Lopez, D. S. (2015b). *The Norton Anthology of World Religions. Buddhism*. New York: W. W. Norton and Company.

Lopez, D. S., Jr. (2016). *The Lotus Sutra. A Biography*. Princeton: Princeton University Press.

Mair, M. (1989). *Between Psychology and Psychotherapy: A Poetics of Experience*. New York: Routledge.

Maitreyabandhu. (2015). *Journey and the Guide*. Cambridge: Windhorse Publications Ltd.

Masuzawa, T. (2005). *The Invention of World Religions*. London: University of Chicago Press.

McGuire, B. (2019). Analogous Activities: Tools for Thinking Comparatively in Religious Studies Courses. *Teaching Theology and Religion*, 22, 114–26.

McGuire, B. (2021). Pedagogical Possibilities: A Review of Approaches to Undergraduate Teaching in Buddhist Studies. *Religions*, 12(231), 1–23.

McGuire, M. (2008). *Lived Religion. Faith and Practice in Everyday Life*. Oxford: Oxford University press.

McLeod, M. (2022, July 28). No Self, No Suffering. *Lion's Roar*, pp. 37–50.

McMahan, D. (2002). *Empty Vision: Metaphor and Visionary Imagery in Mahayana Buddhism*. London: Routledge.

McMahan, D. L. (2008). *The Making of Modernist Buddhism*. Oxford: Oxford University Press.

Mello, R. (2001). The Power of Storytelling: How Oral Narrative Influences Children's Relationships in Classrooms. *International Journal of Education & the Arts*, 2(1), 1–6.

Metraux, D. A. (1992). The Dispute between the Sōka Gakkai and the Nichiren Shōshu Priesthood: A Lay Revolution against a Conservative Clergy. *Japanese Journal of Religious Studies*, 19(4), 325–36.

Molloy, A. (2014, March 7). Dalai Lama Says Gay Marriage Is 'Ok'. *The Independent*. https://www.independent.co.uk/news/world/americas/dalai-lama-says-gay-marriage-is-ok-9175947.html

Moudgil, M. (2017, June 17). Dalits Are Still Converting to Buddhism, but at a Dwindling Rate. *The Quint*. https://www.thequint.com/news/india/dalits-converting-to-buddhism

Mueller, M. (1894). *Sacred Book of the East Translated by Various Oriental Scholars* (Vol. 49). Oxford: Clarendon Press.

Mullen, E. (2014). Buddhists. In G. Harvey (Ed.), *Religions in Focus: New Approaches to Tradition and Contemporary Practices* (pp. 315–34). Abingdon: Routledge.

Mullin, G. H. (2001). *The Fourteen Dalai Lamas: A Sacred Legacy of Reincarnation*. Santa Fe: Clear Light Publishers.

Murcott, S. (1991). *The First Buddhist Women: Translations and Commentary on the Therigatha*. Berkeley: Parallax Press.

Nagarjuna. (2015). Verses on the Middle Way (The Madhyamakakarika). In D. S. Lopez (Ed.), *The Norton Anthology of World Religions. Buddhism* (pp. 368–74). New York: W. W. Norton and Company.

Nakamura, H. (1964). *The Ways of Thinking of Eastern Peoples: India-China-Tibet-Japan*. Honolulu: University of Hawaii Press.

Nan, H.-C. (1997). *Basic Buddhism: Exploring Buddhism and Zen*. New York: Samuel Weiser.

Narada. (1992). *A Manual of Buddhism*. Taipei: Buddha Educational Foundation.

Nattier, J. (1995). A Prophecy on the Death of the Dharma. In D. Lopez (Ed.), *Buddhism in Practice* (pp. 249–56). Princeton: Princeton University Press.

Neale, M. (2011). *McMindfulness and Frozen Yoga: Rediscovering the Essential Teachings of Ethics and Wisdom*. https://static1.squarespace.com/static/5a8e29ffcd39c3de866b5e14/t/5b5303d91ae6cf630b641909/1532167130908/McMindfulness.pdf

NKT-IBU. (n.d.). *Studying Modern Buddhism*. Modern Kadampa Buddhism. https://kadampa.org/study-programs

NKT-IBU. (2022a). *The Lineage of Modern Kadampa Buddhism*. Modern Kadampa Buddhism. https://kadampa.org/lineage

NKT-IBU. (2022b). *Modern Kadampa Buddhism: The Founder*. Modern Kadampa Buddhism. https://kadampa.org/what-is-modern-buddhism

Notton, C. (1932). *The Chronicle of the Emerald Buddha*. Bangkok: Bangkok Times Press.

Office for National Statistics. (2003). *Census 2011: National Report for England and Wales*. London: TSO.

Office for National Statistics. (2004). *Census 2011: National Report for England and Wales* (Part 2). London: TSO.

Oldmeadow, H. (2004). *Journeys East: 20th Century Western Encounters with Eastern Religious Traditions*. Bloomington: World Wisdom Inc.

Oliver, I. P. (1979). *Buddhism in Britain*. London: Rider.

Oppenheim, M. (2017, May 12). 'It Only Takes One Terrorist': The Buddhist Monk Who Reviles Myanmar's Muslims. *The Guardian*. https://www.theguardian.com/global-development/2017/may/12/only-takes-one-terrorist-buddhist-monk-reviles-myanmar-muslims-rohingya-refugees-ashin-wirathu

O'Sullivan, J. (2018, November 19). *Mudita Bhavana: Cultivating Happiness through the Joy of Others*. Medium. https://satijen.medium.com/mudita-bhavana-cultivating-happiness-through-the-joy-of-others-dfb7faf19ebc

Page, T. (2007). *The Mahayana Mahaparinirvana Sutra*. lirs*ru. http://lirs.ru/do/Mahaparinirvana_Sutra,Yamamoto,Page,2007.pdf

Pew Research Center. (2021). *Religion in India: Tolerance and Segregation*. Washington, DC: Pew Research Center.

Pruden, L. M. (1991). *Abhidharmakosabhasyam of Vasubandhu* (Vol. 2). Berkeley: Asian Humanities Press.

Purser, R. (2019). *McMindfulness. How Mindfulness Became the New Capitalist Spirituality*. London: Repeater.

Rahula, W. (1997). *What the Buddha Taught*. London: One World.

Ranatunga, A. C. (2021). What Is Nirvana? In E. Harris (Ed.), *Buddhism in Five Minutes* (pp. 112–15). Sheffield: Equinox.

Rawlinson, A. (1997). *The Book of Enlightened Masters. Western Teachers in Eastern Traditions*. Chicago: Open Court.

Ray, R. A. (2004). *In the Presence of Masters: Wisdom from 30 Contemporary Tibetan Buddhist Teachers*. Boston: Shambala.

Reeves, G. (2008a). *The Lotus Sutra*. Somerville: Wisdom Publications.

Rinpoche, C. T. (2005). *Meaning of Sangha*. Ripa Ladrang. https://www.abuddhistlibrary.com/Buddhism/A%20-%20Tibetan%20Buddhism/Authors/Chagdud%20Tulku/The%20Meaning%20of%20Sangha/Ripa%20Ladrang%20Foundation%20The%20Meaning%20of%20Sangha%20%28by%20Chagdud%20T.htm

Rinpoche, T. T. (2006, May). The Power of Positive Karma. *Shambhala Sun*, pp. 60–5.

Robinson, R., Johnson, W., Wawrytko, S. A., & Bhikkhu, T. (2005). *Buddhist Religions: A Historical Introduction* (5th ed.). Belmont: Wadsworth/Thomson.

Roeder, E. (1999). *The Origin and Significance of the Emerald Buddha. Explorations in Southeast Asian Studies*. Honolulu: Center for Southeast Asian Studies, University of Hawai'i at Manoa.

Routine Day. (n.d.). His Holiness the 14th Dalai Lama of Tibet. https://www.dalailama.com/the-dalai-lama/biography-and-daily-life/a-routine-day

Saddhatissa, H. (1978). The Saddha Concept in Buddhism. *The Eastern Buddhist*, 11(2), 137–42.

Saddhatissa, H. (2016). *Facets of Buddhism*. Kandy: Buddhist Publication Society.

Sahni, P. (2007). *Environmental Ethics in Buddhism: A Virtues Approach* (1st ed.). Abingdon: Routledge.

Sangharakshita. (n.d.). *Lecture 61: Tibetan Buddhist Meditation*. Free Buddhist Audio. https://www.freebuddhistaudio.com/texts/lecturetexts/061_Tibetan_Buddhist_Meditation.pdf

Sangharakshita. (1978). *Lecture 135: A System of Meditation. Lecture Given on March 29th 1978 on the Order Convention Held at Vinehall School, Robertsbridge, Sussex, UK*. Free Buddhist Audio. https://www.freebuddhistaudio.com/texts/lecturetexts/135_A_System_of_Meditation.pdf

Sangharakshita. (1990). *My Relation to the Order*. Glasgow: Windhorse.

Sangharakshita. (1992). *Buddhism and the West*. Glasgow: Windhorse.

Sangharakshita. (2012). *The Purpose and Practice of Buddhist Meditation: A Sourcebook of Teachings*. Ibis: Ledbury.

Sayadaw, M. (2015). How to Meditate. Practical Vipassana Techniques. In D. S. Lopez (Ed.), *The Norton Anthology of World Religions. Buddhism* (pp. 761–70). New York: W. W. Norton and Company.

Schaeffer, K. R. (2015). Introduction. In T. Chogyel (Ed.), *The Life of the Buddha* (pp. vii–xxvi). New York: Penguin.

Seager, R. (2006). *Encountering the Dharma*. Berkeley: University of California Press.

Senchu, M. (2003). *Two Nichiren Texts. Risshøankokuron* (Taishø Vol. 84, No. 2688) *Kanjinhonzonshø* (Taishø Vol. 84, No. 2692). Berkeley: Numata Center for Buddhist Translation and Research.

SGI. (1996). *Soka Gakkai International*. Tokyo: SGI.

Shantideva. (1961). *Siksamuccaya*. Darbhanga: Mithila Institute.

Shantideva. (2015). *A Guide to the Bodhisattva's Way of Life*. Translated by Stephen Batchelor. Dharamsala: Library of Tibetan Works and Archive.

Smith, J. Z. (2004). *Relating Religion: Essays in the Study of Religion*. Chicago: University of Chicago Press.

Snellgrove, D. (1959). *The Hevajra Tantra* (Two vols. T. 417–8. Taishō 892). Sanskrit Text with English Translation. Oxford: Oxford University Press.

Soeng, M. (2021, April 20). Beyond Self & Other. *Lion's Roar*. https://www.lionsroar.com/exploring-the-heart-sutra/

Soka Gakkai. (n.d.). *Sangha*. Soka Gakkai Dictionary of Buddhism. https://www.nichirenlibrary.org/en/dic/Content/S/25

Stone, J. (1999). *Original Enlightenment and the Transformation of Medieval Japanese Buddhism*. Honolulu: Kuroda Institute.

Stone, J. (2003). *Original Enlightenment and the Transformation of Medieval Japanese Buddhism*. Honolulu: University of Hawaii Press.

Strong, J. (1983). *The Legend of King Asoka: A Study and Translation of the Asokavadana*. Delhi: Motilal Banarsidass Publishers.

Strong, J. (2001). *The Buddha: A Short Biography*. Oxford: Oneworld.

Strong, J. (2015). *Buddhisms. An Introduction*. London: One World.

Subhuti. (2009). *The Just Sitting Practice – An Introduction*. Free Buddhist Audio. https://www.freebuddhistaudio.com/audio/details?num=OM814

Sujato, B. (2012a). *Sects and Sectarianism: The Origins of Buddhist Schools*. Santipada: Santi Forest Monastery.

Sujato. (2012b, March 21). *Why Buddhists Should Support Marriage Equality*. Sujato's Blog. https://sujato.wordpress.com/2012/03/21/1430/

Suzuki, D. T. (1907). *Outlines of Mahayâna Buddhism*. London: Luzac & Company.

Suzuki, D. T. (1946). An Interpretation of Zen-Experience. In C. A. Moore (Ed.), *Philosophy-East and West* (pp. 109–29). Princeton: Princeton University Press.

Takakusu, J., & Nagai, M. (1975). *Samantapasadika*. Oxford: Pali Text Society.

Tan, P. (2018). *The Miraculous Life of Gotama Buddha. A Study in the Psychology of Mythology of the Historical Bodhisattva*. Singapore: The Minding Centre.

Thanissaro, P. N. (2011). A Preliminary Assessment of Buddhism's Contextualisation to the English RE classroom. *British Journal of Religious Education*, *33*(1), 61–74.

Thapar, R. (1997). *Asoka and the Decline of the Mauryas*. Delhi: Oxford University Press.

Theos Think Tank (2021) *Nobody Stands Nowhere*. https://www.youtube.com/watch?v=AFRxKF-Jdos (accessed 20 April 2023).

Thera, N. M. (1979). *A Manual of Abhidhamma* (5th ed.). Kandy: Buddhist Missionary Society.

Thondup, T. (1998). *The Healing Power of Mind: Simple Meditation Exercises for Health, Well-Being, and Enlightenment (Buddhayana)*. Boston: Shambala.

Thurman, R. (1976). *The Holy Teaching of Vimalakirti: A Mahayana Scripture*. Pennsylvania: Pennsylvania University Press.

Tomalin, E., & Starkey, C. (2016). *A Survey of Buddhist Buildings in England*. Leeds: The Centre of Religion and Public Life, University of Leeds.

Trainor, K. (2004). *Buddhism: The Illustrated Guide*. Oxford: Oxford University Press.

Tricycle. (2019). What Is Buddhanature? *Tricycle: The Buddhist Review*. https://tricycle.org/beginners/buddhism/what-is-buddhanature/

Triratna Buddhist Community. (2018). *Triratna: How Are We Doing Now? A Triratna Interkula Survey to Assess How the Triratna Community Feels Now about Allegations of Past Misconduct.* Triratna.

Tshering, G. (2015). Foreword. In Shantideva, *A Guide to the Bodhisattva's Way of Life* (p. iii). Dharamsala: Library of Tibetan Works and Archive.

Ubeysekara, A. (2020, July 15). *Nirodha Samapatti in Theravada Buddhism.* Drarisworld. https://drarisworld.wordpress.com/2020/07/15/nirodha-samapatti-in-theravada-buddhism/

Vajragupta. (2010). *The Triratna Story. Behind the Scenes of a New Buddhist Movement.* Glasgow: Windhorse Publications.

Vetter, T. (1988). *The Ideas and Meditative Practices of Early Buddhism.* Leiden: Brill.

Victoria, B. D. (2006). *Zen at War* (2nd ed.). Lanham: Rowman & Littlefield Publishers.

Voon, C. (2016, December 13). *The Raw Expression of a Rare, Emaciated Buddha.* Hyperallergic. https://hyperallergic.com/344879/the-raw-expression-of-a-rare-emaciated-buddha/

Wallis, G. (2007). *Basic Teachings of the Buddha: A New Translation and Compilation, with a Guide to Reading the Texts* . New York: The Modern Library.

Wallis, G. (2020). Gautama vs Buddha. In A. Miller (Ed.), *The Essential Guide to the Buddha* (pp. 65–75). Nova Scotia: Lions Roar.

Wang, R. (2021). How Does One 'Read' a Buddha-Image? In E. Harris (Ed.), *Buddhism in Five Minutes* (pp. 55–9). Sheffield: Equinox.

Waterhouse, H. J. (1997). *Authority and Adaptation: A Case Study in British Buddhism* [PhD Thesis]. Bath: The University of the West of England.

Wawrytko, S. (2007). Holding Up the Mirror to Buddha-Nature: Discerning the Ghee in the Lotus Sutra. *Dao, 6*, 63–81.

Wells, D. (2016, November 9). The Buddhist Life of Benedict Cumberbatch. *Lion's Roar.* https://www.lionsroar.com/the-buddhist-life-of-benedict-cumberbatch/

Whitaker, J., & Smith, D. (2018). Ethics, Meditation and Wisdom. In D. Cozart & J. M. Shields (Eds.), *The Oxford Handbook of Buddhist Ethics* (pp. 51–76). Oxford: Oxford University Press.

Williams, D. (2020, December 10). It's Great That the Government Are Asking Questions about Faith and Religion but Are They Asking the Right Ones? *Faithroots.* https://faithroot.com/2020/12/10/its-great-that-the-government-are-asking-questions-about-faith-and-religion-but-are-they-asking-the-right-ones/

Williams, P. (2009). *Mahayana Buddhism. The Doctrinal Foundations* (2nd ed.). Abingdon: Routledge.

Williams, P., Tribe, A., & Wynne, A. (2012). *Buddhist Thought. A Complete Introduction to the Indian Tradition.* Abingdon: Routledge.

Wilson, B. (2000). The British Movement and Its Members. In D. A. Machacek (Ed.), *Global Citizens: The Soka Gakkai Movement in the World* (pp. 349–74). Oxford: Oxford University Press.

Wintersgill, B. (2017). *Big Ideas in Religious Education.* Exeter: University of Exeter.

Wood, B. (2020). *What Has the Idea of 'Worldview' Contributed to My Curriculum Thinking?* https://www.reonline.org.uk/2020/07/21/what-has-the-idea-of-worldview-contributed-to-my-curriculum-thinking/

Wright, D. S. (2009). *The Six Perfections: Buddhism and the Cultivation of Character.* Oxford: Oxford University Press.

WRN Editorial Staff. (2015, May 15). *Thich Nhat Hanh Talks Violence and How Buddhists and Judeo-Christians are Connected*. World Religion News. https://www.worldreligionnews.com/religion-news/christianity/thich-nhat-hanh-talks-violence-and-how-buddhists-and-judeo-christians-are-connected/

Yun, H. (2012). *Four Insights for Finding Fulfillment: A Practical Guide to the Buddha's Diamond Sutra*. Los Angeles: Buddha's Light Publishing.

Glossary

The glossary will include Pali and Sanskrit transliterations as appropriate, followed by the meaning of the word. Other languages are identified, apart from the English terms.

Pali	Sanskrit	Meaning
Abhidhamma	Abhidharma	The 'higher' teaching of the Buddha. A range of literature is identified as Abidhamma.
Abhidhamma Pitaka	Abhidharma Pitaka	The third section of the Tipitaka (Tripitaka). It is a systematic outlining of the teachings of the Buddha Shakyamuni.
Ahimsa	Ahimsa	'Non-violence'. Inherently linked with the First Precept.
Amitabha	Amitayus also, Amida (Japanese).	'The Buddha of eternal light'. The primary focus of Pure Land Buddhism.
Ananda		One of the ten primary companions of the Buddha. He is believed to have memorised the teachings of the Buddha and is said to have recited them at the First Council, prior to which he had become Awakened.
Anapanasati	Anapanasmriti	'Mindfulness of the breath', which is a practice associated with Vipassana, which brings calm.
Anatta	Anatman	'No permanent self'. One of the Three Marks of Existence.
Anicca	Anitya	'Impermanence'. One of the Three Marks of Existence.
Arahant	Arhat	'Enlightened disciple'. The fourth stage of awakening in the Theravada tradition. An enlightened/awakened being.
Avijja	Avidya	Ignorance and a lack of perception of the reality of the physical world. One of the Three Poisons that drives the cycle of rebirth.
Bardo (Tibetan)		The intermediate stage between death and rebirth.
Bhava	Bhava	'Becoming'. The tenth of the links of dependent origination.
Bhikkhu	Bhiksu	A fully ordained Buddhist monk.
Bhikkhuni	Bhikshuni	A fully ordained Buddhist nun.
Bodhi Tree		The tree under which Shakyamuni Buddha attained enlightenment. In many Buddhist places of devotion there will be a bodhi tree.

Pali	Sanskrit	Meaning
Bodhisatta	Bodhisattva	In Theravada this refers to a Buddha in waiting. Someone who has made the vow to become a Buddha and help others escape the cycle of samsara. Through numerous aeons and lifetimes Shakyamuni Buddha was such a bodhisattva, and since his life on earth, Maitreya has been a bodhisattva waiting in Tusita heaven.
Brahma Viharas		'Divine abidings', of which there are four: immeasurable friendliness, compassion, sympathetic joy and equanimity
Buddha	Buddha	'Enlightened one' or 'awakened one'
Buddha-nature	Buddhadhatu	This suggests that every person has the potential within themselves to become a Buddha.
Buddharupa	Buddharupa	'Form of the awakened one', often used as a focus for meditation, or worship.
Buddhayana		'The Buddha vehicle'. In the modern world it is used as an attempt to unify the traditions.
Dalai Lama		Within Tibetan Buddhism the Dalai Lama is the manifestation of the bodhisattva Avalokitesvara whose role is to protect the Tibetan people. The title, Dalai Lama, was not used until over a hundred years after the first Dalai Lama's death. It is seen that the first 'incarnation' was Gendun Drup (1391–1474), a monk from the Kadampa tradition.
Dana	Dana	'Generosity'. One of the ten virtues.
Dependent origination		See *Pratityasamutpada*
Dhamma	Dharma	The teachings of the Buddha. One of the Three Refuges. Usually translated as 'universal law' or 'universal truth'.
Dhammapada	Dhammapada	One of the most popular Buddhist texts. Part of the Khuddaka Nikaya. It is a collection of the sayings of the Buddha.
Dukkha	Duhkha	Usually translated as 'suffering' but is a much more expansive term that may include 'stress', 'unsatisfactoriness' or 'unease'. The First Noble Truth and one of the Three Marks of Existence.
Four Noble Truths		Truths that are grasped by the noble. They lie at the heart of Buddhist teaching, and are dukkha, tanha (and samudaya), nirodha (nirvana) and magga.
Four Sights		The four things Siddhartha Gautama saw when he left the palace: an old man, an ill man, a dead man and a holy man. Many believe this is where the Buddha realised the truth of dukkha.
Gompa (Tibetan)		Monastery or a place of meditation.

Glossary

Pali	Sanskrit	Meaning
Gotama	Gautama	The family name of Shakyamuni Buddha
	Hinayana	'Lesser vehicle'. Often used to describe the earlier paths of Buddhism prior to Mahayana. Is seen by many as pejorative and the term Nikaya is now preferred.
Jara-marana	Jara-marana	'Old age' and 'death'. One of the links of dependent origination.
	Jataka	Birth story, or more widely known as the stories of the previous lives of the Buddha.
Jati	Jati	'Rebirth'. One of the links of dependent origination.
Jhana	Dhyana, also Ch'an (Chinese) and Zen (Japanese)	Meditative concentration.
Kadampa		An ancient Tibetan Buddhist tradition from the eleventh century. It was later absorbed into newer schools. The New Kadampa Tradition was founded in 1991 under the direction of Kelsang Gyatso.
Kamma	Karma	'Action' or 'doing'. Karma is not an immutable law that is controlled by the universe or by a deity, rather it is something that drives the cycle of rebirth, but also something that is directed by intentional action.
Karuna	Karuna	'Compassion'. One of the qualities to be developed on the bodhisattva path. In Theravada it is one of the divine abodes.
Kesa (Japanese)		A white length of cloth/scarf that is worn around the neck of a Triratna Mitra. On each end is embroidered the Three Jewels as a reminder of the refuge they have taken.
Khandha	Skandha	'Aggregate' or constituent part. The belief in the five khandas is an integral part of anatta. A person is made up of five constituent parts: form, sensations, perceptions, mental activity and consciousness.
Ksanti	Kshanti	'Patience'. One of the paramitas.
Kilesa	Klesa	Mental states that cloud the mind such as fear and anger.
Koan (Japanese)		A question or riddle that becomes a focus for meditation/concentration. Usually in Zen Buddhism.
Lama (Tibetan)		'Teacher'. Usually seen as a leader within Tibetan Buddhism.
Loka	Loka	Realm of rebirth.

Pali	Sanskrit	Meaning
Lotus Sutra		'Wonderful Dharma lotus flower sutra'. *The Lotus Sutra* is a text that has significant meaning within different traditions of Mahayana Buddhism. It tells of the teaching of Shakyamuni Buddha's teaching on Vulture's Peak. In this sutra the teaching prior to the Vulture's Peak Sermon is revealed to be an example of skilful means and that the true or higher teaching of the Buddha is taught by the Buddha to the assembled bodhisattva.
Magga	Marga	The Fourth Noble Truth known as the Middle Way or the Eightfold Path.
	Mahayana	'Greater vehicle'. The largest tradition of Buddhism containing many schools. Believed to have developed in India somewhere between the second century BCE and the first century CE; however, many may suggest that it goes back to the time of the Buddha.
Mala	Also Juzu (Japanese)	Aid to worship. A string of beads.
Maya		Mother of Buddha Shakyamuni/Siddhartha Gautama.
Metta	Maitri	'Loving kindness'. A pure love.
Metteya	Maitreya	The future Buddha, currently a bodhisattva ruling in the Tusita heavens.
Mindfulness		The beginning and basis of meditation. This is the ability to focus on the here and now rather than the future, which is uncontrollable.
Mitra		An ordained member of the Triratna Buddhist order.
Mudda	Mudra	A ritual gesture, usually of the hands, shown in images of the Buddha.
Mudita	Mudita	'Joy'.
Nama-rupa		Name and form is indicative of when the name (the mind) and the form (matter) coalesce to bring together the five khandas to form a being. One of the links of dependent origination.
Navayana		'New vehicle'; often used synonymously with Ambedkar Buddhism, this is, however, only one expression.
Nibbana	Nirvana	Often translated as 'blowing out', sometimes as 'going out'. Signifies the end of rebirth together with the ending or cessation of craving and dispassion. Sometimes identified as the Third Noble Truth.

Pali	Sanskrit	Meaning
Nichiren Buddhism (Japanese)		One of the largest schools of Buddhism within Japan was established based on the teachings of Nichiren in the thirteenth century. The main focus of Nichiren's teachings surrounded the Lotus Sutra, and in the centuries since then there can be seen to have been divisions within the Nichiren community that led to different groups. These divisions have often surrounded the assimilation of Japanese traditions and thoughts into the practice of Buddhism.
Nirodha	Nirodha	'Cessation or 'extinction'. The Third Noble Truth that dukkha can be ended by stopping desires and cravings.
Panna	Prajna	'Wisdom' or 'insight'. One of the characteristics of a bodhisattva.
Parami	Paramita	'A transcendent action'. Within Mahayana there are six paramitas: dana, sila, ksanti, virya, dhyana and prajna. There are sometimes seen to be ten.
Parinibbana	Parinirvana	Final and complete nirvana. Occurs when a Buddha dies.
Phassa	Sparsa	'Contact'. This is the contact between each of the individual senses and the outer environment. One of the links of dependent origination.
Phowa (Tibetan)	Utkranti	The transference of the karmic consciousness at the time of death/rebirth.
Pitaka		'Basket'. Collection of scriptures (see Tipitaka).
Pratityasamutpada	Paticcasamuppada	Dependent origination. Everything is interconnected, and dependent (i.e. not independent), on other aspects and events in the universe. Everything that occurs does so dependent on causes and conditions that pre-exist.
Puja		Devotion or worship.
Pure Land		The Pure Land tradition generally focuses on Buddha Amitabha (Japanese: Amida; the Buddha of Infinite Light) and his Pure Land of Sukhavati (land of bliss and happiness).
Rahula		Son of Siddhartha Gautama.
Rupa	Rupa	'Form'. One of the five aggregates referring to the body. The word is used in other areas such as rupa jhanas.
Salayatana	Sadayatana	The six ayatanas are sometimes referred to as senses or sources. They are inextricably linked with the six consciousnesses. One of the links of dependent origination.
Sakadagamin	Sakadagramin	A 'once-returner'. The second stage to awakening as an arahant.

Pali	Sanskrit	Meaning
Sakyamuni	Shakyamuni	'Of the tribe/clan of the Sakyas/Shakyas' indicating Siddhartha Gautama's family heritage. He is often known as Shakyamuni Buddha.
Samadhi	Samadhi	'Meditation' or the way of meditation. Samadhi is the way of right mindfulness, concentration and effort.
Samatha	Samatha	'Serenity'. A type of meditation sometimes called tranquillity meditation.
Samsara	Samsara	Cycle of birth and rebirth.
Samudaya	Samudaya	'Arising'. Generally refers to the arising or cause of suffering. The Second Noble Truth.
Sangha	Samgha	'Assembly' or community of Buddhists. One of the Three Refuges. Often split into the lay and ordained sangha.
Sankhara	Samskara	'Formations'. Refers to mental formation, one of the five khandas.
Sanjna	Samjna	'Perception'. One of the five khandas.
Satori (Japanese)		'Awakening'. Used in Zen Buddhism.
Siddattha	Siddhartha	Given name of Shakyamuni Buddha. Means 'Wish fulfilled'.
Sila	Sila	'Morality'. Part of the Threefold Way.
Soka Gakkai (Japanese)		A form of Nichiren Buddhism with a large following in the UK. Developed in the twentieth century.
Sotapanna	Srotapanna	'Stream enterer'. The first stage to awakening as an arahant.
Suddhodana		The father of Siddhartha Gautama.
Sunnata	Sunyata	'Emptiness'. Sunyata is an important aspect of existence and the nature of dependent origination.
Sutta	Sutra	'Text'. Usually refers to the words of the Buddha.
Sutta Pitaka	Sutra Pitaka	The second of the three baskets/collections of the Tipitaka.
Tanha	Trsna	'Thirst', 'craving' or 'desire;. The Second Noble Truth that is the source of dukkha.
Tathagata	Tathagata	'One who has thus gone'. A title of the Buddha.
Theravada	Sthaviravada	'Way of the elders'. One of the main traditions of Buddhism. Seen by many as the only surviving form of Nikaya Buddhism.
Thupa/Cetiya	Stupa	'Reliquary'. Usually a burial mound containing remains of the Buddha or other important Buddhists.
Tipitaka	Tripitaka	'Three Baskets'. The Pali Canon containing three sections: Abhidhamma Pitaka, Sutta Pitaka and Vinaya Pitaka.
Tiratana	Triratna	'Three Jewels' or 'Three Refuges' of Buddhism: the Buddha, the dharma and the sangha.

Pali	Sanskrit	Meaning
Triratna Buddhism		Formerly the Friends of the Western Buddhist Order. A Buddhist tradition developed in the twentieth century, initially in the UK.
Tulku (Tibetan)		The rebirth of a Lama.
Tusita	Tushita	A deva realm, where the Buddha was before his birth in this world. The Buddha taught his mother here, and Maitreya is waiting for his birth in Tusita.
Upadana	Upadana	'Grasping'. Linked very much with the idea of craving, grasping to sensual pleasures, to wrong views, the efficacy of rules and practice and the idea of the self. One of the links of dependent origination.
Upaya	Upaya	'Skilful means'. Usually appended to any skilful action. In forms of Mahayana Buddhism it can refer to the Buddha's disguising of his higher teaching.
Upekkha	Upeksa	'Equanimity' or 'evenness of mind'.
Uposatha	Upavasatha	'Entering to stay'. Monthly days of observance.
Vajrayana		'The Diamond Vehicle'. A form of Tantric Mahayana Buddhism. Vajrayana highlights the importance of the teacher who shows the student the path to enlightenment and the possibility of buddhahood in this lifetime.
Vassa	Varsa	Three month rainy retreat usually observed by Theravada Buddhists.
Vedana	Vedana	'Feeling'. One of the five Khandas.
Vihara	Vihara	Usually refers to a Buddhist monastery or place of worship.
Vinaya	Vinaya	'Discipline'. Rules for ordained Buddhists.
Vinaya Pitaka		The first of the three baskets of the Tipitaka. Mainly containing rules of the ordained sangha.
Vinnana	Vijnana	'Consciousness'. One of the five Khandas.
Vipassana	Vipashyana	'Insight' meditation. In vipassana the various stages are to help a person gain insight into the nature of all things.
Viriya	Virya	'Effort' or 'vigour'. One of the six paramitas.
Wesak or Vesak	Vaisakha	Buddha day. A festival celebrating the birth, enlightenment and death of Shakyamuni Buddha.
Wheel of Life	Bhavachakra	A Mahayana thangka representing the cycle of samsara and the realms of rebirth.
Yasodhara	Yasodhara	The wife of Siddhartha Gautama. Later ordained as a bhikkhuni.
Zazen (Japanese)		Sitting meditation. A practice typically associated with Zen Buddhism.
Zen (Japanese)	Chan (Chinese)	A form of Mahayana Buddhism developed in China from the sixth century.

Index

Abhidhamma 122–4, 159, 231
Abhidhamma Pitaka 122–4, 231, 236
abortion 170, 171–2, 178
Aggregates see Five Khandas
ahimsa 232
Alara Kalama 83–4, 87
Ambedkarite Buddhist Movement 44
Ambedkar, Bhimrao Ramji 44–5, 133, 198
Amitabha/ Amida
Amitayurdhyana Sutra (Contemplation Sutra) 129, 132, 151–2
anagami 113, 115–16
Ananda 7, 22, 77, 87, 112, 120, 121–2, 126, 183, 231
anatman see anatta
anatta 14, 26, 35, 47, 49, 50, 51, 52, 54, 115, 231
Anguttara Nikaya 122
anicca 25, 29, 35, 47, 50, 231
animals 36, 55, 56, 63, 157, 172, 174–5, 176, 177
Annata-Kondanna 84
Apple, James 106, 107
Appleton, Naomi 74–5, 184
arahant/ arhat 3, 40, 64, 94, 100–1, 105, 112–16, 117–18, 125, 213, 231
    seven purifications of 114
    stages of becoming 60, 87, 112–16
Armstrong, Karen 3
Arupaloka 58, 60
Ashoka 6, 9, 68, 124
Asokavadana 68–9
Assaji 85
Atisha 42
authority 121, 136, 138–9, 165–6, 185, 187, 190, 192, 194–5, 204–5
Avalokita 27, 49
Avalokitesvara 15, 54, 111, 151, 156, 166, 232
Avatamsaka Sutra 131–2
avidya see ignorance

Awakening 31, 39–40, 41–2, 51, 56, 57–8, 64, 75, 77, 80, 83–4, 85–7, 91, 92–3, 96, 97, 98–9, 105–6, 107–8, 110–13, 117, 126, 130–1, 137, 143, 151, 159, 165–6, 201, 210, 236
ayatanas 29, 33–4, 235

bala 109, 168
bardo
Batchelor, Stephen 9, 190, 198, 207
becoming see bhava 31, 33, 34, 36, 37–9, 165, 231
Bhaddiya 84
bhava-tanha 37–8
bhavachakra see Wheel of Life 52, 231
bhikkhu 83, 87, 135–6, 145, 158, 169, 174, 179, 231
Bhikkhu, Thanissaro 25, 50, 65, 187
bhikkhuni 87, 135–6, 145, 158, 179, 182–5, 231
bhumis see bodhisattva, stages of becoming
Bloom, Colin 1
Bluck, Robert 77, 190, 196, 198, 202, 207
Bodhi, Bhikkhu 92, 94, 113, 115, 123
Bodhidharma 149
bodhisattva 7, 37, 61, 89, 100–1, 105–12, 117, 124, 126–7, 128, 130, 131–2, 137, 151, 152, 158, 167, 170, 198, 201, 232, 234
    examples of 9, 27, 49, 54, 111–12, 128, 131, 156, 184, 188, 189, 232
    practices of/ ideal 41–2, 56, 94, 100–1, 103, 105–10, 126–7, 201, 213, 233
    stages of becoming 43, 101, 106–8
    vow of 106–7, 129, 167
Budai 15, 133–4
Buddha xiii, 1, 2–4, 5–8, 11, 21, 22, 23–5, 28, 36, 38–42, 44, 50, 53, 54, 62, 64–5, 67–90, 91–2, 95, 99, 101, 106–7, 109–10, 112, 113, 115, 119, 129, 130, 131, 132–3, 134, 135, 145, 149, 151, 152, 153–7, 165, 167, 171, 174, 178, 183–5, 188, 193, 196, 198, 200, 204, 211, 231, 232, 233, 236

authentication of sayings 7–8, 12, 70–1, 121–4, 138–9, 188–9, 195
Awakening of 85–7, 97, 232
birth of 6, 10, 68, 76–80
as a bodhisattva 60, 72–6, 83, 86, 133, 174
childhood of 80–1
death of 6, 87–8, 121–2, 125–7, 153
identity of 3–4, 16, 67, 72–6, 105, 120–1, 188–9
leaving the palace 81–83
life as an ascetic 83–5, 155
past lives 13, 73–4, 109, 170
retelling of his life story 35, 45–6, 67–71, 135
sources for his life story 67–71
Teachings of *see* dharma
buddha-nature 50–1, 56, 58, 131, 136–7, 177, 192, 232
Buddhaghosa 112, 114, 123, 155, 173
buddharupa 143, 152–8, 232
Buddhism
  definition of xii, 1–17, 21–2, 23, 89
  development of 6–11, 12–15, 82–3, 125–7, 132–4, 208–10
  different forms of 5–6, 7, 10–11, 12–17, 21, 24, 41–5, 57, 103, 116–18, 121, 148–9, 165, 174, 187–205
  in the UK 185–6, 187–205, 207–213
buildings 10–11, 203, 211–12

Census of England and Wales 207–8
Chodron, Thubten 5, 25, 27, 28, 29, 60, 75, 95, 97, 137
Chogyel, Tenzin 70, 75, 80, 83, 86
colonialism xi-xiii, 1–3, 21, 58, 117, 132, 141, 208
Commission on RE xiii-xiv
consciousness 2–3, 29, 30, 31, 33–4, 48, 52–4, 57, 60, 64, 129–30, 131, 143, 144, 149, 171–2, 200, 233, 236, 237
contact 29, 30, 33–4, 235
Conze, Edward 109
cosmology Mahayana 54–7, 57–8, 65–6, 91
cosmology Theravada 58–64, 91
craving 30, 33, 34, 35–9, 40, 41, 55, 64, 75, 85, 97, 144, 153, 179, 182, 201, 234, 235, 236, 237
Cush, Denise 155, 207

Dalai Lama 15, 54, 55, 112, 232
Dalit Buddhist Movement 44, 45
dana 14, 61, 108–9, 167, 168, 175–6, 232, 235
demigods 55, 56

dependent origination 25, 26–35, 36, 37, 43, 45, 49, 53, 55, 86, 99, 110, 123, 127, 200, 231, 233, 234, 235, 236, 237
devas 55–6, 60–2, 64, 87, 91, 171
Dhamma/ dharma 4, 5–6, 7, 11, 21–2, 26–7, 39, 42–3, 56, 57, 71, 75, 84, 86–7, 91, 97, 99, 105, 106, 107–8, 119–134, 138–40, 149, 156, 157, 160, 167, 180, 183, 196–7, 198, 203–4, 209–10, 232
  decline of 125–7, 132–4, 139, 180, 183
dhyana 108–9, 148–9, 150, 168, 200–1
Diamond Sutra 109, 128, 197
Digha Nikaya 122
Dipamkara 72, 73
ditthi 38, 92, 100, 114
Dorje Shugden 193
Dossett, Wendy 58
Drup, Gendrup 54, 55, 232
dukkha 23–35, 36–39, 39–40, 49, 60, 64, 82–3, 89, 91, 167, 232
dukkha-dukkha 25

Edicts of Ashoka 68
Eightfold Path *see* Middle Way
emptiness 24, 26, 27–8, 35, 38, 41, 43, 45, 49, 53–4, 99, 109–10, 127–8, 131, 146, 213, 236
Engaged Buddhism 176–7, 180
Enlightenment *see* Awakening
environmentalism 175, 176–7, 185
essentialism xiv
euthanasia 170, 171, 172–3, 186

false speech 94–5, 180–1, 199
Ferguson, Gaylon 49
festivals 140, 141–2, 158–9, 212
five khandas/ skhandas 23, 29, 31, 39, 42, 47–50, 52, 64, 111, 114, 233, 234, 236, 237
Five Precepts 95, 102, 165–6, 167–85, 199
Flower Sermon 149–50
formation 28–9, 33, 34, 48–9, 236
Four Noble Truths 22–45, 45–6, 64, 86, 87, 91, 97, 98–9, 99–100, 117, 119, 122, 123, 127, 132, 144, 146, 152, 154–5, 213, 232, 234, 235, 236
Four Sights 81–3, 232

gandhabba 62, 172
Gautama, Siddhartha *see* Buddha
Gelugpa 17, 193
Gethin, Rupert 6, 33, 38, 39, 40, 100, 116, 123, 124, 148

Gohonzon 190–1, 192
Gombrich, Richard 2, 4, 64
Gotami, Krisha 35
Gotami, Mahapajapati 80, 87, 136, 183
grasping 30, 33, 34, 36, 49, 115, 237
Gyatso, Kelsang 194–5, 233

Hanh, Thich Nhat 21, 24, 26–7, 49, 53, 81, 82, 96, 126–7, 132, 141, 146–7, 161, 166, 168–9, 177, 179, 181, 182, 187
Harvey, Peter 8, 9, 37, 53, 64, 71, 101, 143, 172
Heart Sutra 27, 109, 127–8, 194–5
hell 55, 56–7, 59, 63, 171, 172
Holt, James xiv-xv, 1, 3, 21, 45, 102, 141, 159
Humanists UK xv
Humphreys, Christmas 185, 207, 209
hungry ghosts 55, 56, 62, 79

ignorance 23, 28, 33–4, 35–6, 37, 43, 55, 116, 130, 137, 144, 153, 157, 199, 231
intoxicants 96, 136, 168, 169, 181–2, 195, 199

Jackson, Robert xiii
Japan 5, 9, 11, 12, 58, 110, 137, 148, 162, 188–90, 192, 196, 209, 210
Jataka Tales 70, 72, 74–5, 77, 122, 170, 172, 184
jhana 60–1, 98, 142–3, 144, 202
jnana 109, 168

kama-tanha 36
Kamaloka 61–2, 63
kamma *see* karma
karma 26, 29, 30, 31, 37, 44, 50, 52, 53, 55, 56–7, 58, 60–114, , 86, 94, 99, 137, 165, 169, 170, 174, 233
karuna 93–4, 147, 148, 156, 166–7, 233
Kassapa 73, 74, 75
Kennett, Jiyu (Peggy) 185, 29
Keown, Damien 37, 41, 44, 56, 99, 109, 112, 170, 172, 173
Khuddaka Nikaya 122, 232
koan 127, 150, 233
ksanti 72, 105, 108, 109, 122 168, 233

Lankavatara Sutra 55, 131
Lingwood, Dennis *see* Sangharakshita
Longer Sukhavativyuha Sutra (Infinite Life Sutra) 129, 132
Lopez, Donald xii, 4, 9–10, 39, 56, 76, 122, 123, 150, 161, 170, 188, 197

Lotus Sutra 7–8, 11, 42–3, 51, 75–6, 105–6, 112, 127, 188–9, 190–2, 234
loving kindness *see* metta
Lumbini 10–11, 68, 77, 211

magga *see* Middle Way
Mahanama 84
Mahayana 7–8, 9–10, 12, 14, 16, 28, 29, 41–2, 43, 50, 54–8, 63–4, 65–6, 69–70, 75–6, 88, 91, 100–1, 103, 105–112, 116–18, 124–34, 136–8, 146, 148–9, 159, 167–8, 174, 184, 188, 199, 202, 204–5, 234
Maitreya 15, 44, 61, 75, 105, 111, 125, 132–4, 156, 232, 234, 237
Majhima Nikaya 122
malas 158, 161, 234
mandalas 65–6, 111, 150–1, 158, 159, 161, 192
mantras 9, 58, 111, 119, 157–8, 195, 198
Mara 61, 69, 85–6, 97, 153, 182
Masuzawa, Tomoko xii
Maya 76–7, 234
Mcleod, Melvin 25
McMahan, David 5, 12, 13–14, 155
McMindfulness 160–1
meditation 13–14, 23, 27, 37, 44, 53, 58, 60–1, 65, 84, 85, 92, 94, 96–8, 124, 125, 127, 128, 130, 131, 135, 141, 142–52, 153, 157–8, 159–61, 166, 182, 188, 194–5, 200–3, 210, 232, 233, 234, 236, 237
merit transfer of 37, 58, 109, 112, 162, 167
metta 145, 147–8, 166–7, 168, 169, 234
metta bhavana 147–8, 169, 200, 201
Middle Way 37, 40–1, 56, 62, 85, 87, 91–103, 109, 115, 116, 122, 141, 142, 143, 155, 165, 234
mindfulness 30, 57–8, 60, 84, 92, 94, 96–7, 97–8, 102, 114, 143–4, 144–7, 155, 159–62, 169, 182, 201, 203, 210, 212, 231, 234, 236
Modern Buddhism 12–13, 16, 210
morality *see* sila

nama-rupa *see* name and form
name and form 29, 33–4, 234
Navayana Buddhism 44–5, 133, 234
nembutsu 58, 188
New Kadampa Tradition 17, 188, 192–5, 204, 211, 233
nibbana *see* nirvana
Nichiren 11, 188–9, 235
Nichiren Buddhism 11, 17, 42–3, 127, 132, 137–8, 174–5, 188–92, 235, 236
Nikaya Buddhism 7, 9, 136, 233, 236

nirodha 39–40, 232, 235
nirvana 26, 39–41, 60, 62, 63, 64–5, 88, 105–6, 108, 113, 116–18, 120, 126, 137, 139, 144, 149, 153, 161, 211, 232, 234, 235
no-self see anatta

Pali Canon 109, 120, 121–5, 126, 236
paramitas see Ten Perfections
parinirvana/ parinibbana 42–3, 64, 75, 87–8, 100, 106, 112, 117, 133, 153, 167, 235
Paticcasamuppada see dependent origination
patience see ksanti
Pew Research Senter 2, 11
power dynamics 140, 177–8
prajna/ panna 11, 40, 43, 55, 61–2, 72, 92, 94, 98–100, 101, 105–6, 107–10, 116, 117, 122, 127–8, 137, 146, 150, 156, 165, 167, 168, 185, 195, 199, 235
pranidhana 106, 109, 168
pratityasamutpada see dependent origination
Pratyutpanna Samadhi Sutra 128
prayer wheels 157–8
puja 141, 142, 152–8, 203, 235
Pure Land Buddhism 17, 57–8, 129, 150, 151, 188, 189, 204–5, 231, 235
Pure Lands 57–8, 106, 112, 118, 128–9, 151–2, 188

Questions of King Milinda 47

Rahula 77, 81, 235
Rahula, Walpola 24–5, 36, 39, 119–20
Rajagaha 83
realms of rebirth see cosmology
rebirth 14, 28–9, 30, 31, 33–4, 36, 37–8, 39–41, 42, 44, 47, 51–66, 75, 86, 89, 99, 106, 108, 111, 113, 115, 116, 117, 126, 128–9, 165, 172, 188, 233
Refuges 5–6, 71, 73, 75, 87–8, 119–20, 134, 135, 137, 139, 157, 192, 193, 195, 196, 197, 198, 203, 210–11, 232, 233, 236
religion xi-xv, 1–2, 4, 6, 13, 14, 21, 67, 121, 134, 139, 141, 181, 183, 208, 211
right concentration 92, 94, 97, 98, 103, 115
right action 92, 93–4, 95–6, 98, 115
right effort 92, 94, 97–8, 103, 115
right livelihood 92, 93–4, 95–6, 102–3, 115, 170, 203
right mindfulness 92, 94, 96–8, 100, 103, 115, 143, 236
right resolve 92, 94, 99, 100, 103, 115
right speech 92, 93–5, 102–3, 115

right view 38, 62, 92, 94, 99–100, 102–3, 115
Rinpoche, Shugseb Jetaun 184
Rinpoche, Wangyal 50
Rupaloka 58–9, 60–1

sadhana 111, 198
sakadagamin 113, 115, 235
samadhi 62, 92, 96–8, 125, 236
samatha 60–1, 143–4, 201, 236
same-sex relationships 178–9, 185
samskara see formation
samudaya 35–9, 40, 232
Samyutta Nikaya 3, 122
Sandhinirmocana Sutra 129–30
sangha 5–6, 7, 8, 11, 14, 63, 87, 106, 119, 134–8, 138–40, 157, 158, 165, 183–4, 192, 196, 198, 202–4, 204–5, 210, 236
  founding of 87, 89
  in Mahayana 136–8
  in Theravada 134–6
Sangharakshita 45, 196–8, 200, 201–2, 204
sankhara-dukkha 25, 236
sasana 4
sattha 4
savaka 4
self 14, 26, 27–8, 30, 35, 37, 47–50, 51, 52, 53–4, 86, 106, 108, 113, 115, 127–8, 130, 142, 171, 175, 182–3, 200–1, 231
sensation 30, 33–4, 48, 143, 233
sexual misconduct 95, 136, 168, 169, 177–80, 195, 199, 204
Shakyamuni Buddha see Buddha
Shantideva 9, 49, 101, 106, 126, 139
Shorter Sukhavativyuha Sutra (Amitabha Sutra) 129, 132
shrine 152–8, 178
Shurangama Sutra 131
Sikhism xii-xiii, xiv, 89
sila 62, 92, 93–6, 108–9, 114, 168, 235, 236
Simpsons 15, 211
six paramitas 108–10, 235
skillful means see upaya
Smih, Jonathan Z. xi-xii
Smith, Wilfred Cantwell 2
social justice 176–7, 190, 210
Soka Gakkai/ Soka Gakkai International/ Soka Gakkai International UK 17, 137–8, 188, 190–2, 204, 236
Soma 182
sotapanna 62, 113, 115, 135, 236
sparsa see contact
stealing 95, 175–6, 195

storytelling 35, 75, 89–90, 139
Strong, John 2, 10, 12, 68, 71, 72, 74, 211
Suddhodana 76, 236
Sukhavati see Pure Lands
Sumedha 72, 73
sunyata see emptiness
Sutta Pitaka 122–5, 236
Suzuki, D. T. 126, 149, 209
syncretism 11, 12, 15, 210–11

tanha see craving
Tantra 110–11, 159, 195
Tathagata see Buddha
ten perfections of a Buddha 73
Ten Positive Precepts of Triratna Buddhism 199
ten precepts 136, 199
thangka 150–1, 158, 159
Theos Think Tank xiii
Theravada 3, 7, 8–9, 12, 16–17, 28–9, 33–4, 35–6, 41, 52, 54, 56, 58–64, 65, 72, 74–5, 87, 91, 100, 105, 112–16, 116–18, 121–3, 126, 131, 132–3, 134–6, 137, 138, 146–7, 155, 167, 172, 184, 187–8, 199, 204–5, 208, 211–12, 236
Thirty-two marks of a Great Being 77, 78, 150
Thirty-two portents of the Buddha's birth 77, 79
Three Marks of Existence 25, 26, 28, 47, 231, 232
Three Refuges/Jewels see Refuges
Three vehicles 7–8, 12, 16
Threefold Way see Middle Way
Tibetan Book of the Dead 52
Tibetan Buddhism 54, 107, 111, 131, 137, 151, 157, 158, 187, 192–5, 197, 209
Tipitaka 121–125, 138, 231, 235, 236, 237
Triratna (formerly Friends of the Western Buddhist Order) 11, 45, 96, 188, 196–204, 210, 211, 233, 234, 236
trsna see craving
Tsongkhapa 193, 194
Tusita heaven 75, 80, 105, 132, 159, 232, 234, 237
Twelve Nidanas 28–34, 38, 45, 53, 66

Uddaka Ramaputta 83–4, 87
upadana see grasping
upaya 101, 108, 109, 168

Vajravarahi 184
Vajrayana 7, 8, 9–10, 16, 17, 37, 57, 110–11, 118, 150–1, 158, 159, 187, 202, 237
Vappa 84
Vasubandhu 52, 178
vedana see sensation
vegetarianism 168, 173–5
vibhava-tanha 38
vijnana see consciousness
Vimalakirti Sutra 130–1
Vinaya 8, 123, 126, 169, 178, 195, 237
Vinaya Pitaka 69, 121–2, 236, 237
viparinama-dukkha 25
vipassana 97, 144, 144–8, 201–2, 231, 237
virya 108–9, 168, 235
visualization 106, 111, 150–2, 158, 159, 198, 201

Wheel of Life 31–3, 36, 45, 54–7, 63, 65–6, 111, 118, 237
Williams, Paul 11, 41, 43, 100, 110–11, 115, 129
wisdom see prajna
Women role of 87, 110, 125, 135, 136, 138, 182–5, 210
World Religions Paradigm xi, xiv, 1, 16, 141
worldviews x, xi, xiii, xiv, xv, 4, 13, 14, 46, 142, 159, 162, 180, 185, 187–8, 210

XIV Dalai Lama 5, 25, 27, 28, 54, 75, 106, 112, 117, 118, 137, 151, 167, 170, 173, 174, 178–9, 187, 192–3, 210

Yasodhara 81, 82, 184, 237

Zen Buddhism 14, 16–17, 118, 130, 131, 137, 148–50, 166, 175, 185, 187, 204–5, 209, 233, 236, 237

www.ingramcontent.com/pod-product-compliance
Lightning Source LLC
Chambersburg PA
CBHW081841230426
43669CB00018B/2773